LOST LEGACIES

Cover design by Leaven Agency.
Author photographs by Evangelos Photography Ltd., Vancouver, B.C.
Book designed and typeset by Leaven Agency.
Edited by Keith Henderson.

Legal Deposit, Bibliothèque et Archives nationales du Québec
and Library and Archives Canada, 3rd trimester, 2024.

Library and Archives Canada Cataloguing in Publication
Title: Lost legacies : learning from ancestral stories for inspiration and policy-making today /
    Margaret V. Ostrowski.
Names: Ostrowski, Margaret V., author.
Description: Includes bibliographical references.
Identifiers: Canadiana 20240388631 | ISBN 9781927599624 (softcover)
Subjects: LCSH: Ostrowski, Margaret V.—Family. | LCSH: Polish people—Canada—
Biography. | LCSH:
    Immigrants—Canada. | CSH: Polish Canadians—Biography. | LCGFT: Autobiographies.
Classification: LCC FC106.P7 O88 2024 | DDC 971/.0049185—dc23

For our publishing activities, DC Books gratefully acknowledges the financial support
of SODEC and of the Government of Canada through Canadian Heritage and the
Canada Book Fund. Nous reconnaissons l'aide financière du gouvernement du Canada.

Société
de développement
des entreprises
culturelles
Québec   Canada

Printed and bound in Canada.
Interior pages printed on Enviro Book, an environmentally responsible paper
containing 100% post-consumer recycled fibre, processed chlorine-free and
manufactured using biogas energy.
Distributed by LitDistCo.

DC Books
5 Fenwick Ave., Montreal West
Quebec H4X 1P3
www.dcbooks.ca

MARGARET V. OSTROWSKI

LOST LEGACIES

LEARNING FROM ANCESTRAL STORIES FOR INSPIRATION AND POLICY-MAKING TODAY

To my dear sons, Simon and Kevin
and my lovely grandchildren
Evelyn, Charlotte, Theo, Henry, Spencer and Taylor
Knowing your heritage will make you stronger

To the memory of Joanna Pietkiewicz
Your resilience and kindness have not been forgotten

CONTENTS

INTRODUCTION

This book originated from my insatiable curiosity about how our world works. From explorations of people, places and things, I often derive great excitement, comfort, and peace. I might learn about the plumbing system in my house or how to cure Achilles tendonitis; what it is like in Tuktoyaktuk, Lardeau, South Africa, Sri Lanka, and Bhutan; how our legal and political systems work (or not); why my father painted a portrait of a goose. The list is ongoing. And of course, I sometimes am surprised at how things really don't work well, and this surprise in itself triggers a creative quest to fix something or at least rethink it. Relatively recently, I realized there were two adjacent doors as yet unopened in my explorations: my ancestral history and our Canadian immigrant history. What could I learn? And would my discoveries be at all important for me or anyone else? This book answers those questions.

Primarily, I describe the journey of looking into my ancestral history by researching one person: my Polish grandmother who immigrated to Canada in 1914 with her husband and three children, one of whom was my father. What I found led me to write about someone who would otherwise be lost in the passage of time. But her story is only meant as an example of the richness of who we all are today. For in the process of that exploration, it became very clear to me that I was expanding my understanding of my own personal context here on the planet – developing a four-dimensional view involving the past – and that this approach of joining the past to the present not only was useful to me but also enriched my view of others in my community, my province, and my country. There was much more to look at besides my own ancestral history of immigration. These sorts of fascinating stories are all around us, hidden in the routine and conformity required by our daily lives.

I then thought it would be meaningful to include some examples of other remarkable groups and individuals who had struck me as memorable and who made my daily life far more significant and interesting after I came to understand their "background." Having been a legal decision-maker for the Immigration and Refugee Board of Canada, in order to highlight some of the individuals' struggles to settle in this country, I selected two examples of the stories I had heard when adjudicating applications of immigrants in Canada who were challenging a deportation order or wanted to bring a family member here. I also wrote about some communities that had been part of my life experience: the Irish in Canada, as I have an Irish relative by marriage; the Doukhobors in Castlegar in whose museum I had volunteered when living there; the inhabitants of Lasqueti Island where I had visited a friend and others. All my research yielded amazing stories and histories of vision, heroism, eccentricity, determination, adventure, challenge, and disappointment.

Early in my career before I studied law, I was a Registered (Social) Psychologist and with that background, it was important to me not only to hear the stories and marvel at the challenges and adventures, but also to actually reflect on the significance of narratives, backgrounds, and histories in a more expansive sense – the "takeaway" from it all. I came across other writers who had reflected in similar and different ways and who had recognized the importance of such reflection. I have included their commentaries and work alongside mine as sort of a synthesis of our collective regard for the legacies of our ancestors – their fortitude and bravery, their different ways of approaching life challenges, and the possible reasons for the feeling of disconnectedness we sometimes experience and for the unusual fears that seem unexplainable.

In a final chapter, I reflect on how important it is to retrieve those who have been lost or forgotten in history so that we may build on what they have left. From their legacies, we may appreciate having a variety both of views on reality and of choices about how to live our lives, and we may begin to understand current cultural challenges in our society. We need reminding that we exist along a continuum in time, both individually and societally, with many deep roots that can be comforting as well as worthy of respect and admiration. In one sense, it is a complex notion, but in another, it is also very simple and deeply worthwhile to understand the importance of our context, our history, our story.

CHAPTER ONE: STORIES

The universe is made of stories, not atoms.
  —Muriel Rukeyser, "The Speed of Darkness"

The divine art is the story.
  —Isak Dinesen, "The Cardinal's First Tale"

For several years, as a member of the Immigration and Refugee Board, I listened to many stories and I made hundreds of decisions about whether a person could stay in Canada or be deported as well as related decisions such as whether they could bring family members into Canada. The overriding tasks in my role as an adjudicator/ judge were to listen carefully to the stories, determine their truthfulness, and then apply the law as set out in the *Immigration and Refugee Protection Act of Canada*. Some of the stories were heart-rending, changing the way I think and the way I view an anonymous person walking down a street. Let me share some of these stories so you can see what I mean.[1]

A middle-aged Canadian citizen who had been born in South Asia and arrived in Canada in the 1980s was applying to bring his daughter to Canada. He had first applied a few years earlier, but his application had been denied, so he had appealed that decision to the Immigration Appeal Board. He had been waiting several years for a hearing date. At the hearing, he told me his story of coming to Canada. He had escaped Vietnam by boat in 1985 because he opposed the communist regime. His wife was pregnant, and they planned to meet later. He was eleven days at sea during which time

---

1   Most immigration appeal hearings are open to the public. The applicant in an appeal hearing is referred to as "the appellant."

---

the boat encountered pirates; he was beaten and tortured, and all his personal possessions were stolen by the pirates. Reaching a small village in Thailand, he was interviewed by an officer from the United Nations High Commissioner for Refugees (UNHCR). His wounds were treated for two months; then he was moved from one to another of three refugee camps in Thailand. In one of those camps, a Vietnamese-speaking UNHCR officer asked whether any family members had accompanied him in the boat, and he said no. He was then asked to sign an immigration document written in English, which he could not read as he knew only Vietnamese. Sometime later, he was accepted as a government-sponsored refugee for resettlement in Canada. He stated definitively that at no time had he been asked whether he had a wife or dependents at home. Upon his arrival in Canada, he signed a Record of Landing written in English, and again he was not offered a translator. In Canada, he tried to contact his family members in Vietnam but received no reply. Ultimately, he was able to visit Vietnam in 1999 to see his father and wife after fourteen years; he also met his daughter for the first time. He visited them again in 2000, 2001 and 2004. He had applied to sponsor only his daughter because he had been told he did not have the required income to sponsor his wife. At the time of the hearing, he was employed in shift work and put in long hours at a local canning factory.

The counsel for the Ministry of Citizenship and Immigration argued that there had been a fatal lack of disclosure of the family member (that is, his daughter) when the appellant entered Canada, and that the lack of intention to deceive was irrelevant. Ministry counsel further submitted that by law, the Immigration Appeal Division had no humanitarian and compassionate jurisdiction to grant relief. Credibility was one of the pivotal issues. Was he telling the truth?

In my decision I concluded that there was no motivation alleged during the hearing for him to hide the fact that he had a wife and possibly a child. After hearing the details of his escape and viewing his demeanour, I also found that his experiences escaping from Vietnam and coming to Canada were credible and traumatic such that he'd been at a point in his arrival where he would do exactly as he was told. He had suffered much abuse in his escape, including being hung by a fishhook implanted in his back. (During the hearing, he took off his shirt and exhibited a large, deep scar or gouge on his back.) On arrival in Canada, he described how he and others were put up for a few days in a hotel and given canned food to eat. He testified that unfortunately they were not given a can opener, so they opened the cans with their teeth.

I concluded that he was not given a reasonable opportunity to declare his non-accompanying family members, and that as natural justice, humanitarian, and compassionate relief could be granted as fairness must apply for the particular section to be held applicable. In other words, I allowed his appeal to sponsor his daughter. I still remember what I felt when I saw the deep gouge in this man's back, the result of pirates hanging him on a hook like a large fish. He presented as a very hard-working, quiet man who had gone through much strife and great suffering. If you saw him on the street, he might appear tired; he might not look at you, and his overalls and shirt might smell like the fish-packing plant where he worked. Yet his was an amazing, moving story of survival.

A fellow from the Roma culture was also accused of breaching a condition of entry to Canada. In this case, he was appealing his deportation order. The appellant was a young man in his thirties, slated for deportation because, on his immigration application, he had denied ever being detained or incarcerated. This was not true, but for the sake of his child who had been born in Canada, he was seeking permission to stay on humanitarian and compassionate grounds. A previous case decided by the Immigration Appeal Division had set out factors to be considered when misrepresentation as to detention or incarceration had occurred. Those factors included the seriousness of the offence that had led to the deportation order, the possibility of rehabilitation, the degree to which the appellant was established in Canada, family in Canada who would be dislocated, and the degree of hardship that would be caused to the appellant by his return to his country of nationality.

The appellant had been raised in a small village in Hungary in a poor Roma family of five children. Three of his siblings were intellectually challenged and one sister had been taken from the home to be raised in a more prosperous family. He had been trained as a tool and die maker in Hungary and had worked in construction. After being laid off, he had gone to Germany to work on a farm, but after three years, he was deported for staying in the country illegally. Back in Hungary, he became involved in one incident of car insurance fraud and was detained by the police for six months, but he was eventually released without a conviction. In admitting to this offence at the hearing, he said he was very sorry for his wrongdoing.

He then visited Canada where he got married and decided to stay, living with his wife for ten years until they separated. Subsequently, he met his common-law wife, a Roma, and they had one child who by virtue of being born in Canada was a citizen. At the time of the hearing, a second child was due in a few months. The appellant had been employed in several jobs since coming to Canada and presented a letter from his current employer, stating he was making $60,000 per year and that his full-time job was expected to last for another five years.

In his testimony, the appellant said that if he were required to leave Canada to return to Hungary, his common-law wife and their son would accompany him. However, he claimed the prospects for housing and employment were dim. They could not live with her parents who were barely surviving. His parents had disowned him because he had involved his brother in the insurance fraud, and his sister had no room for him, let alone a pregnant wife with a small child. The appellant's legal representative provided evidence that prospects for already poor workers in Hungary were worsening and that the situation particularly impacted children. Further evidence also indicated that many Roma residing in rural areas lived below the poverty line. There was no evidence that he had violated any laws in Canada.

In my decision, I found the appellant had been candid in admitting to his earlier misrepresentation and was genuinely ashamed. There was no evidence of a conviction for the alleged insurance fraud, and he had been law-abiding in Canada. I also noted that he had described barely eking out an existence in Hungary even if it meant not adhering to local laws, and that he cited this as the reason for working illegally in Germany. I found from his common-law wife's testimony that he had a solid family life here and dependable income and that if returned to Hungary, he would have little family support and bleak employment prospects. It would be in the best interest of the son and the new child to have a father providing an income. I allowed him to stay in Canada.

I found his story credible – a struggle for survival by an individual from a group traditionally oppressed and discriminated against in Hungary and beyond. I was moved by what he had done to rehabilitate after transgressions elsewhere, to follow Canadian societal norms, and to settle in Canada and make a life for his family that was not possible in his country of birth. I felt an onus

------

upon me to be cognizant of other groups in our world that have traditionally had little opportunity for a decent life. This Roma man's story had widened my world view. After that hearing, I bought and read the fascinating book *The Gypsies in Poland: History and Culture*, by Jerzy Ficowski.

I have since found that my grandmother had an intriguing story in the same vein. She was born in the Russian Partition of Poland in 1888, the youngest of twelve children, and grew up in a *folwark,* an agricultural village, in an area that is now in Belarus. It has been suggested by a renowned Polish historian that her maiden name, Pietkiewicz, has noble origins and that accordingly the family had prestige and power in Poland before 1795, which I learned only after writing the first draft of this book.

Although Polish, her village was under Russian rule and hence subject to Russification, but old traditions survived. Education and opportunities for advancement were very limited, so after enduring a rough journey across the Atlantic in steerage class, she, my grandfather and their three small children, including my father, immigrated to Canada to start a new life in 1914, just before the outbreak of the First World War. Arriving in Halifax, they found the undertaking challenging, as they could not speak English; medical care was virtually unavailable to them because of the cost, and they had no large extended family for support. Three children born in Halifax died very young; family members were injured in the Halifax explosion, and my grandfather left the family to search for a better homeland in Argentina but ultimately returned to Poland. How she managed to become a dignified, wealthy businesswoman in Canada is an inspiring and unforgettable story.

Though I will be setting out many details of her life in subsequent chapters, this book is not meant to be a memoir of her life. My Polish grandmother is simply one example of how an examination of the past, especially through ancestral stories and histories, can lead to an enlightened understanding of ourselves and our society and to the recognition that our ancestors have left important legacies for us to build on.

CHAPTER TWO: THE IMPORTANCE AND POWER OF STORIES FROM THE PAST

Study the past if you would divine the future.
— Confucius (551–479)

We live in a culture that, for the most part, appears to lack any real interest in the past. Yes, there has been an increased curiosity about genealogy – the names of our ancestors and the countries from which they came. However, I'm talking about a real understanding of life back then, why we now live the way we do, and how our current society came to be the way it is, our context. For instance, in May, we in Canada celebrate the Victoria Day holiday with fireworks. As a child, I remember calling it "firecracker day." Why do we celebrate that? We decorate trees and exchange presents at Christmas; we get a day off work on Labour Day; our children dress up and go door to door for treats on Hallowe'en. Why? Few know the intricate histories of how these dates and celebrations came to be. We rarely know much beyond our own personal experience and what we may remember from compulsory "social studies" classes in grade school. Stories of those times and guidance from elders are rarely sought. Like others who have spoken of the importance of knowing our past, I see this omission as a loss.

In her 2016 book *The New Politics of Immigration and the End of Settler Societies,* lawyer and professor of law Catherine Dauvergne commented: "Losing the past does of course rob us of its insights."[2] That same year, political scientist Jennifer Welsh noted in her Massey Lectures that "the twenty-first century has not seen

---

2   Catherine Dauvergne, *The New Politics of Immigration and the End of Settler Societies* (Cambridge: Cambridge University Press, 2016), p. 17.

unfettered progress towards peace and a single form of government, but the reappearance of trends and practices many believed had been erased: arbitrary executions, attempts to annihilate ethnic and religious minorities, the starvation of besieged populations, invasion and annexation of territory, and the mass movement of refugees and displaced persons."[3] Is this, I wonder, in part because we have lost interest in our pasts? In his foreword to the book *Passages: Welcome Home to Canada*, Michael Ignatieff opined that we should not assume immigration ever meant assimilation in the strict sense of discarding identity: "new identities never obliterate old ones, and new identities are unlikely to be authentic and strong if they are built on forgetting. Moreover, to ask new Canadians to forget old selves would be to squander their unique contributions to their adopted country."[4]

In the introduction to an excellent book entitled *Our Forgotten Past: Centuries of Life on the Land*, Jerome Blum wrote: "That past [of the way people lived on the land] is where the roots of our civilization and our own roots lie, and the more we know about those roots the more we know about ourselves."[5] In *The End of the Old Order in Rural Europe*, he emphasized the agricultural roots most of us with European ancestry share:

---

3   Jennifer Welsh, *The Return of History: Conflict, Migration, and Geopolitics in the Twenty-First Century* (Toronto: House of Anansi Press, 2016), cover flap.

4   *Passages: Welcome Home to Canada* is a collection of writings by eleven Canadian authors in a project initiated by Westwood Creative Artists and The Dominion Institute. It was published in Toronto by Doubleday in 2002; this quote is from Michael Ignatieff's foreword, which appears on page 9.

5   Jerome Blum, *Our Forgotten Past: Seven Centuries of Life on the Land* (London: Thames & Hudson, 1982), p. 8.

In the last quarter of the eighteenth century over a hundred million people or about two-thirds of the population of all Europe, lived in [mainland Europe]. . . . Of these many millions at least seven, and in some countries more than nine, out of every ten persons lived on the land. Nearly all of these country dwellers drew their living from agriculture; a relatively small number were occupied in other callings, such as handicraft production, forest industries, mining and the like. Whatever their source of their livelihoods, they belonged to that order of society known as the peasantry. Through the accident of their birth into that lowest of estates, they were denied by the society in which they lived freedoms and privileges possessed by members of orders with higher status, compelled to be subservient to and dependent upon persons in these higher status groups, and required to render certain payments and services demanded of no other order of society. . . . Peasants in western Europe enjoyed much personal freedom but were not truly free. Most of them still lived in dependence upon, and owed servile obligations to, their seigniors. Those who lived in eastern Europe endured a serfdom that often was scarcely distinguishable from chattel slavery.[6]

The sort of lives that our ancestors led is almost entirely foreign to many of us and scant views of the past are often relied on to direct our current economic, political, social, and cultural frameworks. For instance, recently there have been movements to rename schools and streets and tear down monuments commemorating

---

6   Jerome Blum, *The End of the Old Order in Rural Europe* (Princeton: Princeton University Press, 1978), p. 3.

our founding fathers. In a recent *Financial Post* column, Stephen R. Brown wrote:

> Our current national narrative holds that Canadian colonists were – universally – despicable, racist thieves who sought the extinction of Indigenous people and discriminated against vulnerable populations whenever they could. . . . These new narratives fail as actual history because they lack a grounding in fact.[7]

He went on to state that blaming Sir John A. Macdonald for the entirety of the residential schools ignores that he died before they were greatly expanded and placed under church authority. If we lose our ancestors' stories that are grounded in fact – their stories and their histories – we lose a part of who we are and how we got that way.

It should be noted that the author Thomas King pointed out that stories can be wondrous, empowering phenomena, or they can actually be limiting and strict. We should realize that in certain stories we have had a choice. For example, in his 2003 Massey Lectures entitled *The Truth about Stories*, Thomas King, of Cherokee and Greek descent, conveyed a key message: "The truth about stories is that that's all we are."[8] King told two stories of creation, one from an Aboriginal point of view and the other from the Christian Bible.[9] The Woman Who Fell from the Sky is a long tale of a curious

---

7   Stephen R. Brown, "Canada Needs a Revival of Popular History," *Financial Post*, December 19, 2023, p. 10.

8   Thomas King, *The Truth about Stories: A Native Narrative*, CBC Massey Lectures Series, 9th ed. (Toronto: House of Anansi Press, 2003), p. 2. (This is a great book!)

9   Thomas King, pp. 10–21.

woman who was pregnant and hungry. Disregarding a badger's warning not to dig too deep, she dug around the base of an old tree, until she dug to the other side of the world and fell right through and into the sky. She tumbled through the sky and saw a dot – a blue dot just covered with water: the earth. The animals that lived there in the water saw she was coming and worked on figuring out a way to protect themselves from a big splash. Ultimately, an otter dove down, brought up some mud, and with the help of others, formed land and rivers, waterfalls, trees with fruits and nuts, summer, winter, sunshine and shadows. And then the woman had twins, a girl and a boy.

Next, King set out the Christian story of creation in Genesis and said this is a story that captures the imagination:

> God creates night and day, the sun and the moon, all the creatures of the world, and finally, towards the end of his labours, he creates humans. Man first and then woman. Adam and Eve. And he places everything and everyone in a garden, a perfect world. No sickness, no death, no hate, no hunger. Of every tree of the garden thou mayest freely eat. But of the tree of knowledge of good and evil, thou shalt not eat of it. . . . One rule. Don't break it.
>
> But that's exactly what happens. . . . If you like the orthodox version, you can blame Eve. She eats the apple and brings it back to Adam. Not that Adam says no. A less misogynist reading would blame them both, would chalk up the debacle that followed as an unavoidable mistake. A wrong step. Youthful enthusiasm. A misunderstanding. Wilfulness. But … that is the end of the garden. God seals it off and places an angel with a fiery sword at the entrance and tosses Adam and Eve into a howling wilderness to fend for themselves, a

wilderness in which sickness and death, hate and hunger are their constant companions.[10]

King talked of these two creation stories, one a tale where the universe is governed by a series of co-operations that celebrate equality and balance, and the other where all creative power is vested in a single deity – omnipotent, omniscient, and omnipresent – and the world is at war: God versus the devil, humans versus the elements. King then asked why we tell our children that life is hard when we could just as easily tell them that it is sweet. "What if the creation story in Genesis had featured a flawed deity who was understanding and sympathetic rather than autocratic… someone who was willing to accept a little help with the more difficult decisions? What kind of world might have been created with that story?"[11] Should we re-examine our stories and find truths and new, positive meanings therein?

With these various perspectives in mind as I sought to better understand what little I knew of my grandmother's life and the clarifying facts of that life's story, I looked first at the story of Canada's immigration history.

---

10   Thomas King, pp. 21–22.

11   Thomas King, pp. 26–28.

CHAPTER THREE:
CANADA'S IMMIGRATION STORY

The most effective way to destroy a people is to deny and obliterate their own understanding of their history.
> Attributed to George Orwell

A person who has no past, only a future, is a person with little reality.
> —Octavio Paz

Anthropological research has determined that many thousands of years ago, Indigenous peoples arrived in North America by crossing over the frozen Bering Strait or, as some have speculated, by boat from the Pacific. During the last two thousand years, Irish monks landed in Newfoundland as did the Vikings from Norway and seaman from Europe for the bountiful fishing. Some Portuguese came, some Italian explorers, and then in 1534, Jacques Cartier who actually journeyed up the St. Lawrence River and initiated European settlements in Canada. Others followed in the early 1600s, such as the enterprising trader Pierre Dugua de Mons and his employee Samuel de Champlain, and others seeking fish and beaver fur for fashionable hats. In these early decades, though, there was nothing to attract serious colonization in what was called New France, particularly as the First Nations peoples did all the work to supply the furs.[12]

---

12   The brief description in this paragraph is but a very short summary of chapter 1, "The Beginnings," in Valeri Knowles, *Strangers at Our Gates: Canadian Immigration and Immigration Policy, 1540–2006* (Toronto: Dundurn, 2007). Her text contains many more interesting facts.

Mention must be made here of the early European explorers' total reliance on the First Nations peoples who led the newcomers along the mountain trails, down the rivers, and through the forests. Those explorers were taught the important skills of how to eat, dress, travel, and survive. An excellent example of this is set out in the travels of Samuel Hearne (born 1745 and died 1792),[13] the first European to make an overland excursion across northern Canada to the Arctic Ocean along the Coppermine River in the 1770s. In his account of travels, he described the various tribes, including the Cree hunters, the Dene, and a band of Chipewyans who guided the way and saved him and his companions from starving to death. He gave particular gratitude to a Chipewyan named Matonabhee who was a leading caribou hunter with exceptional Indigenous knowledge of travel and living off the land and who actually made Hearne's trip possible. Hearne also documented ruthless massacres between tribes. An intriguing account by a European about daily living in a First Nations village on Nootka Sound was written by John R. Jewitt who described his captivity there from 1803 to 1807.[14]

European ideas about economics and trade were changing to the notion that a nation's wealth and power were best served by increasing exports and reducing imports. As France only had fish and fur from their colonial interests, the natural resources and raw materials of New France became important and workers were needed. Four thousand French Catholics arrived there between 1627 and 1643, including merchants, professionals, landless nobles drawn by the prospect of cheap properties (called *seigneuries*), and

---

13   Samuel Hearne, *A Journey to the Northern Ocean: The Adventures of Samuel Hearne*, Foreword by Ken McGoogon (Surrey, British Columbia: Touchwood Editions, 2007).

14   John R. Jewitt, *The Adventures and Sufferings of John R. Jewitt*, annotated and illustrated by Hilary Stewart (Vancouver: Douglas and McIntyre, 1995).

skilled workers such as blacksmiths and carpenters who might have been influenced by the reports from the Jesuits who encouraged them to come and settle.[15] As most of these ambitious immigrants were single males and wanted wives, a substantial number of young unmarried women were also persuaded to come to the new land. In a clear move to prevent interracial unions with Indigenous women, the law forbade bachelors in the colony to hunt, fish, or participate in the fur trade until all the arriving European women were married. Having a large family was favoured, and parents were rewarded with a family allowance bonus. Canada's population in 1700 comprising new arrivals was 15,000.[16]

In 1760 Canada became British territory, and for the following forty years, immigration to Canada was not regulated as Britain had no explicit emigration policy; there was a view at the time that emigration would drain the nation's vitality.[17] In the late 1700s, certain political factors resulted in immigrants coming from the United States. Fortifications in Halifax, established to prevent French attacks against New England, became a home for Loyalists escaping from the American Revolution, particularly in 1783 and 1784. These Loyalist refugees – Highland Scots, Germans and native-born Americans – had been loyal to Great Britain in the American War of Independence and did not want to become citizens of the new United States of America; in some cases, they feared punishment for their allegiance.[18]

---

15   Taken from Knowles, *Strangers*, pp. 15–17.

16   Knowles, *Strangers*, pp. 22–24.

17   Graeme Wynn, "On the Margins of Empire (1760–1840)," in *The Illustrated History of Canada*, ed. Craig Brown (Toronto: Key Porter Books Limited, 2002), p. 211.

18   Knowles, *Strangers*, pp. 36–41.

Overpopulation and changes in agricultural land use generated a great exodus from Great Britain and Europe, not only to North America but also to South America, South Africa, and Australasia after the 1815 end of the Napoleonic wars.[19] But in 1855, immigration numbers to the developing Canada decreased because of a revival in United Kingdom trade, the need for British men to serve in the Crimean War, and immigration to the United States. So in the later 1850s, the Province of Canada initiated an immigration promotion program (the precursor to more extensive campaigns later in the century) targeting small farmers and agricultural labourers, particularly in the UK and, later, Germany. It was thought that it was time to discourage workers such as mechanics, clerks, and house servants, who were not lacking in the new lands.[20] By Confederation in 1867, two-thirds of the population in British North America had British origins.[21]

A group of immigrants who did not come here by choice during these earlier days of immigration were slaves. Historian Constance Backhouse in her book *Colour-Coded: A Legal History of Racism in Canada, 1900–1950*[22] reminded us that wealthy merchants brought slaves to New France. Joseph Mensah, author of *Black Canadians*[23] described Jean Talon, the Intendant of New France, importing slaves from Africa. In 1793, a phase-out of slavery began in Canada after it was legislated that no further slaves could be brought;

---

19   Knowles, *Strangers*, p. 49.

20   Knowles, *Strangers*, pp. 66–67.

21   Knowles, *Strangers*, p. 49.

22   Constance Backhouse, *Colour-Coded: A Legal History of Racism in Canada, 1900–1950* (Toronto: University of Toronto Press, 1999).

23   Joseph Mensah, *Black Canadians: History, Experience, Social Conditions, Revised Edition* (Winnipeg: Fernwood Publishing, 2010).

however, children born to "negro mothers" were to remain slaves to their mother's owners until the age of twenty-five. In the middle of the 1800s, thousands of slaves escaped to Canada from the United States after a law was passed compelling authorities in the northern states to return them to their owners.[24]

In every decade of the 1800s, particular social, economic, and political circumstances were reflected in immigrant numbers and reactions to immigrants in British North America. For instance, there was a large number of immigrants to Quebec in 1832 with about 52,000 arriving in that year alone. However, many contracted cholera, and the French in Quebec, thinking this was a deliberate attempt to exterminate them, became suspicious and fearful of new immigrants, and at one time even threatened to fire on any steamers that did not turn back from the banks of the St. Lawrence.[25] In 1847 came a major influx of starving immigrants, many suffering from typhus and dysentery, and bringing disease to Montreal, Kingston, and Toronto, with great loss of life. Many of these immigrants were Irish. The death toll was about 30,000 people.[26]

From 1846 to 1854, Ireland experienced the emigration of many due to the great potato-blight famine – an estimated one million Irish died. Ireland in the 1800s was one of the poorest Western nations, dependent on agriculture in the form of peasants farming small tracts of land owned by the Protestant English and the Anglo-Irish hereditary ruling class. The potato had been introduced to Ireland in 1590 from Peru and it grew well in the cool, moist soil, yielding an annual crop sufficient to feed a family with a relatively

---

24   Penni Mitchell, "Women Led Freedom Quests," *Herizons*, March 22, 2015, www.thefreelibrary.com/Women+led+freedom+quests.-a0415108684.

25   Knowles, *Strangers*, pp. 60–61.

26   Knowles, *Strangers*, p. 65.

nourishing staple that could survive in storage over the winter; often large meals of boiled potatoes were served daily. Other crops were sold for export to pay rent. However, in September 1845, an airborne fungus (*Phytophthora infestans*), originally transported on ships from North America to England, was blown from southern England to an area near Dublin. The blight spread very quickly, causing the potato leaves to blacken and the potatoes to rot within days. At first, just a one-year blight was anticipated, but for years it destroyed the crops, causing malnutrition, typhus, dysentery, and death. There were many reports of emaciated men, women, and children dying and being buried in huge trenches.[27]

Evictions (estimated to be about one-half million) by heartless landlords caused many to escape from the land; some landowners would even pay the ship's passage to send a poor family to British North America, and gave false promises that money, food, and clothing would be waiting at their destination. Such vessels were referred to as "coffin ships," as many passengers were severely sick or died at sea and others drowned when their vessel was sunk by icebergs in the Atlantic. The survivors settled after quarantine[28] in places such as Quebec City, Montreal, Kingston, and Toronto. Some French Canadians kindly offered homes to those orphaned by the coffin ships as evidenced by the abundance of Irish family names among succeeding generations of French Canadians.[29] Their

---

27   I relied on "The Irish Potato Famine," *The History Place*, www.historyplace.com/worldhistory/famine/, for some of the facts in this paragraph. The larger story in that article is fascinating as well as disturbing.

28   Many died of typhus and dysentery in quarantine on Grosse Ile, a quarantine station for the port of Quebec.

29   Facts are from "The Irish Potato Famine: Coffin Ships," *The History Place*, www.historyplace.com/worldhistory/famine/coffin.htm. Another helpful article

stories are both inspiring and heart-breaking, leaving no doubt that those who lived must have been extraordinarily strong.

One exceptional Irish Catholic immigrant who was a significant contributor to the formation of a Canadian confederation was Thomas D'Arcy McGee, more commonly known as D'Arcy McGee. He was born in 1825 in Carlington, Ireland, and learned the basics about Ireland's history and politics from his mother's side of the family who ran a bookstore. His mother died in 1833. He spent from 1842 to 1845 in the United States to distance himself from his stepmother and worked at the *Boston Pilot* newspaper with a specialty in Irish issues. On his return to Ireland, he became politically active as the editor of *The Nation*, the voice of the Young Ireland movement which advocated strongly for Irish independence. In 1848 to avoid arrest, he fled Ireland disguised as a priest and returned to the United States, earning his living there as a journalist. However, he became quite disillusioned with the politics there and moved to Montreal in 1857 to assume the editorship of *The New Era*. In Montreal he found a milieu of liberty and tolerance that was quite different from what he had experienced in the United States; his political beliefs matured, and in 1861, he received a law degree from McGill University. Together with his ability as a convincing editorialist and his reputation as a visionary as well as his exceptional charm, he cultivated a significant supportive audience for his views: he encouraged immigration and promoted both the building of a railway to facilitate economic development and a high tariff to protect manufacturing.[30]

---

is "Coffin Ships: Death and Pestilence on the Atlantic," *Irish Genealogy Toolkit*, www.irish-genealogy-toolkit.com/coffin-ships.html.

30   Many facts herein are from Josephine Phelan, *Ardent Exile: The Life and Times of D'Arcy McGee* (Toronto: The Macmillan Company of Canada Limited, 1951). This book is easy to read and has lots of personal details.

Mention should be made of the Fenian Brotherhood, an Irish republican organization based in the United States that focused on the takeover of the Canadian colony in order to put pressure on the British government to withdraw from Ireland in exchange for the return of the colony. Raids on Canadian soil in 1866 and from 1870 to 1871 terrorized the settlers.[31] McGee strongly denounced the Fenian Brotherhood and opposed separatist movements.[32] He became a strong spokesperson for a unique Canadian identity and culture, not one that favoured particular cultures (often referred to as multiculturalism). He was the Minister of Agriculture, Immigration and Statistics in the Conservative government of 1863, and over time became not only a colleague of Sir John A. Macdonald but a strong friend.

McGee was elected to the first Canadian Parliament in 1867 and is regarded as one of the Fathers of Confederation. It has been postulated by some historians that the only reason that the vote on Confederation of Canada passed was to counter the Fenian attacks.[33] Unfortunately, McGee's strong stance against the Fenian Brotherhood may have cost him his life – he was assassinated in 1868 by a Fenian sympathizer. There are buildings, streets, schools, an electoral district, and villages named in his honour, acknowledging his exceptional legacy and his contribution to the founding of the Dominion of Canada.

---

31   For a description of the Ridgeway Raid, see Peter Vronsky, *Ridgeway: The American Fenian Invasion and the 1866 Battle That Made Canada* (Toronto: Penguin Canada, 2012).

32   For commentary, see Keith Henderson, "Not as Crazy as You'd Think: Fenians and Thomas D'Arcy McGee," Personal Thoughts and Views (blog), March 25, 2021, www.thespecialcommittee.com/blog/history/not-as-crazy-as-you'd-think/

33   See quote of P.B. Waite in Henderson, p. 13.

After Canadian Confederation in 1867, more focus was directed to settling the Prairies and British Columbia (B.C.) to prevent their loss to the United States. Up until the First World War, "immigration salesmen would target farmers with capital, agricultural labourers, and female domestics, preferably from Great Britain, the United States, and northern Europe, in that order."[34] In 1869, the first *Immigration Act* set no limits on who was to be allowed in. However, this was changed in 1885 by an act to restrict Chinese immigration – a head tax was imposed to regulate those coming to B.C. to work on the Canadian Pacific Railway. Groups of Mennonites reached Manitoba in the 1870s and 1880s; Icelanders came after volcanic eruptions in their country in 1873; Jewish settlers arrived, especially in the 1880s after the assassination of Czar Alexander II initiated pogroms in Russia, and Hungarians came to Manitoba from industrial slums in the United States. Overall, though, settlement in the Western regions was slow, and many immigrants preferred the American West.[35]

But in the late 1800s, with a new hardy wheat strain, developments in agricultural technology, and the diminishing supply of good free land in the United States, this preference was about to change. The newly elected Prime Minister Wilfrid Laurier appointed Clifford Sifton as Minister of the Interior in 1896 (a post he held until 1905), with a mandate to set new immigration goals. As Sifton described it:

> Our desire is to promote the immigration of farmers and farm labourers. We have not been disposed to exclude foreigners of

---

34 Knowles, *Strangers*, p. 69.

35 Knowles, *Strangers*, pp. 71–79.

> any nationality who seem likely to become successful agricul-
> turalists. . . . It is admitted that additions to the population
> of our cities and towns by immigration [are] undesirable
> from every standpoint and such additions do not in any
> way whatsoever contribute to the object which is constantly
> kept in view by the Government of Canada in encouraging
> immigration for the development of natural resources and
> the increase of production of wealth from these resources.[36]

One group of farmers and labourers who immigrated to Canada in the later 1800s were the Doukhobors. The word means "spirit-wrestlers," and their immigration has been referred to as a utopian experiment, one of many in B.C. An extensive and informative history, far beyond the simplification I set out here, was written by Ivan Avakumovic and George Woodcock in their 1968 book *The Doukhobors*, which is highly worth reading. Briefly, the Doukhobors were a group of Russian pacifist dissenters from the Caucasus Mountains region who came to Canada to escape militarism, the bearing of arms, and the teachings of the Russian Orthodox Church. In their home country, they had replaced the Bible with orally transmitted psalms and hymns and refrained from the use of religious symbols. As they developed their teachings, they adopted vegetarianism, communal living, and abstinence from alcohol. In 1895 in Russia, one group of them publicly and overtly burned their weapons – their guns, knives, and swords –suffering arrests, beatings, and forced dispersal, and were subsequently persecuted by the government's Cossacks. The international attention around this incident put pressure on the Russian government, which then

---

36   Knowles, *Strangers*, p. 85. The quote here in Knowles was taken from a memo that Sifton wrote to Laurier in 1901.

agreed to let them leave the country. Funded by the Quakers, Count Leo Tolstoy, the Tolstoyan movement, and the Russian activist Peter Kropotkin, about 6,000 emigrated to Manitoba and Saskatchewan in 1899 and were later followed by additional individuals. By 1930, there were about 8,700 Doukhobors settled in communal agricultural settlements. Some issues emerged in Canada, as they were obliged to swear allegiance to the Crown and to register births and deaths, but they were not required to participate in military service, and over time, they became an accepted and respected part of the surrounding communities.[37]

I write about this group because I lived for a few years in Castlegar in the West Kootenays of B.C. A large group of Doukhobors (the Christian Community of Universal Brotherhood) had moved there from the Prairies. The locals in Castlegar told me of the Doukhobors' jam factory that had existed at one time just across the Kootenay River and produced many wonderful fruit jams. The Doukhobor community had built numerous pairs of large, two-storey brick buildings, each having many windows and a big porch, as well as small wooden outbuildings arranged in a U-shape to form a courtyard area. These buildings often were situated in a lovely pastoral setting—sometimes in a sunny open area surrounded by orchards and farmed fields, sometimes on a small rise of land.

When I lived there in the mid-1970s, there was a Doukhobor museum in the works. I was so impressed with their history of non-violence, non-smoking and non-drinking, as well as their vegetarianism and their welcoming manner that I volunteered for their historical society and came to have very fond feelings for their ideals. I learned about their saunas, many medicinal herbs,

---

37   Facts are from Ivan Avakumovic and George Woodcock, *The Doukhobors* (Toronto: Oxford University Press, 1968).

fields of sunflowers and borscht recipes, and about their acappella singing and their genuine, calm, and loving manner. They exemplified one of their slogans: "Toil and a peaceful life." Though they no longer live communally and are quite integrated into the local community, this group brought and still brings a message of peace and love. I was grateful for their presence in Canada. Their legacy is often forgotten because of the Orthodox Doukhobor resistance to conventional education and the many disruptions and troubles perpetrated by the minority anti-materialist sect of the Doukhobors called the Sons of Freedom. In hindsight, though the arson and nude marches by the Sons of Freedom were certainly over the line in our cultural context, their message that we are consumed by materialism has since been highlighted by others in our society as a valid concern.

Others seeking utopia also came to Canada. As Justine Brown writes in *All Possible Worlds*, there were Scandinavian settlers who in the spirit of utopian socialism came to the Pacific Northwest for a new life.[38] A Norwegian colony was established at Bella Coola, one that smoothly adapted to form the basis of a very pleasant town. She highlights both a settlement of Danes at Cape Scott that because of harsh weather conditions existed only from 1897 to 1909, and a group of Finns who came to Malcolm Island; unfortunately, they suffered from a fire in their meeting hall that killed eleven people, and from a leader, Kurikka, who by entering into unprofitable financial contracts on behalf of the community precipitated the settlement's demise. Today, the little village of Sointula on Malcolm Island still has some reminders of their experimental utopia. There are well-groomed residences, as well as a co-op store that

---

38   Justine Brown, *All Possible Worlds: Utopian Experiments in British Columbia* (Vancouver: New Star Books, 1995).

seems to sell virtually everything you need, and a lovely museum of Finnish artifacts.

The book *Accidental Eden*, Douglas L. Hamilton and Darlene Olesko describe the settlement, in the early 1970s, of a relatively small island in the Georgia Strait off the coast of B.C. – Lasqueti, only seventy-two kilometres north of Vancouver.[39] In the book, the authors set out its history: archaeological investigations unearthed village sites on this island that had been inhabited for thousands of years; middens of bones and shells suggest the inhabitants had hunted deer, seabirds, and sea mammals, and gathered shellfish and fish. Spanish conquistadors in the 1500s and other European explorers who followed brought deadly diseases, including smallpox, and left, for the most part, a relatively empty island. In the later 1800s, a few settlers thought sheep farming would be a good idea. Then logging and salmon fishing were tried, but the distance to a market was problematic. A small number of settlers endured for a number of decades, but by the late 1950s and the 1960s, many had left, deserting their homesteads. So Lasqueti in the late 1960s and early 1970s became a small-time mecca for back-to-the-earth people seeking an idealized country life, many from the United States disillusioned with their lifestyle and the politics of the Vietnam War.[40] Hamilton and Olesko's book contains lovely stories describing many of the inhabitants, their families, their freedom, and the challenges of eking out an existence on the land. Many didn't stick with it. But the book highlights that some of the old-timers remain today, and the island still has no hydroelectric hook-up, no public water system, no sewage disposal, few paved roads, and

39   Douglas L. Hamilton and Darlene Olesko, *Accidental Eden: Hippie Days on Lasqueti Island* (Qualicum Beach, British Columbia: Caitlin Press, 2014).

40   Hamilton and Olesko, pp. 24–30.

no police detachment. And to many they say, that is the beauty of Lasqueti – a place unique for those who know about it as having a history of supporting environmental values, peace, and eclecticism.

There are numerous other instances of distinctive immigrant communities in Canada's history, but now, I would like to look more closely at a story of my own heritage, a tale whose discovery was triggered by a painting of a goose.

CHAPTER FOUR: THE GOOSE AND THE RIBBON

The ancient people perceived the world and themselves within that world as part of an ancient continuous story composed of innumerable bundles of other stories.
—Leslie Marmon Silko, "Love Poem"

Take a look into any random old Polish cookbook to understand the culinary abundance of goose dishes. Besides the classical goose roasted with apples (probably the most popular goose recipe in Poland), goose would also be stuffed with sour cabbage, groats or chestnuts, goose breasts would be served in sour cream, and smoked sausages would be made of chopped goose meat.
—Magdalena Kasprzyk-Chevriaux, "Polish Food 101 – Goose"

It was the acrylic painting that my father gave me – of a farm goose followed by four fluffy white goslings – that started me thinking years after he had passed away. Why would my father, at the time a seventy-eight-year-old retired chemical engineer, paint geese? The piece had been one of his first attempts at art after an eight-week "painting for seniors" course at the local community centre. He had worked in pulp and paper mills most of his life and had an engineer's highly practical mind, combined with a strong drive to survive. I knew of no goose in the family history, and I had no inkling whatsoever that my father had any sense of "cuteness." Yet he had painted a picture of this lovely waterbird. There had to be a story.

I did some research and discovered that the geese in the painting were a domesticated form of the Greylag goose, a species found across Eurasia, including where my father had lived as a toddler, but not in Canada. Greylags swim in rivers, lakes, and marshes and have a short, stout bill that enables them to feed on leaves, stems, and roots. Alert and suspicious, they are supposedly not an easy animal to raise because they mate for life, one gander with one to four geese; in addition, they graze on pastures and field stubble, so they need to be herded – no kitchen scraps for these birds! But for rural dwellers in the past, geese had much to offer: tasty, high-fat flesh, feathers for writing instruments and arrows, down for quilts, pillows and clothing, and wings for brooms. In medieval times and later, they were a typical part of agricultural village life on the plains and lowlands of Europe.[41]

They remain a delicious part of traditional Polish cuisine. Zofia Czerny's *Polish Cookbook*[42] contains three recipes for goose: Goose à la Polonaise, Goose with Liver Stuffing, and Goose with Groats Stuffing. For Goose à la Polonaise, her instructions are:

> Soak tenderized goose in cold water for 2–3 hours, rub in salt, divide in half, pour boiling water over goose and cook slowly. Clean mixed vegetables. When meat is half cooked, add vegetables, onion and cook slowly, reducing liquid to 3 cups. Prepare roux with fat and flour, dilute with the stock from the goose, add salt, nutmeg and marjoram to taste. Stir while cooking. Carve goose into serving pieces, place in sauce, heat, mix with egg yolks before serving, arrange on platter with fluffy, parched barley.[43]

Apparently a real treat!

---

41   "Greylag Goose," *iNaturalist*, www.inaturalist.org/taxa/7018-Anser-anser.

42   Zofia Czerny, *Polish Cookbook*, trans. by Christina Cękalska and May Miller (Warsaw: Państwowe Wydawnictwo Ekonomiczne, 1975).

43   Czerny, pp. 260–261.

I'm not sure whether the goose my father painted for me had been a pet or a meal-in-waiting, but Polish food is certainly known for being hearty. When we visited my grandmother's home, she would make for us the most delicious meals: sauerkraut, ham, dumplings *(kluski),* sausage, and Easter bread (lots of buttery smells) are some of the special foods I remember.

The oldest Polish cookbook on record was written by a soldier, chef, and author named Stanislav Czerniecki in 1682 titled *A Collection of Dishes.* From the Middle Ages to the 1800s, Polish food was based on grains such as rye, millet, buckwheat, wheat, meats of wild and farm animals, along with fruits, herbs, local spices, and many vegetables. Potatoes arrived in Europe from the Andes region in the second half of the sixteenth century, but only in the later 1700s was potato growing introduced to Poland.[44] The cottage gardens of Rozpaszka would have yielded cabbage, potatoes, turnip, beets, peas, beans, kohlrabi, and fruits, all of which could be either preserved by canning and salting (pickling) or stored in a root cellar for three or four months. Additionally, there would be herbs, berry producing bushes, flowers, and shrubs and, of course, fruit trees (especially pear and cherry).[45] My two sets of grandparents and my mother always had wonderful gardens. I particularly remember the gooseberries and rhubarb in my grandmother Joanna's garden. In Poland, women often gathered berries, nuts, and mushrooms in the later summer months and the fall.

---

44   Fernand Braudel, *The Structures of Everyday Life: The Limits of the Possible,* vol. 1, *Civilization and Capitalism 15th–18th Century* (New York: Harper and Row, 1985), p. 167.

45   I have relied on Sophie Hodorowicz Knab, *Polish Herbs, Flowers & Folk Medicine: The Peasant Garden* (New York: Hippocrene Books, 1995), pp. 66–71, for some facts, as well as past family gardens.

Sophie Hodorowicz Knab's *Polish Customs, Traditions, and Folklore*[46] contains numerous descriptions of special meals for festive events which were quite frequent in the Polish tradition. At a wedding, for instance, it was a classic universal custom that the first food a married couple ate was *kasza jaglana*, a cereal or porridge made of millet, served unsalted and cooked in milk so that their married life would be sweet. Chicken was also frequently served at Polish weddings, as were peas which were a symbol of fertility. Local foods were always prominent, "but the meal always included sauerkraut, beet soup with noodles, and then *kolacz*, the wedding bread."[47]

The foods were very festive and satisfying – homegrown and homemade, something to be admired. The drink of the Polish peasants was beer, made from brewing wheat, oats, barley, rye, or millet; old recipes also included other ingredients, such as poppy seeds, mushrooms, aromatics, honey, sugar, and bay leaves.[48]

In the Polish-Lithuania Commonwealth, a traditional dish considered to be a Polish national dish is *bigos*, also known as hunter's stew. Occasionally, my mother would make it. I learned from her that it is a combination of various kinds of chopped meats such as pork, beef, poultry, and sausage, sauerkraut or fresh cabbage, fried onions, mushrooms, seasonings such as pepper, allspice, and bay leaves, and other spices as the cook desires or as are common in local custom. In typical Polish fashion, other ingredients were added such as tomato paste, potatoes, prunes, even rye bread – and

---

46   Sophie Hodorowicz Knab, *Polish Customs, Traditions, and Folklore* (New York: Hippocrene Books, 1993).

47   Knab, *Polish Customs*, p. 209.

48   Braudel, p. 238.

---

other suitable leftovers from the fridge. The wide range of ingredients meant there were many recipes for *bigos*.

When my grandmother, then in her seventies, was laid up at her home after an accident, in Barrie, Ontario, the beautiful aroma of the herb wintergreen[49] permeated the house. Knab's *Polish Customs, Traditions, and Folklore* describes the Polish tradition of herbal healing. It was the housewife's job to grow and collect herbs, wildflowers, and other plants from open meadows or the wayside and prepare them for a variety of uses. Such knowledge and skills had been passed down from generation to generation as doctors rarely came to small rural villages.[50] There was sometimes a link to religious folklore and tradition. Here are a couple of examples of herbs that she lists:

> *Bez Czarny* (Sambucus nigra), commonly known as elderberry, or as the Polish people called it, the black, or wild, lilac. The ripened berries were crushed and made into a syrup which was drunk during times of high fever. It also healed whooping cough. The soft, white, inner core of the branch was dug out, and after drying was placed on hot embers. The sick individual was instructed to breathe in the smoky fumes to reduce a cough. Aside from its medicinal properties, however, the elderberry was not favorably looked upon. When the women went into the fields to gather plants, grains, herbs, and flowers to be blessed on the day of Our Lady of Herbs, they gathered all that grew except for the branches of

---

49   Wintergreen is a strong anti-inflammatory and antiseptic herb and is sometimes used as a remedy for rheumatic and arthritic problems.

50   I have relied on Knab, "Brief History of Medicine and the Healing Arts in Poland," in *Polish Herbs*, pp. 33–46. A chapter I highly recommend.

the black lilac, for it was believed that Judas hanged himself on a black lilac tree.[51]

Zywokost (Symphytum officinalae). Commonly named comfrey, this plant was one of the best loved of all healing herbs. This tall, hairy leaved plant was used for all broken bones and also for the aches of rheumatism and the troubles of tuberculosis. The root was cut into small pieces, and then cooked in a small amount of fat and a spoon of honey. This "pap" was applied to the bad bruise, sore, or broken bones to promote healing. Another method of using the root was to soak it in alcohol for a few weeks. The root was then strained out, and the mixture poured into a bottle. The mixture was then used as a liniment and applied to aching areas afflicted with arthritis.[52]

The history of medicine and the healings arts in Poland – indeed, in all of Europe – is a fascinating one and goes back to the influence of Greek and Roman herbal medicine practices which reached many lands. In AD 60, Dioscorides had written a classic text on medicinal cures that included 600 plants, which remained an important source of information until the 1500s. Additionally, Poland was uniquely positioned with respect to travelling merchants and peddlers passing through, and healing methods and plants were exchanged by this means. For many centuries, it was the monks who wrote down medicinal herbal knowledge in manuscripts that were then delivered to other monasteries throughout

---

51   Knab, *Polish Customs*, p. 161.

52   Knab, *Polish Customs*, pp. 164–165.

the continent. These healing practices were used in the areas administered by the monastic settlements.[53]

A medical academy was established in Krakow in 1364, which enabled the translation and expansion of herbal texts and knowledge. Barber-surgeons – who repaired broken bones, carried out bloodletting, prepared medicines, and performed surgeries – formed a guild in 1626. In 1789 the first medical school was founded in Warsaw, but as educating students was slow and costly, there remained an abundance of uneducated practitioners and others from foreign lands in Poland. And of course, fraudsters also plied their trade. Always though, there were folk healers – women, and sometimes men, who knew traditional herbal and other remedies and would apply these for small fees. Often manors had their own stocks of healing herbs and compounds, the recipes passed down from mother to daughter. Later, small pharmacies arose, carrying a much greater assortment of plants (including from India, China, and the Americas), as well as candles, alcoholic beverages, cheese, and other such products. In the 1700s and 1800s, travelling salesmen (often from Hungary) carried rucksacks of medicinal cures, soaps, and perfumes, though sometimes they were regarded as nuisances. For example, in 1774, the town of Kozmin issued an edict to stop travelling salesmen from selling their products. In the later 1800s, as literacy increased, books of herbal remedies were popular and widely available. Many immigrants to America during this time brought with them the book *Herbal or Atlas of Healing Plants*, by Sebastian Kneipp.[54]

---

53   Knab, *Polish Herbs*, pp. 33–35.

54   This history is but a very short selection of facts taken from Knab, *Polish Herbs*, pp. 36–48.

Although Christianity was accepted in Poland in 966, some pagan practices and beliefs continued, including the "evil eye," curses, spells, and superstitions related to preserving one's well-being. Here is an example of a superstition:

> A way to protect one's baby against the influence or potential harm intended by witches is by the use of red, silky ribbons. At home, lightly tying one around a newborn's waist, with the knot around the navel, is said to protect him or her against bad influences and dark spirits. Outside the home, where dangers grow, a ribbon is also tied to the stroller, usually to the handle, with a flowery knot. This functions as a sort of shield to ensure the baby's safety when out and about discovering the world.[55]

Perhaps my father's gift to me of a painting of a goose was a type of red ribbon, a message from a survivalist, of what in his early life served as delicious nourishment that fortified his body, kept him warm with feathers and down, and provided household implements – all which served as protection against want and harm for him in those early days.

---

55   Charles Black, "Babies vs Crones: Red Ribbon Shields," *A Guide to Good and Bad Luck Omens in Poland*, accessed September 14, 2022, www.goodlucksymbols.com/superstition-in-poland/.

CHAPTER FIVE: A HISTORY OF AN ANCESTRAL HOMELAND

I belong to a nation which over the past centuries has experienced many hardships and reverses. The world reacted with silence or with mere sympathy when Polish frontiers were crossed by invading armies and the sovereign state had to succumb to brutal force.

    —Lech Wałęsa, *The Struggle and the Triumph*

The awareness of one's origins is like an anchor line plunged into the deep, keeping one within a certain range. Without it historical intuition is virtually impossible.

    —Czeslaw Milosz

There was no Poland per se from approximately 1795 to 1918 – a hundred and twenty-three years! November 11, 1918 has been regarded as Poland's day of independence. There was some form of government between 1918 and 1921, but during this time, things were not settled entirely as Poles had to fight the Soviet Union, Lithuania, Ukraine, Czechoslovakia, and Germany to define the borders of Poland. In 1920, the Polish Army destroyed the Red Army in the west, which ended in the Treaty of Brest Litovsk and solidified Poland's eastern boundaries. By 1921, all other boundaries were secured.[56]

The present Polish nation is sandwiched between Russia and Germany – two large, powerful and historically aggressive nations.

---

56   Chester M. Sadowski, Ph.D., personal correspondence, December 20, 2022. Much credit must be given to Chester Sadowski who helped me immensely with this chapter. I have used his suggestions in many places. He is a retired chemistry professor who is very knowledgeable of Polish history.

Poland has ocean port cities on the Baltic Sea, including well-known Gdansk. A large river, the Vistula, runs from south to north with its origins in Cieszyn near the Czech border in the Tatra Mountains; the river connects Krakow and Warsaw to the Baltic near Gdansk. The country is predominantly fertile plain, but the south has the beautiful Tatra Mountains (part of the Carpathian range), which form a natural border between Slovakia and Poland.

The greater Poland area has been inhabited by various tribes since the Paleolithic era. There is an archaeological museum at Biskupin located west of Warsaw and north of Poznan detailing a site there of a late Bronze Age and early Iron Age (1800 to 1700 BC) forti-fied settlement, actually a village over a lake. The reconstructed settlement includes a bridge, a tower and rampart, a gateway, and houses for a village that once had about 700 to 1,000 inhabitants.[57]

Mention should be made of the Sarmatians, speculated to be peoples from Iran who migrated between the sixth and fourth centuries BC to parts of Eastern Europe before any modern Slavic people.[58] They were regarded as exceptionally strong and war-like, though there is no conclusive evidence that they were related to the Slavs.[59] Their strength was significant. In the 1500s to 1700s, some Polish nobles came to believe that they were united as nobles because their putative ancestors were Sarmatians. That blood-line gave them military superiority along with the right to shape Polish nationality and to distinguish themselves from peasants who were thought to have no Sarmatian ancestry. These nobles wore

---

57   For further description of this site, see Wieslaw Zajaczkowski, *Biskupin: A Guide to the Archaeological Reservation*, trans. by Alicja Petrus-Zagroba (Wroclaw, Poland: ZET Publishers, 1994).

58   See Tadeusz Sulimirski, *The Sarmatians* (London: Thames and Hudson, 1970).

59   Sadowski, personal correspondence, December 20, 2022.

---

distinctive clothing with an oriental flair and unusual haircuts, but in the 1700s, they increasingly became looked on as obscure and out of touch.

From about the fifth century AD, various Slavic tribes started settling in the area and began banding together. These tribes included the Biezunczanie, Bobrzanie, Dziadoszanie, Goleszyce, Goplans, Lendians, Lubuszanie, Lubuszyce, Masovians, Opolanie, Polans, Pomeranians, Pyrzyczanie, Silesians, Slezanie, Trzebowianie, Vistulans and Wolinanie. The name "Poland" comes from the Polanie tribe – a name meaning the people of the fields[60] – who lived along a river near the modern-day city of Poznan, in central Poland. Poles are considered Western Slavs.

The origin of the term "Slav" is in dispute. There are quite a few opinions. Here are a couple. The word originated from the word "slovo" meaning "word" – Slowian means the person who speaks the language;[61] "Slav" comes from the Indo-European root *kleu* meaning "to hear" occurring in derivatives of fame and glory. A name like Miroslaw means one who attains glory or fame through peace.[62]

The Piast ruling dynasty was established in about 940 AD, named after the semi-legendary leader Piast the Wheelwright who united together a number of smaller tribes. Piast's great-great-grandson, Duke Mieszko I, became the first documented Polish monarch of that dynasty, and he reigned for over six decades from 930 to

---

60   Adam Zamoyski, *The Polish Way: A Thousand-Year History of the Poles and their Culture* (New York: Hippocrene Books Inc., 1987), p. 8.

61   Sadowski, personal correspondence, December 20, 2022.

62   *Word History:* "Slave," in *The American Heritage Dictionary of the English Language,* 5th ed. (New York: Harper Collins, 2022), www.ahdictionary.com/word/search.html

992, the country's boundaries similar to the current ones.[63] He was renowned for the Christianization of Poland and accepted Roman rather than Greek Orthodox Christianity in 966, a "turning point in the history of the culture."[64] It became part of the mainstream civilization of Roman Catholic Europe, and Mieszko was recognized by the pope as a king. He had churches built and was skilful in his foreign relations and military prowess in establishing boundaries. By around 1050, Krakow was the capital.

When pagan "Old Prussians" attacked in north-eastern Poland, the Teutonic Knights, a German military and religious order, assisted Poland at the request of the Duke of Mazovia for intervention on a religious basis. However, the Teutonic Knights turned it into a political opportunity to gain control of the Baltic shore. They took over the port of Gdansk and claimed northern Poland. Later, a horrific invasion of Europe by the Mongols was met by a combined force of the Germans and Poles at the Battle of Legnitz in 1241.[65] It is apparently in dispute as to who were the victors.

In the mid-1300s, King Casimir III the Great (1333–1370), the last of the Piast rulers, reunified some areas and restored Polish rule in the region. Under his rule, Poland became prosperous and powerful, though concessions were made to Bohemia in the southwest and the Teutonic Knights in the north. An enlightened ruler, he established legal, economic, commercial, and educational foundations in the country and promoted Poland as a safe place

---

63 Neal Bedford et al., *Poland* (Fort Mill, South Carolina: Lonely Planet, 2008), pp. 29–30.

64 Ignacy Wieniewski, *Heritage: The Foundation of the Polish Culture*, 2nd ed. (Toronto: Polish-Canadian Women's Federation in Canada, 1981), p. 7.

65 Sadowski, personal correspondence, December 20, 2022.

for Jews.[66] By the end of the sixteenth century, Poland had a larger Jewish population than all of the rest of Europe.

Jews had previously arrived in Poland from several directions. In the 900s, the first Jews, merchants known as Radhanites, came along trade routes to Kiev and Bukhara. Jews banished from Prague arrived in Poland about 1097. The reign of King Boleslaw III (1102–1139) saw religious tolerance and more Jewish immigration from Western Europe. (Interestingly, because many Jews were employed as engravers, some coins minted in the early medieval period had Hebrew inscriptions.) There were times when the Roman Catholic Church pushed for persecution of the Jews but Polish rulers protected them. The Polish–Lithuanian Commonwealth was the only major state in Europe that consistently allowed freedom of religion. However, after the fall of the Commonwealth and the partition and the destruction of Poland as a state in 1795, Polish Jews were subject to new governing powers which were often anti-Semitic. Interestingly, Jews were not persecuted in China or in India.

By the late 1300s, there was dynastic alliance (Lithuanian Grand Duke Jogaila married Queen Jadwiga of Poland) with Lithuania "where Poland gained a partner in skirmishes against the Tatars and Mongols, and Lithuania received help in the fight against the Teutonic Knights."[67] Poland, Lithuania, and various allies defeated the Teutonic Knights in 1410 in the Battle of Grunwald and killed their Grand Master. The Knights, however, still continued to influence northern Poland until their final defeat by Polish forces in the 1500s.[68]

---

66 Bedford et al., *Poland*, p. 30.

67 Bedford et al., *Poland*, p. 31.

68 Sadowski, personal correspondence, December 20, 2022.

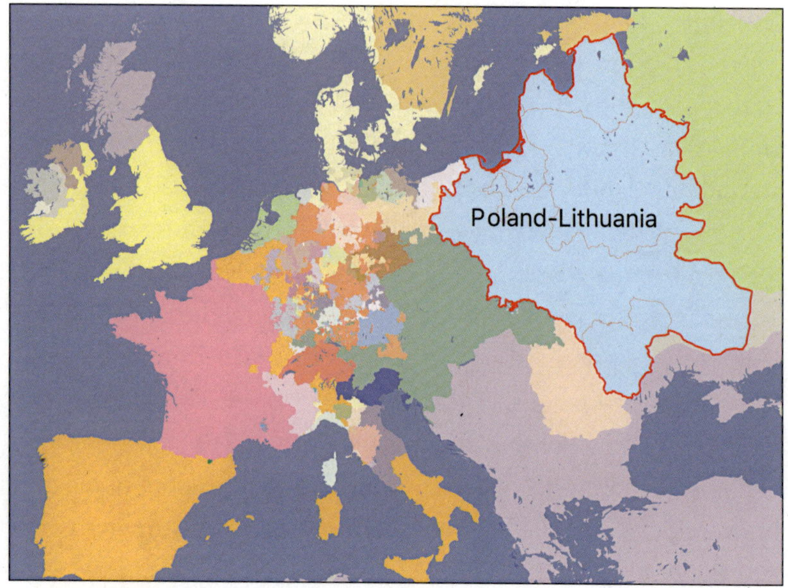

Figure 1: Map of Poland in the 1600s

It has been said that the Golden Age of Poland began in the 1500s during the Jagiellonian Dynasty (1382–1572), when on July 1, 1569, the Union of Lublin was signed by the Crown of the Kingdom of Poland and the Grand Duchy of Lithuania to create the single state, the Polish–Lithuanian Commonwealth. This union, reaching from the Baltic to the Black Sea, included the territories of Podlachia, Volhynia, Podilia, the Bratslav region and the Kviv region. The nobility of those territories were given the same rights and privileges as the Polish nobility. Poland and Lithuania ruled as one but retained their separate ministries, treasuries, and armies. The Polish heavy cavalry, the Hussaria (the Winged Hussars), was the most successful cavalry in Europe from the 1500s to the early 1700s, winning many battles against overwhelming odds. One example of their might was the decisive win at the Battle of Kirchholm, where in twenty minutes they defeated a Swedish army that was three times their size.[69]

Figure 2: Hetman's Guard. Painting of W. Pawliszak

69   Sadowski, personal correspondence, December 20, 2022. It has been referred to as the greatest defeat in Swedish history.

It is important to mention that, during the Golden Age, there was a cultural richness in Poland that was second to none. There were hundreds, perhaps thousands of gorgeous palaces and castles that celebrated the richness of the many peoples that were free to inhabit the country.

Figure 3: Polish Castle Interior, circa 1750

The Age also produced such luminaries as Nicolaus Copernicus (Mikolaj Kopernik) who was born in 1473 in Thorn (Torun), Kingdom of Poland, and died in 1543. He is still regarded as a "Renaissance polymath" – a person with wide-ranging knowledge. He had been an astronomer, a mathematician, and a Catholic canon, and was also a physician, governor, diplomat, and economist. Copernicus formulated the revolutionary theory that the earth revolved around the sun, rather than vice versa, as was then believed. As he feared ridicule, his findings were published at the time of his death. "The condemnation of Copernicus's ideas by the Roman Church, which would have devastated the Catholic canon had he lived to hear of it, probably served to make his book more popular."[70] He was subsequently regarded to have made an extraordinary contribution to the Scientific Revolution.[71]

The union of Poland and Lithuania proved difficult to maintain over the longer term for various reasons. The growing feudal nobility (wealthy landowners) who caused uprisings for civil rights in 1594, 1648, and 1768 as well as use of the parliamentary convention that allowed a single vote to veto an act of Parliament, made legislative progress very difficult. Apparently, foreign agents paid huge bribes to prevent the removal of the veto by the Polish Parliament.[72] Additionally, succession to the Polish throne was uniquely determined by the nobility through a voting process that permitted foreigners to be considered. From 1573 to 1795 (when the Commonwealth ceased to exist), only four of the eleven kings who ruled Poland were native Poles. Others came from countries such as Austria, Denmark, and Sweden.

Special mention must be made of Jan Sobieski, a Pole, who reigned as King of Poland and Grand Duke of Lithuania from 1674 to 1696. He is often regarded as Poland's most illustrious ruler. To his surprise, author Miltiades Varvounis found that no English-speaking author had made this known for many decades, so he wrote a definitive biography of Jan Sobieski which

---

70   Dana Sobel, *A More Perfect Heaven: How Copernicus Revolutionized the Cosmos* (New York: Walker Publishing Company, 2011), p. 226.

71   Other well-known Polish-speaking nobility included the Radziwills and Czartoryskis. See Marek Rostworowski, ed., *The National Museum in Cracow, the Czartoryski Collection: A Historical Outline and Selected Objects* (Warsaw: Arkady, 1980).

72   Iwo Cyprian Pogonowski, *Poland: An Illustrated History* (New York: Hippocrene Books Inc., 2000), pp. 15–16.

was published in 2012.[73] He had a strong need to present to the English-speaking reader

> the achievements of one of the most fascinating men ever to sit on a throne or command an army. A king that lived in an era when the heroic age of warrior kings had almost gone, though not for him, this last European of his kind personally exercised in war after war the supreme military command he had gained; he exercised it with such skill and won with his sword such renown, that he was acclaimed as the greatest soldier of his time.[74]

73 Miltiades Varvounis, *Jan Sobieski: The King Who Saved Europe* (Bloomington, Indiana: Xlibris Publishing, 2012). I have relied on this work by Varvounis for my description of Jan Sobieski and his legacy. My paragraph is, however, very brief and there are many key omissions by myself for the sake of brevity. The book is very thoroughly researched and I consider it a "must read."

74 Varvounis, p. 14.

Figure 4: *Portrait of John III Sobieski (1629–1696), King of Poland*

Jan Sobieski was born in 1629 as a member of the Polish nobility in the Commonwealth city of Olesko (now in Ukraine). He attended college in Krakow in 1643 and graduated from the philosophical faculty of the Jagiellonian University[75] in 1646. After travelling

75   The Jagiellonian University in Krakow is the second oldest university in Central Europe. The oldest is the Charles University in Prague.

for two years in Europe, he joined the army with his brother. He fought in various sieges (at Zamosc, Zboriv, and Beresteczko), received promotions, and was sent by King John II Casimir Vasa as an envoy to the Ottoman Empire where he learned the Tatar and Turkish languages, which served him well in later years. He was active in the Polish regiments when the Swedes invaded, was a commander of a large Tatar cavalry, was elected deputy and later became a member of the Sejm (the Parliament of the Kingdom of Poland), fought against a Russian invasion, and was a treaty negotiator. With more military successes, he became renowned as a military leader and achieved the rank of Grand Hetman of the Crown, the highest military rank in the Commonwealth. Though there was a period of complex politics within the Commonwealth when Sobieski was vilified, partially for his pro-France stance, his victories against the invading Tatars in 1671 put him in good stead with others. Shortly after Sobieski had led a defeat of the Ottomans in the Battle of Khotyn, the king died and Sobieski was elected Monarch of the Commonwealth.

As king he faced huge challenges. After half a century of military actions and defences by the Commonwealth, the treasury was depleted. There were still military threats from the north, but the Ottomans' Muslim empire was the biggest concern as it vied for supremacy in Central and Western Europe. There were many complex battles, alliances made and broken, and fierce fighting during those times, but the most notable was the Battle of Vienna in 1683. King Sobieski was in joint command of the Polish and German troops against the invading Ottoman Turks under Kara Mustafa. It was a very vicious battle, but as a result of the military genius of King Sobieski, the invaders were defeated. Pope Innocent XI and other foreign dignitaries hailed him as the saviour not only of

Vienna but also of Western European civilization and Christianity in Europe.

By the early 1700s, though, Poland was in decline and the Russian tsars began intruding into the country's politics; by the middle of that century, their involvement had become more apparent. *The Last King of Poland* by the historian and author Adam Zamoyski sets out in great detail all that led up to the tragic loss of a country.[76] In 1755, a twenty-three-year-old Pole named Stanislaw August Poniatowski was working as the secretary to the English ambassador in St. Petersburg, Russia. He was introduced to and shortly thereafter became romantically involved with the then Grand Duchess Catherine Alekseyevna. Their romance affected Stanislaw's view of and relationship with Russia for the duration of his life. In his memoir, he recorded that "at that moment [when he became involved with Catherine] I forgot there was a Siberia," referencing the fact that those who incurred imperial displeasure were punished with banishment.[77]

Following a *coup d'état* in 1762 that overthrew her husband, Peter III, the grand duchess became Catherine the Great, Empress of Russia. Through her help, Stanislaw became King of Poland in 1764 and enjoyed some good years. However, Catherine proved to be a powerful leader and was set on expanding her empire through both conquest and diplomacy. Stanislaw would later be accused of naively believing that he and Catherine had a special relationship and that she would respect his views and wishes regarding Poland. This was not the case. Around 1768, Catherine designated herself

---

76   Adam Zamoyski, *The Last King of Poland* (London: Phoenix Giant, 1998). I learned a lot from this book and the material below is substantially from that excellent work.

77   Zamoyski, *The Last King of Poland,* quoting Stanislaw III, *Memoires Secrets et Inedits de Stanislas Auguste,* 1762, pp. 56–57.

the protector of the political rights of dissidents and peasants in the Commonwealth which provoked anti-Russian uprisings in Poland.[78]

Increasingly weak, Poland was ultimately partitioned in 1772, losing one-third of its territory and two-fifths of its population to Prussia under Frederick II, to Russia under Catherine the Great, and to Austria under Empress Maria Theresa. Stanislaw had attempted other alliances with Great Britain and France but had been unsuccessful. Access to the Baltic Sea was now in the hands of Prussia, which imposed high tariffs. Some in Western Europe regarded Poland as unsophisticated and ungovernable and hence had little interest in protecting it. Meanwhile, Frederick II of Prussia referred to it as a "royal cake" for the taking.

In 1775, a new constitution was presented and the Sejm was changed. The new government consisted of a Permanent Council and a Commission of National Education. In essence, Stanislaw became president, and many of the former Crown appointments were now the prerogative of the Council. The Russian Empire supervised the Council through its ambassadors and envoys. This new arrangement did result in some economic revival and resurgence of culture and education in Poland, but complications and strife continued.

Then on May 3, 1791, a remarkable constitution, supported by Stanislaw, was enacted to redress long-standing defects in the Polish-Lithuanian Commonwealth.[79] It was the first constitution of its type in Europe and created a constitutional monarchy, supplanting

---

78   See Zamoyski, *The Last King of Poland*, pp. 152–172.

79   May 3 is still celebrated in Poland as Constitution Day.

---

the anarchy fostered by powerful magnates.[80] Unfortunately, it survived for just one year. Concerned that this constitution might regenerate the power of the Commonwealth, Catherine provided support to a Polish anti-reform group called the Confederacy of the Bar[81], which defeated Polish loyalist forces in 1792 and 1794. In 1795, Catherine succeeded in the second partition of Poland, again among Russia, Prussia, and Austria, and the country of Poland per se disappeared off the map for 123 years.[82] (It is of some heart-warming consolation that the Ottoman Empire and Persia did not recognize the Partitions of Poland.) Stanislaw was summoned to St. Petersburg in Russia to establish residence there. Catherine died in 1796 and Stanislaw August Poniatowski, the last King of Poland, died the following year. He is not well regarded by many Poles even though he was a progressive ruler who favoured the arts and culture in Poland.

---

80   The Commission for Education set up by the 1791 constitution was the first Department or Ministry of Education in Europe.

81   Sadowski, personal correspondence, December 20, 2022.

82   My father and his family came from the Russian Partition of Poland; my mother's family came from Galicia, in the Austrian Partition.

Figure 5: Map of Central and Eastern Europe in 1900 showing the extent of the three empires that partitioned the Polish-Lithuanian Commonwealth.

Jerome Blum's book *In the Beginning: The Advent of the Modern Age: Europe in the 1840s*[83] describes how nationalism in Polish communities sprang up in the Romantic period of the late 1700s and early 1800s. A popular belief circulating at the time was that God had divided the human race into nationalities, each with a role to play in a divine plan, often one with messianic overtones.[84] For instance, certain Polish nationalists called Poland the Christ among nations – crucified and martyred through no fault of its own, but who, through its struggles and suffering, would redeem and liberate all other nations.[85] Adam Mickiewicz was viewed as a

---

83   Jerome Blum, *In the Beginning: The Advent of the Modern Age Europe in the 1840's* (New York: C. Scribner's Sons, 1994), c. 3.

84   Blum, *In the Beginning*, p. 89.

85   Blum, *In the Beginning*, pp. 8–90.

messianic nationalist who promoted the union of all Slavic people under the leadership of Poland.[86]

The Poles tried their best to continue as a cultural entity, and several unsuccessful insurrections occurred during the 1800s and early 1900s, the most significant being the November Uprising in 1830-1831, the January Uprising in 1863-1864 (both uprisings initiated and organized by nobles), and the Revolution of 1905. (The uprising in the major Polish industrial centre of Lodz in 1905 was precipitated by a strike of Polish textile workers because of poor working conditions. A large general protest that followed was eventually crushed, and many hundreds of Poles were killed or wounded.) Uprisings and protests continued throughout Russia from 1905 to 1907.[87] Unfortunately, these attempts resulted in even greater loss of liberty for the Poles.

Less than a decade later, the First World War broke out. Much of the fighting was on Polish lands, resulting in great loss of lives and livelihoods. Many Poles were conscripted into the Russian, German, or Austrian armies, which meant that some Poles had to fight against each other. In 1917, Russia became preoccupied with civil war, and in 1918, the Austrian Empire collapsed, and the German army withdrew from Warsaw. Polish sovereignty was declared by Marshall Jozef Pilsudski who became a hero to all Poles.

An insightful memoir was written by Professor William Rose (1885–1968), who lived in Poland for a number of years and learned the Polish language.

---

86   Blum, *In the Beginning*, p. 90.

87   Much more beyond my very brief description of the 1905 uprising is fully described in Abraham Ascher, *The Revolution of 1905: Russia in Disarray* (Stanford, California: Stanford University Press, 1988).

The years 1914–19 completely altered my outlook on European civilization, whether the culture of the individual or of the group. It amounted to an introduction to the "submerged" half of Europe, in particular to people and peoples numbering nearly 100,000,000 souls who had been living in a state of arrested development for centuries and whose lives had been violently interrupted more than once through the ages while the West had been going on in relatively undisturbed fashion. . . . It had remained almost totally a rural, agricultural society, and so was looked down on as "backward."[88]

Given the Poles' lengthy history of cultural and political oppression, I can see why there was extensive emigration from cities, towns, and the countryside in the late 1800s and early 1900s. As well, the countryside in Poland became overcrowded and there was no work in the cities as some cities had passed laws preventing peasants from settling there.[89]

---

88   Daniel Stone, ed., *The Polish Memoirs of William John Rose* (Toronto: University of Toronto Press, 1975), p. 4.

89   Sadowski, personal correspondence, December 20, 2022.

CHAPTER SIX: A FARM/VILLAGE IN THE RUSSIAN PARTITION

I believe that each person has a favorite place, a tree, a mountain, or a beach which they want to come back to, even if the return can only take place in the boundaries of their imagination.
—Sana Szewczyk, *Under a Ginkgo Tree and Other Stories*

I grew up knowing that I had some Polish heritage and a Polish last name, which I thought was easy to spell and pronounce (though it tripped up many others despite not containing "szcz," "rzy," or other such combinations). I was taught to refer to my grandmother as *babcia* and my grandfather as *dziadek*, but that was about the extent of the Polish I knew. On visits to my grandparents, just a few words to us children were exchanged in English; there were lots of hugs, and then we ran out to play in the backyard while my parents and grandparents spoke in Polish. I attempted to learn some Polish in recent years through a university night course. I soon found that the Latin courses I excelled at in high school and that were helpful in learning French and Spanish, were of no help in learning Polish. Though Polish has a Latin-based alphabet with diacritics on certain consonants and vowels, the vocabulary was very foreign. My oldest brother had been taught Polish as a child by my parents, but he was beaten up by some boys for speaking Polish when my family lived in La Tuque, Quebec. None of the rest of us was taught to speak Polish so that we would not be subject to such bullying. My parents came to realize that it was best to raise us to fit into the predominantly British culture of southern Ontario where we moved soon after leaving La Tuque. Because I was white and spoke English, as a child I didn't hesitate to conclude that I should be like the rest of my friends and school chums, and I bought right into all of Canada's British-based culture. I came to think that I was just an Anglo-Saxon with a funny last name and parents who weren't quite in step with the times. But why were we not like the family in *Father Knows Best*, a popular 1950s program that I watched weekly as a young girl? At the time, it didn't occur to me that there could be extraordinary reasons for our differences. Only later in life did I become inquisitive about my heritage, especially as I came across stories from immigrants to Canada.

I vaguely knew of my father's childhood from a scant and rarely discussed memoir he had written in his later years. In that memoir I discovered that he had been born in a small Polish village farm at a time when Poland as a country did not exist. This, I subsequently learned, was why, in the ship's manifest I found on a library microfilm reel, Russia was listed as his country of birth. Looking at my father's painting of the goose, I wondered whether he recalled geese from his childhood, summoning from his memory this distant trace of his earliest roots. I was intrigued and wanted to know more, not just about him but about my grandmother as well.

This is the story of Rozpaszka, the agricultural farm enterprise where my grandmother and grandfather, and their three children (one of whom was my father) lived until 1914 when they immigrated to Canada. My father never spoke about Rozpaszka, so for most of my life I knew nothing about this farm or how and why the family left. Until I began my investigations, it was simply a name on the back of two photos from a trip he had made in 1934 to his birthplace, one of which showed him visiting with his paternal grandfather on the Ostrowski farm.

When I first heard of Rozpaszka, I scoured a current map of Poland, but it was nowhere to be seen. Although I subsequently learned it was about ninety-sixty kilometres east of Vilnius, the capital of Lithuania, I could find out nothing more. On a tour to the Baltic countries in 2016, I was in Vilnius and asked a tour guide for help. With that assistance and some more online searching, I finally found the name "Folwark Rozpaszka" on an old map. The location had become a great mystery for me so this was a substantial find.

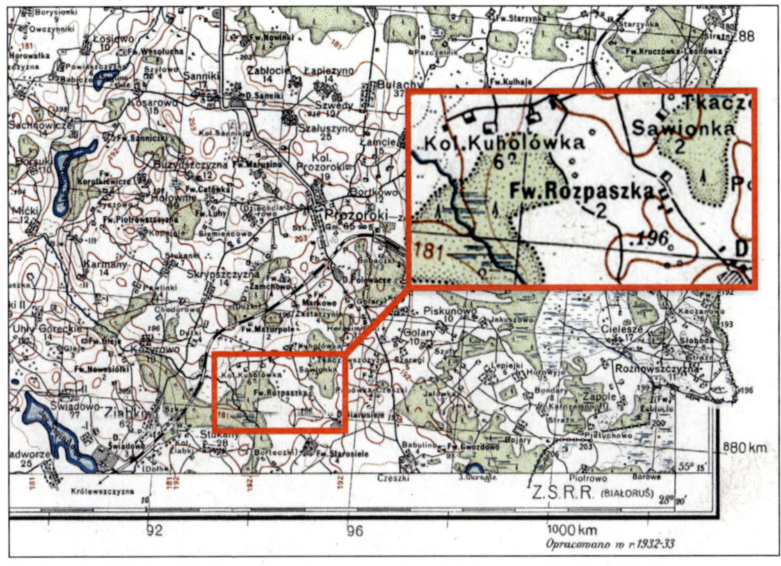

Figure 6: Map showing location of *Folwark* Rozpaszka

In pre-partition Poland, these lands were part of the Polish-Lithuanian Commonwealth and were divided between two voivodships[90] – the Vilnius and Polock governorates. In 1793, these lands came under Russian rule. Rozpaszka is now in Belarus, but when my grandmother and father were born in 1888 and 1911, respectively,

---

90   A voivodeship is the highest-level administrative division of Poland, similar to a province in Canada.

it was in the Russian Partition of Poland, Dzisna county, Prozoroki parish and the Vilnius governorate. It was a multinational area consisting of Poles, Polonized Lithuanians, and Belarusians, who comprised over 50% of the population, as well as Ukrainian noble elites, Jews, Armenians, Tatars, gypsies, and others.[91] It was an agricultural area with lots of marshes and wetlands and relatively poor soil. Accordingly, it was one of the least populated areas in Poland and one of the least developed urban populations. Even in 1921, none of the district towns had more than 5,000 inhabitants.[92]

The designation "folwark" on the old map described a large agricultural farm as part of a larger estate worked by serfs, possibly near a village or inside a village. *Folwarks* were prevalent in Polish lands from the 1300s, in Lithuania from the 1400s, in the Polish-Lithuanian Commonwealth, and after the partitioning of the Commonwealth, in the Russian Partition until the early 1900s.[93] In the earliest days, *folwarks* were centred on church grounds; later, becoming part of the feudal manorial system, they were taken over by the nobility and rich peasants. The purpose of these large agricultural enterprises was to produce surplus food for export and profit by the feudal lords.

The crops varied, depending on the nature of the region's soil. There were clay soils in the lowlands and sandier soils in the uplands.

---

91   Interestingly, in the 1919 census surveys, there was a large number of people undecided about their nationality.

92   Many facts from this paragraph are taken from Zbigniew Zalas, "Powiat dziśnieński województwa wileńskiego w latach 1919–1939" ("Today's district of the Vilnius voivodeship in the years 1919-1939"), *Lituano-Slavica Posnaniensia: Studia Historica* 13 (2008): 169–215, as translated with internet help by Andrzej Mankowski, September 30, 2020.

93   George Orwell's *Animal Farm* (London: Secker and Warburg, 1945) was intended as a satire of these large agricultural entities.

Rye, oats, wheat, barley, potatoes, sugar beets, peas, apples, various berries, cucumbers, and tomatoes seem to have been common. Recipes from the late 1800s also incorporated mushrooms, dill, marjoram, caraway, venison, and cabbage. Farm animals included cattle, pigs, horses, goats, and free-ranging poultry. Fertilization with chemical fertilizers was almost non-existent.[94]

In the Middle Ages peasants who had their freedom worked on rented lots on a lord's manor and owed the lord a few days of unpaid labour each year. But in the 1500s, the labour requirement was increased and new legislation stipulated strict conditions for the peasants, including a ban on them moving away. At this point, they were regarded as serfs (the lowest rung in the peasant class). In the 1600s, when the prices of agricultural goods fell, the serfs' situation worsened, and they essentially were in a regime of exploitation by and dependency on the lord of the manor. The Russian peasants' experience of serfdom has been regarded as the most severe and oppressive in Europe. Scholar Jerome Blum in *Lord and Peasant in Russia* wrote: "The serf lived always at the mercy of the whims, appetites, and temper of his owner."[95] Serfs also were burdened with paying taxes to the state and being drafted into the army.

Blum provided a useful description of the basic labour economy of the western provinces that had been annexed from Poland in the 1700s,[96] in particular White Russia (an old name for the lands of Belarus), Lithuania and the southwest. Under Polish rule, the lord of each agricultural estate and the peasants living there had to draw up an "inventory" that set out the size of the peasants'

---

94   Zalas, p. 194.

95   Jerome Blum, *Lord and Peasant in Russia: From the Ninth to the Nineteenth Century* (Princeton: Princeton University Press, 1961), p. 437.

96   Blum, *Lord and Peasant*, pp. 461–462.

holdings and the fixed amount of dues they accordingly had to pay; each peasant family's obligations varied in proportion to the size of its holdings. A full holding consisted of ploughland, meadow, house lot, and garden. Apparently, few peasant families had a full holding; some had only a house lot and garden, and some were landless, living as boarders in the homes of other peasants. When Russia took over those lands, there were a number of complicated changes over the following decades regarding the obligations of peasants and lords, including the introduction of taxes, but what was constant was serfdom.

The agricultural land holdings of serfs were presided over by a noble who lived in a manor house called a *dwor*, an arrangement that continued until the communist takeover of Poland and the end of nobility by a decree in 1944. *Dwors* had originally been built by knights in a castle-like defensive style, but they later became the homes of the nobility and other landowners. Nobles apparently disliked city life, preferring their homes in the countryside and retaining only apartments in the city. As most of these manor houses were made of wood, many have deteriorated but a few still remain. Some *dwors* were not particularly large, but others had many guest rooms and even private chapels. Besides benches, cupboards, tables, beds, and chairs, *dwors* might have chests and wardrobes made from linden wood, often painted green, inlaid, and engraved. The decorations were elaborate.

> The walls were covered with tapestries, rugs, and gaudy Italian *coltrine*. Persian and Turkish carpets were highly prized. Ancient weapons and hunting trophies hung in places of honor to stress the noble virtues.[97]

---

97 Norman Davies, *God's Playground: A History of Poland*, vol. 1, *The Origins to 1795* (New York: Columbia University Press, 1982), p. 249.

Needless to say, the homes of the serfs and peasants were basic and bore little resemblance to the *dwors.*

Figure 7: Manor House (Dwor)

The history of serfs in the Russian Partition in the 1800s varies with place and time – in the provinces of Kiev, Volynia, Grodno, and Kovno, serfs' obligations were lighter than elsewhere. Conditions in greater Russia generally were harsh and revolts were not unusual; for instance, "between 1835 and 1854 rioting peasants killed 144 estate owners and twenty-nine of their stewards," and troops were called to restore order 381 times.[98] Emancipation came slowly. In Russia in 1861, the Emancipation Manifesto granted freedom to many millions of serfs, but it was years later before legislation was

---

98   Blum, *In the Beginning,* p. 312.

enacted to end all service obligations. In *Our Forgotten Past*, Blum wrote that "in most lands the decree hailed as the law that freed the peasantry did not really end their servile status. Despite the ringing declarations of freedom, much of the old servitude remained."[99] Prior to this, freed peasants in some areas were granted land but had to pay indemnifications for it. In the Baltic, peasants were freed but without land. The People's Republic of Poland in 1944 finally abolished *folwarks,* nationalizing them to form state-owned collective rural enterprises or partitioning them, with little or no compensation to the owners.

My grandmother and grandfather and their three children were born on a *folwark*, which they may have owned to some degree. It could have been a poor farm as my grandmother was from a large family, being the youngest of twelve children. Genealogical research has yielded some indications that the Pietkiewicz family (my grandmother's birth name) and the Ostrowski family (my grandfather's birth name) had at one time been in the nobility; both names are associated with a noble title and a coat of arms. Prior to 1578, Polish kings had granted these distinctions to individuals for performing services for the country, distinguishing themselves in battle, holding a prominent position in government and/or owning a landed estate and swearing loyalty to the sovereign. However, this pleasant finding must be taken in context – in the 1600s, nobility made up over 10% of the population as coats of arms and noble status were inherited by all family members. The lesser nobility paid little in taxes "but often owned such tiny holdings that they lived at a subsistence level and were no better off than the peasantry."[100]

---

99   Blum, *Our Forgotten Past*, p. 71.

100   Blum, *Our Forgotten Past*, p. 91.

Figure 8: Photo of Henry and his grandfather, Ignacy Ostrowski, at the Ostrowski home in Rozpaszka 1934

As generations of families expanded, land was divided and households were supported by working fathers, but there were still privileges associated with coming from a noble family, and minor nobility could serve wealthy citizens who owned large tracts of land, castles, towns, and factories. However, once part of Poland came under Russian rule in 1795, and particularly after the Polish uprising in 1830, the tsar reorganized the remnants of Polish central and regional authorities and reformed the laws governing the nobility. By 1836, the number of nobles had been greatly reduced, as the reforms eliminated those who could not produce full and verifiable heraldic documentation and who did not own entire villages. Rebel nobles from the uprising and those convicted of crimes were also excluded. The new model was based on the Russian system of aristocracy, where privileges such as exemption from taxes and shortened military service were given to those who had been outstanding in military and civilian professions.[101] Further Russification occurred after the 1863 January uprising, which resulted in additional reduction in the number of nobles. The character of what had been Poland was being decimated.

The First World War brought a big change to Poland because the partitioning powers – the German, Russian and Austrian-Hungarian Empires – had changed through defeat or collapse. The five lands around the Baltic Sea – Finland, Estonia, Latvia, Lithuania, and Poland – were finally allowed to become independent republics after the war. Poland, though diminished in size with the actual borders settled in 1922, was back on the map. However, its location between Germany and Russia was still problematic as the events in the 1930s showed. Poland now was two-thirds Polish speaking, but included five million Ukrainians, three million Jews, and about 750,000 Germans.

One might well ask what lay ahead for those Poles who chose not to emigrate before the First World War, which was the case for many of my relatives from Poland. The years following were extremely violent as I learned from reading *Bloodlands: Europe between Hitler and Stalin*, by Yale historian Timothy Snyder.[102] Though I had known that Poland and the surrounding areas were not good places

---

101 Iwona Dakiniewicz, "How the Tsar Decimated the Polish Nobility," *Rodziny* 40, 4 (Fall 2017): 3–4. I have relied on this well-regarded article in my writing on this subject but there is much more in this article that interested readers should consult, including some lists of applications for nobility in the 1800s.

102 Timothy Snyder, *Bloodlands: Europe between Hitler and Stalin* (New York: Basic Books, 2010). For a horrific story of the early life of a child during these times, see Wesley Adamczyk, *When God Looked the Other Way: An Odyssey of War, Exile and Redemption* (Chicago: University of Chicago Press, 2004).

to be during the last few hundred years, I was shocked to hear that masses of people had been terribly treated, starved, and killed there. Snyder describes the "bloodlands" as extending from central Poland to western Russia, through the Soviet Ukraine, Belarus and the Baltic States. After extensive research, Snyder concluded that fourteen million people in this area were murdered between 1933 and 1945 while both Hitler and Stalin were in power, and "not a single one of the fourteen million murdered was a soldier on active duty. Most were women, children and the aged; none were bearing weapons; many had been stripped of their possessions, including their clothes."[103] According to Snyder, this was a period of political mass murder. "Both regimes shot educated Polish citizens in the tens of thousands and deported them in the hundreds of thousands." And it was not concentration camps that claimed most of the victims; more than half died because they were denied food. "The two largest mass killing actions after the Holocaust… [were] Stalin's directed famines of the early 1930s and Hitler's starvation of Soviet prisoners of war in the early 1940s."[104] Indeed, "[t]he bloodlands were no political territory, real or imagined; they are simply where Europe's most murderous regimes did their most murderous work."[105] Snyder's is a unique perspective in that before his book, there had been no definitive history of the "bloodlands" as places of mass killings excluding the Holocaust and Stalin's artificial famine in the Ukraine.

The "bloodlands" are where many of my relatives who did not emigrate lived, eking out some semblance of a life and dying who

---

103 Snyder, p. viii.

104 Snyder, p. xiv.

105 Snyder, p. xviii.

knows how. According to Snyder, "[i]n the Soviet Ukraine, Soviet Belarus, and the Leningrad district, lands where the Stalinist regime had starved and shot some four million people [from 1931 to 1939], German forces managed to starve and shoot even more in half the time."[106] It's hard to imagine such lands as your ancestral home, scarred with such suffering, hatred, fear, and death. I learned from a Pietkiewicz cousin that my great-uncle, his grandfather, was a forest warden who had been shot dead by the Russians in 1939 because he was wearing a forestry jacket; his son was sent to a Russian gulag. Many Ostrowskis and Pietkiewiczs are listed on the memorial for those murdered in the 1940 Katyn massacre of nearly 22,000 Polish military officers and intelligentsia prisoners of war. My maternal Polish relatives' ancestral home in Makeniska near Podkemien was filled with villagers; doors were locked and the house was burned to the ground by Ukrainian Nationalists (the Ukrainian Insurgent Army) and Russians in about 1944. The catastrophic massacre of an estimated several hundred thousand Poles has been described in *Ethnic Cleansing of Poles in Volhynia and Eastern Galicia 1942–1946*, by Mikolaj Terles,[107] and in the *Vengeance of the Swallows: Memoir of a Polish Family's Ordeal*, by Tadeusz Piotrowski.[108] Additionally, hundreds of Jews, Russians, Czechs, Georgians, and Ukrainians who were part of Polish families or that hid Poles were also massacred.

---

106 Snyder, p. xi.

107 Mikolaj Terles, *Ethnic Cleansing of Poles in Volhynia and Eastern Galicia 1942–1946* (Toronto: Alliance of the Polish Eastern Provinces, 1991).

108 Tadeusz Piotrowski, *Vengeance of the Swallow: Memoir of a Polish Family's Ordeal under Soviet Aggression, Ukrainian Ethnic Cleansing and Nazi Enslavement, and Their Emigration to America* (Jefferson, North Carolina: McFarland and Company, 2009).

To this day I am shocked and horrified at how Poland, once a strong, vibrant entity in Europe was reduced to a weakened, struggling, bullied country. My first taste of the hardships endured by the Poles since the decline of their Golden Age was a trip I took to Poland in July 1979 when it was under communist Russian rule. Poland came under Russian rule by way of an agreement in 1945 at the Yalta Conference, which provided for the formation of a provisional government of Poland to be orchestrated by Stalin who demanded Soviet sphere of political influence in Eastern and Central Europe. The Polish government-in-exile based in London, England, since 1940 was ignored.

The trip started from Brussels, Belgium, where we visited my oldest brother and his family who had been living there for a few years. I was looking forward to an adventuresome relaxing train ride from Brussels to Warsaw that would take us through the Iron Curtain and into Berlin. The Iron Curtain or the Berlin Wall had separated Western Europe from Poland, Eastern Germany, Czechoslovakia, Hungary, Yugoslavia, Romania, Bulgaria, Albania, and the Soviet Union since 1946, and the beginning of the Cold War. While waiting at the train station, we saw numerous sleek locomotives and passenger trains stop, load on genteel passengers with leather luggage, and then depart on a smooth accelerated pace from the station – very modern and comfortable looking. However, the train we were to take was not one of those. I was taken aback when a slow-moving, rusty, antiquated train chugged in with passengers hanging out of windows and sitting on suitcases in the doorways and down the aisles. That was our train to Warsaw! Yes, we sat on our suitcases in the aisle or on a cramped bench the whole way to Warsaw (approximately 1,120 kilometres) – the washroom was close to non-functioning, and I will say no more on that. The train stopped for several hours at Checkpoint Charlie, the crossing from

West to East Berlin, during which armed guards passed slowly through the passenger cars and checked all documentation, while their counterparts used large mirrors to search under each train car for stowaways and contraband. It was quite nerve-racking.

Arriving in Warsaw was another education piece for me – the station was sparsely populated, and I did not hear a word of English, French, or any language in which I could recognize Latin vocabulary. An older grey-haired man, looking somewhat anxious, was pacing up and down the train platform – that was my mother's cousin, Janusz, who was looking for us. He spoke not a word of English or French, but he spoke Polish, German, and Russian. As my husband had some background in German, we were able to have an enjoyable visit to his little apartment in a concrete highrise for a simple meal.

Figure 9: Photo of a street in Warsaw, 1979, by author.

We toured reconstructed Warsaw, a city that was almost completely destroyed in the Second World War; we went to the market near the town square where there was not a banana or orange to be found – just turnips, onions, cabbages, and some tomatoes. Janusz explained that most of the local produce was sent to Russia; there were no imported foods. The near-empty local bakery we passed by had a line-up down the block for bread – I doubt many were able to get a loaf. After leaving Warsaw and having visited Auschwitz (the memories of that room full of eye glasses, another room from floor to ceiling filled with shoes still haunt me today), we visited other relatives, including my cousin Teresa Pietkiewicz, her husband, and her daughter in Luban, a city in the southwest of Poland that had been at various times Hungarian, German, and Prussian, as well as a prisoner-of-war camp during the First World War before becoming part of Poland. The Russians had moved many of the Polish inhabitants of eastern Poland/Russia to this city which explains why the Pietkiewiczs lived there and not near Rozpaszka. My cousin Teresa lived with her husband and daughter and her father (my father's first cousin) in a small ageing bungalow with a garden, overshadowed by a concrete grey high-rise apartment. We were given their best for a family dinner party – tomatoes, onions, bread, canned spam, and a few vegetables from their garden. Teresa spoke some French so I was able to converse somewhat with her. I offered to pay for her family to visit us in Canada, but Teresa refused as she was worried that her daughter would never return to her home in Poland after seeing what other countries could offer.

My trip to Poland was very enlightening and it was wonderful to meet relatives I had never met. But I left in sadness to see a country that was isolated, held back, and crippled – so different from its Golden Days. Some years later I came to understand why

education and religion were important values for my family, coming from a country that had been a leader in education centuries
ago and had had high regard for the religious beliefs of all. Family
and community had also been important for Poles as they relied
on each other in their homes and villages.

CHAPTER SEVEN: A VILLAGE SETTING

We have failed to track our formative history across the Atlantic.
  —Ken McGoogan, *Celtic Lightning*

Manorial farm enterprises and peasant villages in the Russian Partition were self-sufficient entities – in their own world – as few villagers travelled. It was a simple world with a fragile existence surviving in a context of oppression. For those who left and endured the many challenges and changes required by emigration, their reflective and sometimes sentimental descriptions of their lost village life can give us insight into the solidity of the Polish character. Such people remembered the beauty of their natural surroundings despite the fact their country was lost to them.

Figure 10: A Village in Russia, 1889

In 1920 a unique sociological study was published in the United States by William Thomas and Florian Znaniecki on Poles from the Russian Partition who immigrated to America between 1880 and 1910. *The Polish Peasant in Europe and America*[109] comprised five volumes totalling 2,244 pages. This work is unique in that the authors studied social change by relying on a new category of sources: life histories, letters, and other documents attesting to the subjective experiences of immigration and the new lives of Polish immigrants in the United States.

Volume III contains a 312-page autobiography of one Polish immigrant who describes in detail his early life in his native village of Lubotyn in the province of Kalisz, just west of Lodz, as well as his immigration to America. His date of birth is not indicated, but I presume from the context that it would have been in the later 1800s. Though his native village was west of Warsaw whereas my grandparents' (and father's) village lay to the east, his was a first-hand description of a Polish village under Russian rule before the First World War,[110] depicting rigid dependency on the manor-owner and the resulting despondency of the inhabitants. He wrote that, in his manorial village,

> all the inhabitants are more or less dependent upon the manor-owner, and there is the most minute social hierarchy from the manor-owner down, in the order of priest, steward, teacher, tavern-keeper, organist, butler, teamster, blacksmith, carpenter, shepherds, etc. and finally the common laborers.

---

109 William I. Thomas and Florian Znaniecki, *The Polish Peasant in Europe and America*, vols. I–II (Chicago: University of Chicago Press, 1918), and vols. III-V (Boston: Gorham Press, 1919). In this chapter, I refer to vol. III.

110 It had previously been under Prussian rule until the defeat of Napoleon in 1814.

There is no real community, no unique and consistent social opinion, no permanence of tradition; servility, desire to climb, with little opportunity to climb."[111]

As set out in the *Polish Peasant*, a manorial village was different than a peasant village in that the peasant village "is a community of equals, in spite of differences of wealth, with a large amount of autonomy in internal matters. There is a religious dependence upon the priest, a remnant of respect for the noble, fear of the official, but the influence of the community is incomparably stronger than any external influences."[112]

His native village however, was set in a charming landscape, a setting perhaps from the Golden Age of Poland.[113] There were ten houses, an old-style brick church on a hill, and the priest's house. To the south was a beautiful orchard belonging to the priest and to the west was the organist's house. Another road led to the cemetery 3,000 feet away and then "the wide world." There was an old but neat wooden school building on the other side of the main road surrounded on three sides by flower beds. Beyond the school were three other houses belonging to the manor, housing two fishermen and a shepherd, four drivers, the land-steward, the cattle-keeper, and the watchman. To the west was the manorial farmyard with buildings arranged in a square and, beyond that, the manorial land. On the right-hand side of the manor was a small wooden chapel, to the east, the manorial garden, and on the south side, a big lake. The old wooden manor house was in the middle of the garden, and

---

111   Thomas and Znaniecki, vol. III, p. 90.

112   Thomas and Znaniecki, vol. III, p. 90.

113   The description of this village below is taken from Thomas and Znaniecki, vol. III, pp. 89–91.

a beautiful alley of lime trees led to the highway. A forge stood on the east side of the garden, and near the forge was a steep footpath that village people used to access the lake for water. And there was a large old tavern built with unburned bricks as well as a stable. "Such," he said, "was my native village."[114]

The village surroundings are described in some detail as well. On the south side, the lake was overgrown with dense reeds inhabited by crested larks, constantly singing; women washed linen on the shore and children bathed. On the north side of the lake was a large, dense forest where mushrooms, strawberries, and blackberries could be picked and nuts gathered. The west and east sides were also forested and good for picking mushrooms.

> But this was not all that adorned Lubotyn. I must add that in the triangle between the church and the tavern was a pond, and around it a meadow from which the tavern-keeper gathered hops. . . . The pond made the village still more beautiful, for on summer evenings it was pleasant to listen to the croaking of frogs, that were not silent until late in the night. And to this must be added the song of the nightingale that made its nest every year in the manorial garden.[115]

Such were the nostalgic memories of a Polish man who immigrated to America and described a sentimental picture of his native village setting.

I was able to find another first-hand description of a village, Ryswianka, near the 1921 Polish–Soviet border in the province of

---

114   Thomas and Znaniecki, vol. III, p. 90.

115   Thomas and Znaniecki, vol. III, p. 91.

Wolyn, which is south of Rozpaszka but relatively close to it. In his opening chapter, Tadeusz Piotrowski, author of *Vengeance of the Swallows*, has romantic memories of the beautiful setting of his village as it existed in the early 1920s:

> Even now, when I hear that long-forgotten name, my thoughts take wing like a startled watch of nightingales launched skyward by the sudden peal of thunder. Rainbow colours flood my imagination. Images of long, winding, country roads, of wooden structures with stucco walls, of thatched roofs, of verdant fields heavy with their bounty, of roaming livestock, harnessed brood mares, and domestic fowl surface in my consciousness…

Call us provincial but to us all the province of Wolyn – with its still enchanted predominately forested and marshy terrain, its numerous Ukrainian and Polish villages, and its far-flung but, by erstwhile standards, prosperous towns, was the whole world although tales abounded of the East – of Moscow, the Ural Mountains, and the great Siberian wastelands; and of the West – of Germany's forbidding Black Forest and of the vast civilized world beyond. Except for the veterans of the foreign wars, few people from our village, at least in living memory, had actually ventured forth into those great beyonds. Except for the roving Gypsies – forever trafficking in relics of the true cross, feathers from the wings of the Archangel Gabriel, and the vials of salty tears from the eyes of the Blessed Virgin Mary – few had ever come to us therefrom.[116]

---

116 Piotrowski, p. 3.

Life in the village was simple and followed the turning of the seasons, overarched by the liturgical calendars of the Ukrainian Autocephalous Orthodox Church, the Ukrainian Byzantine Catholic Church, the Roman Catholic Church, and Judaism – "with a full measure of still more ancient paganism added for sheer relief." According to Piotrowski, a thousand years of Judeo-Christian tradition had not purged the Slavic faith of its preoccupation with the "dark, chthonian demons of its ancestors and the tellurian deities of the nether world. This unique syncretism produced a melancholy people inclined both to fatalistic thoughts and messianic destinies."[117]

Life was soon to change, however; there was the catastrophic massacre of several hundred thousand Poles in Volhynia and Eastern Galicia, including his village in the 1940s as mentioned in Chapter 6 above. In the remaining ten chapters of *Vengeance of the Swallows*, he sorrowfully and painfully documents the complete destruction of his village and the executions of neighbours killing neighbours (Ukranian Nationalists and Russians killing Poles), describing it as an "APOCALYPSE."[118]

Depicted in the short book *My Polish Grandmother*,[119] another village in the Russian Partition was Przezdziecko-Pierzchaly, north-east of Warsaw and near the small, rambling river Maly Brok. The author's grandmother, Anna Chmielewska, born in 1899, lived in a village no longer on maps and that had only seven homes and sixty villagers. The family were descendants of nobility, but their farm was small and the home simple, as the estate had been subdivided

---

117 Piotrowski, p. 8.

118 Piotrowski, p. 23.

119 Stephen Szabados, *My Polish Grandmother: From Tragedy in Poland to Her Rose Garden in America* (Columbia, South Carolina: CreateSpace, 2018).

many times over throughout the generations. The author described how descendants of the nobility retained their special distinction:

> The impoverished nobles, who lost their rights, stood behind an invisible wall that separated them from the peasants who lived nearby. They remained nobility in their minds, and they continued to arrange marriages for their children with partners who were also of "noble birth." They were the... *Szlachta* or nobles whose identity was not recognized. They were marginalized and poverty-stricken. However, they were usually very conservative, patriotic, religious, and stereotyped as provincials.[120]

The village contained only farmers, no merchants. The villagers' homes were in a single line, with a road front and back that divided their homes and farm buildings from the fields. Their farm was five acres and planted in three or four narrow strips. Three kilometres away was the neighbouring town of Andrzcjewo, where the villagers could attend a Catholic church and sell their farm products. The grandmother's extended family grew wheat, rye, barley, and oats as well as corn, beets, potatoes, tomatoes, onions, carrots, cabbages, cucumbers, and beans for their food and to feed the animals. Some of the grains were taken to a miller to be ground into flour for baking.[121]

These descriptions give an idea of the setting of some Polish villages in the Russian Partition. My grandmother Joanna's family *folwark* farm setting may have shared various elements of the three

---

120 Szabados, *My Polish Grandmother*, p. 6.

121 Szabados, *My Polish Grandmother*, pp. 8–13.

villages described above as simple, rustic, but pretty. Her family perhaps leased all or part of their home and some immediate surrounding land and perhaps some other lands in or near the agricultural entity as hers was a family with twelve children. There would have been other families in the agricultural enterprise to form a village or farm complex. Restitution would have been payable in some amount to the *dwor*/manor owner who presided over the lands. The people lived a small farm life with a strict dependence on the manor-owner of the *folwark*.

But how could a family with twelve children (only eight surviving[122]) live and thrive in a cottage with limited plots of land? Some had to leave as the plots became smaller through division among children over the years. What did they need to survive the loss of their family and their community? What was the extent of their schooling? Was their faith something that was strong and helpful in resettling in a new country?

---

122 Joanna, Wladek, John, Dominic, Anna, Paulina, Teofila, and Jozef.

CHAPTER EIGHT: EDUCATION AND RELIGION: CORNERSTONES FOR A FUTURE

Children must be taught how to think, not what to think.
>   —Margaret Mead, *Coming of Age in Samoa*

Just as a candle cannot burn without fire, men cannot live without a spiritual life.
>   —Buddha

EDUCATION

The importance of education was an early emphasis in Poland. Cathedrals and larger churches in the early days, during the 1000s and 1100s, were the first to establish education for the clergy and some schools. In the 1200s, monks were brought from France and Silesia to teach agricultural methods to the peasants,[123] and parish schools were built in new villages and towns. "The network of provincial schools was created but they were generally restricted to nobles, knights and merchants."[124]

The founding of the Jagiellonian University in Krakow in 1364 by King Kazimierz the Great stands out as a milestone in Poland's history. It is the second oldest university in Central Europe and is one of the oldest universities in the world that is still operating. "It became the main centre of education for intellectual elite and a place of academic tolerance. At the beginning the profile of the

---

123   Glenn E. Curtis, ed., "Education," in *Poland: A Country Study* (Washington, DC: GPO for the Library of Congress, 1992), p. 1, www.countrystudies.us/poland/42.htm.

124   Katarzyna Charzynska, Marta Anczewska, and Piotr Switaj, "A Brief Overview of the History of Education in Poland," *Bulgarian Comparative Education Society* (2012), p. 92, www.semanticscholar.org/paper/A-Brief-Overview-of-the-History-of-Education-in-Charzy%C5%84ska-Anczewska/9fb58e4bc969fbd37c81c2e856cd14ea90550038.

---

university indicated that one of its aims was to educate the qualified clerks."[125] After the death of King Kazimierz, development slowed down. However, in the 1390s, the university was reorganized by King Wladyslaw Jagiello; it was expanded and attracted students from many countries. From 1450 to 1500, over 40% of students were outsiders. Notable alumni include mathematician and astronomer Nicolaus Copernicus, poet Jan Kochanowski, chemist Karol Olszewski, King Sobieski, and anthropologist Bronislaw Malinowski. In the Golden Era between 1500 and 1535, it was attended by over 3,000 students. During this time, the foundation for a Jagiellonian Library was commenced.

In the 1700s, additional colleges were founded for the upper classes: in 1741, priests founded the Collegium Nobilium in Warsaw for young men of ruling families, and in 1765, King Stanislaw August established the Knights' School for young men of noble families. Adam Zamoyski described the king as having a "campaign to spread the light" – the king supported a literary society to publish Polish literature; he established the first public theatre and had opera companies booked with French plays, initiated a new periodical to include French writings and Polish poetry and essays, and some of his own writings.[126] King Stanislaw August also created a Commission on National Education (1773–94), the world's first state Ministry of Education which set up a national system emphasizing the study of mathematics, natural sciences, and languages. "The commission also stressed standardizing elementary education, integrating trade and agricultural skills into the elementary school curriculum, and improving textbooks at all

---

125 Charzynska, Anczewska, and Switaj, p. 93.

126 Zamoyski, *The Last King of Poland,* p. 134.

---

levels."[127] These improvements further transformed and expanded education in Poland.[128]

After the final partitioning of Poland in 1795, education in Austria remained under the auspices of the Church; education in (German) Prussia focused on German culture,[129] and in Russia, the schools in the Polish provinces were given little thought. Though schools were allowed to be established in the Polish villages, there was little motivation for such endeavours as teaching was in the Russian language so these schools were rarely set up. [130] Even so, by the early 1800s, Polish education was still well ahead of anything in central Russia.[131]

After the November Uprising of 1830-31 in the Russian Partition, the government changed its policy and intensified Russification of the education system.[132] Russification was the Russian policy of forcing the Polish people to assimilate in all aspects, including language, culture, and religion. For example, the Russian monetary system was adopted in 1841; Poles were prohibited from buying land, and Russian was the only legal language for government administration, including the courts. The university in Vilnius,

---

127 Curtis, p. 1.

128 Many thanks to Dr. Chester Sadowski for his suggestions and assistance in this chapter. His guidance was very much appreciated.

129 Catholics there were targeted in a movement called *Kulturkampf*—a struggle for culture. Chancellor Bismarck focused particularly on Catholics and their leaders until about 1886 because they strongly stood up for Polish rights and culture.

130 Sadowski, personal correspondence, August 7, 2023.

131 Norman Davies, *God's Playground: A History of Poland*, vol. 2, *1795 to the Present* (New York: Columbia University Press, 1982), p. 231. This book is an extraordinary resource that I have used here in an attempt to present a simplified version of Polish history.

132 Davies, *God's Playground*, vol. 2, p. 233.

founded in 1579 as the Jesuit Academy of Vilnius with a curriculum taught in Latin, was closed until 1919.

The Jagiellonian University in Krakow was in an area occupied by the Austrian Empire from 1795; in 1805, it was Germanized; in 1809, it was Polonized once again. From 1815 to 1846, when Krakow was a free city, Poles from the three partitions could attend if approved by their government; in 1846, it came under the auspices of Austria and Germanized,[133] and, for a time, the university's large auditorium was converted into storage areas for grain due to Austrian hostility and threat of closure. There was some relaxing of that threat by Kaiser Ferdinand I of Austria, and the 1870s saw significant improvements with schools. In the Austrian Partition around 1868, Poles gained freedom of education and cultural development; however, this unfortunately changed in about 1880, during a period known as the "Galician Misery" when small farmers lost their land to the nobles.[134] There was no Polish university in Prussia, and students seeking higher education had to attend German universities.[135]

In the Russian Partition after 1864, education was in Russian and private education in the Polish language was forbidden. Young men were liable for conscription as ordinary soldiers in the Russian army if they failed to pass Russian high school exams. All administrative offices, including law courts, were conducted in Russian, and street names were in Russian. Polish newspapers and books could be published but they were censored. If it could be afforded, some

---

133 Krzysztof Stopka, "History of the Jagiellonian University," *Jagiellonian University in Krakow*, accessed February 8, 2024, www.en.uj.edu.pl/en_GB/about-university/history.

134 Andrzej Mankowski, former Polish Consul General for British Columbia, personal correspondence with author, February 2021.

135 Davies, *God's Playground*, vol. 2, p. 231.

went to schools in the Austrian Partition (Krakow and Lwow). By the 1880s, as Russian peasants were in the process of being emancipated, industrialization was on the rise, and cities were becoming more populated (Lodz was the centre for the textile industry; coal and iron/steel industry was being developed), and education became a priority for the people.[136] But Russification remained dominant – research and teaching the Polish language and history and Catholic history were outlawed and students were punished for resisting Russification. "In an era when Polish literature was widely regarded as subversive, book collections had to be preserved in secrecy."[137] Apparently Vincent Dudek (who was later married to my grandmother) studied Polish taught to him by his grandfather in an attic by candlelight, as Polish books were kept hidden.[138] The Poles in the Russian Partition, with strong determination to persevere with Polish education, increasingly turned to schooling their own children.

> In Russia, the typical Polish "patriot" of the turn of the century was not the revolutionary with a revolver in his pocket, but the young lady of good family with a textbook under her shawl.[139]

136 Facts taken from Anna M. Cienciala, "Lecture 6: Poland 1864–1914," lecture for History 557, "Nationalism and Communism in East Central Europe," University of Kansas, Spring 2002 (revised 2004), accessed October 20, 2023, www.acienciala.ku.edu/hist557/lect6.htm.

137 Davies, *God's Playground*, vol. 2, p. 235.

138 Susan Stronberg-Stein, *Louis Dudek: A Biographical Introduction to His Poetry* (Ottawa: Golden Dog Press, 1983).

139 Davies, *God's Playground*, vol. 2, p. 233.

Polish activism rose with growing areas of resistance where teaching and publishing continued in Polish, and there are strong indications that village public life was never successfully Russified because of this Polish resistance. Toward the end of the 1800s, there were numerous private, informal, or "underground" Polish cultural enterprises.[140] Some of the "illegal" groups were called "flying universities" because they moved from place to place to avoid the attention of Russian authorities. Marie Sklodowska-Curie was one of the best-known attendees of this type of education. Campaigns to educate the peasants were disguised as bee-keeping societies or sports associations.[141] Self-education also became very popular. A 1911 report to the Russian Policemaster of Sosnowiec noted at least ten "illegal schools" in the district; a few examples of the reported illegal schools were as follows:

> The mother of Stanislaw Chrzanowski, an official of the "Jerzy" Mine, teaches in her house on Wesola Street;
> Maria Goralska, the daughter of an official of the "Jerzy" Mine, holds lessons in a house belonging to the Company on the other side of the street from the clinic;
> The daughter of a guard on the Warsaw-Vienna Railway called Filak teaches in Duda's house.[142]

An autobiography written in 1898 by Stefan Zeromski (who was short-listed for the Nobel Prize in literature) called *The Labors of Sisyphus* described Polish students in a village school being taught

---

140 Davies, *God's Playground*, vol. 2, p. 235.

141 Davies, *God's Playground*, vol. 2, p. 236.

142 Davies, *God's Playground*, vol. 2, pp. 236–237.

Russian and boys in a Russified high school, which taught that everything Russian was modern and progressive whereas anything Polish was outdated and bad.[143] Polish literature was regarded as subversive. The Poles had a huge challenge to keep their language and culture, but they were determined and continued with their private "underground" schools. Also, about one-third of the population of all ages in the Russian Partition were engaged in some form of home-study in the early twentieth century.

It appears my grandmother could have attended a small schoolhouse in or near Rozpaszka with classes taught in Russian, which attempted to inculcate in the students a belief in the superiority of the Russian culture. But she also would have been living in a Polish-speaking home and taught in Polish about the Polish culture, whether in local homes or by her many older siblings. In an autobiography, Tadeusz Piotrowski wrote about his sisters taking outside work as domestic servants at a young age to earn money for the household.[144] As Joanna lived in a large family on a farm, the children would have been expected to assist with farm work and perhaps would work in the homes of others as domestic help. It was evident that opportunities for schooling in her native language were limited for her.

Education continues to be a top priority for many Canadian immigrants, including Poles, as it opens doors for advancement,

---

143 The Polish title is *Syzyfowe Prace*. "The novel is based on the author's personal experiences as a child and adolescent in the Russian-controlled Poland and describes his school and students' attempts to resist the policy of russification. The title refers to the Greek myth of Sisyphus and portrays the attempts to indoctrinate students as an occasionally successful but ultimately doomed to failure." From *The Labors of Sisyphus*, Stefan Zeromski, LibraryThing, accessed February 8, 2024, www.librarything.com/work/2270643.

144 Piotrowski, p. 5.

both personal and financial, to jobs and professions that would otherwise be closed. When she immigrated to Canada, my grandmother arrived with a deep appreciation of education as she had been denied a substantial education in her home village. She came from a culture whose people broke laws to educate their children, and she probably carried with her an awareness of the importance of education that had been embedded centuries before. She recognized the abilities and interest of her son (my father) in schooling despite his rough start – he failed Grade 1 in Halifax three times because he could not speak English and missed about eight months of school in his early teens because of a serious illness. Through her and my father's hard work and thriftiness, my grandmother arranged for my father to attend the University of Toronto in 1931 where he completed a B. App. Science in Chemical Engineering.[145] I was raised in a household where education was primary in our lives – of the seven of us children in the house, all had at least two university degrees; two of us have three degrees; and one has four degrees. Poland in its Golden Age was one of the top leaders in Europe in education. It is no wonder that the value of education had become a foundational part of the Polish character.

RELIGION

Today, Poland is described as a Roman Catholic nation, but it took centuries for Christianity to be established. Up until about 966, Poland as well as the Baltic nations, were dominated by various pagan religious beliefs – a popular pagan god at that time was

---

145   My mother's parents emigrated from the Austrian partition of Poland. Though my mother didn't speak English until she was five years old, she was one of the few women in the B.A. graduating class of 1935 at the University of Toronto.
Four of my brothers have a B. App. Science in Chemical Engineering.

Svetovid, a Slavic god of war, fertility, and abundance. Christianity took hold along with other belief systems from the time that King Mieszko accepted Roman Christianity in 966. The Church with its clergy became the centre for intellectualism and education. Schools, cathedrals, monasteries, and parishes emerged over time as did many Polish saints such as St. Wojciech who was canonized in the year 1000 and who is regarded as the first great patron of the Christian Polish nation. Religion unified the Polish, particularly during the time of the Tatar invasions.

During the Protestant Reformation in the 1500s, with religious persecution raging elsewhere, Poland became a place of refuge for dissenting sects, including Protestant thinkers and leaders of reformations.[146] The Polish-Lithuanian Commonwealth (1569-1795) was a mixture of Roman Catholics, Jews, Eastern Orthodox Christians, Protestants, Armenian Catholics, and some Muslims. According to Brian Porter-Szucs in his comprehensive book *Faith and Fatherland: Catholicism, Modernity, and Poland,*[147] this amalgam made it one of the most religiously diverse countries in Europe. Poland also had been a refuge for Jews for many centuries. In *From Counter-Reformation to Glorious Revolution*, Hugh Trevor-Roper stated that "Poland [from its founding in 1025 to the 1569 formation of the Polish-Lithuanian Commonwealth] was the most tolerant country in Europe."[148] In the

---

146 Jan Comenius, born in eastern Moravia in the Kingdom of Bohemia, retreated to Poland in about 1628, fleeing persecution in Bohemia. He is renowned for his advocacy for universal education.

147 Brian Porter-Szucs, *Faith and Fatherland: Catholicism, Modernity, and Poland* (Oxford: Oxford University Press, 2011). I have relied on this book extensively, and I highly recommend it. It contains many fascinating details that I am unable to refer to given the scope of my book.

148 Hugh Trevor-Roper, *From Counter-Reformation to Glorious Revolution* (Chicago: University of Chicago Press, 1992), p. 51.

middle of the 1550s, about three-quarters of the world's Jews lived in Poland. However, "[well] into the seventeenth century…many Catholics considered their Church to be in a precarious position, under threat from Protestants, from Jews (some felt that the Jews dominated rural economic life), and in a state too weak or too pathetic to enforce denominational unity."[149] To support and encourage Catholism, Jesuit teachers were invited into the country.[150]

Poland only came to be dominated by Catholicism in the 1800s when it was partitioned and occupied;[151] the struggles for national liberation and social justice strengthened the bond between the Church and the Polish people. "The Church was often the only institution that had a Polish character. Thus, Polish national consciousness came to be more strongly tied to a Catholic religious identity."[152] Regarding the 1900s, Porter-Szucs noted that:

> Any remaining uncertainty regarding the equation between Pole and Catholic was made irrelevant by the Second World War and its immediate aftermath. The postwar boundaries were drawn so as to exclude almost all Lithuanians, Belarusians, and Ukrainians; the Germans and most of the remaining Ukranians were forcibly expelled; and nearly all the Jews perished in the Holocaust.[153]

---

149 Porter-Szucs, p. 5.

150 Sadowski, personal correspondence, August 7, 2023.

151 Porter-Szucs, p. 7.

152 Michael H. Bernhard, *The Origins of Democratization in Poland* (New York: Columbia University Press, 1993) p. 210.

153 Porter-Szucs, p. 9.

What did that Polish faith look like in the later 1800s? According to Porter-Szucs's extensive study, the liturgies of the mass in 1860, 1910, and 1930 were very similar, and "one was very likely to hear a sermon that contrasted the misery of this life with the glories of heaven… messages of fear and guilt overwhelming those of love and hope."[154] Porter-Szucs set out several opinions of others that "every misfortune was to be accepted as a just punishment from God."[155] There developed a strong devotion to Mary, referred to as the Marian cult, which had intensified over the previous two centuries. (In 1656, King Jan Kazimierz had crowned her Queen of Poland.) This devotion continues today. Referred to as the "Miracle on the Vistula" (Battle of Warsaw, 1920) for the unexpected Polish success, according to Polish lore, Mary apparently appeared to the Bolshevik soldiers in the skies and held a shield which made all bullets aimed at Polish troops bounce back and hit the Bolsheviks instead. This miraculous win by the Poles prevented the Bolshevik encroachment into Germany.[156] Thomas Fiddick wrote: "The Battle of Warsaw of 1920 is one of the few phenomena of modern history which has been traditionally explained by reference to the supernatural. . . . What seemed so miraculous was the 'sudden, mysterious and decisive' retreat of the Red Army from the gates of Warsaw."[157]

According to Porter-Szucs, even after the partition of Poland into the three parts, Roman Catholicism was still allowed to exist,

---

154   Porter-Szucs, p. 57.

155   Porter-Szucs, pp. 59–61.

156   For the political and military details, see Thomas Fiddick, "The 'Miracle of the Vistula': Soviet Policy versus Red Army Strategy," *The Journal of Modern History* Vol. 46 , No. 4 (December 1973): 626–643.

157   Fiddick, p. 626.

although this varied from territory to territory. As Roman Catholics had been taught obedience to authorities, the rulers let the religion continue: "The attitude of the Vatican was made clear in 1832 with the publication of Pope Gregory XVI's encyclical, *Cum Primum,* which identified the tsar as the 'legitimate prince' to whom the Poles owed obedience."[158] When Russification was increased in the last third of the 1800s, some priests became more oppositional, but many others reacted by withdrawing to a narrowly delineated understanding of their pastoral duties.[159] After the unsuccessful 1863 Polish uprising against the Russian tsar, new laws included some forced conversion to the Russian Orthodox religion and new heavy taxes. According to Zalas, throughout the entire 19th century, there was dissolution of Catholic orders and the conversion of churches into Russian Orthodox churches.[160]

Roman Catholicism served as a bedrock for the Polish people, especially when they had lost their country for 123 years and their culture was suppressed. The Church brought people together. The Poles were a very proud nation when Karol Jozef Wojtyla, born in Wadowice south-west of Krakow, and Archbishop of Krakow, was chosen to be Pope John Paul II. Celebrations were worldwide. He led the Roman Catholic world from 1978 to 2005 and is credited with contributing to the peaceful end of the Soviet regime in Eastern Europe through private conversations with Polish and Soviet leaders. As well, he had been a great traveller, and his world-wide outreach brought greater visibility to the Church.

---

158   Porter-Szucs, pp. 8–9.

159   Porter-Szucs, p. 9.

160   Zalas, pp, 159–215.

Folwark Rozpaszka belonged to the Prozoroki Roman Catholic parish, but unfortunately, few or no records survive in that archival source. I have no memories of my grandmother Joanna attending church, but it appears that she was raised Roman Catholic. My father told me that she did not attend the Roman Catholic Church in Canada because the masses were in English and she spoke only Polish. Additionally, my father shared a story of why he had been a practising Roman Catholic all his life. In Timmins, Ontario, during August 1925, when he was about fourteen years old, he contracted typhoid fever. The first signs were that he was dizzy and felt weak, but soon he also became delirious, fell into a coma, and had a high fever (106 degrees) for about ten days. He was put on a starvation diet and lost forty-five pounds, dropping down to a mere seventy-five pounds. For months, he was bedridden, during that time developing pneumonia and then pleurisy. He must have already had ties to Roman Catholicism, as he made a pact with God at that time that if he survived, he would attend the Catholic Church mass every Sunday for the rest of his life. He was given the Catholic last rites, but he survived, and he was true to his promise. All his children were raised Roman Catholic, and we were required to attend church weekly with him and our mother.

Roman Catholicism was very important in my family from my infancy. It provided a good basis for instilling willpower (no meat on Fridays, weekly mass), a sense of home and belonging, friendships, confidence in living, and a peaceful death if you followed the rules. It was, however, quite limiting for women who were regarded as secondary, and I know my mother and I had to endure this burden. For example, the Catholic Church was very strict about the use of birth control. My mother had seven children and worked hard in the home all her life to raise them. Some simple advice she gave me was, "Don't have too many children."

These simple outlines of education and religion in Poland made it very clear to me that over the centuries they stood as cornerstones that Poles could rely on to survive the most outrageous attacks on their country and on themselves. On immigrating to new lands, Poles wisely carried with them those values, so very evident in my own family.

CHAPTER NINE: FESTIVALS, TRADITIONS, THE ARTS AND SCIENCES

I want to leave my country, but I don't want to leave my home.
—Kirkpatrick Sale

Our past, more than a millennium old, remains generally speaking unknown and obscure.
—Aleksander Kwasniewski

FESTIVALS AND TRADITIONS

Jerome Blum in *Our Forgotten Past* noted that much of Western history since the end of the Middle Ages has been marked by want, hunger and misery, combined with a rich culture of stories, legends, art, music, dancing, festivals, magic, and witchcraft.[161] Folk beliefs and customs were part of the fabric of the village that served well the needs of the individual, the households, and the community.

Old Poland had a wide range of customs, festivals, and traditions, which were very much centred on the religious calendar but also included midsummer and name-day celebrations, harvest festivities, and birth, wedding, and death rituals. Documented in Knab's *Polish Customs, Traditions and Folklore* are month-by-month descriptions of the many colourful festive traditions and beliefs that structured everyday life. As an example, I will briefly outline a February festival celebrated in Old Poland as set out in that book.

February 2 was the Feast of the Purification of the Blessed Mother (also called the Presentation of Christ in the Temple; referred to as Candlemas by the English), "commemorating the

---

161 Blum, *Our Forgotten Past*, p. 8, referring to chapter 5 in that book entitled "The Struggle to Survive" by Dr. Diedrich Saalfeld.

ancient law of Moses that excluded Jewish mothers from public worship for forty days after giving birth to a son." This celebration took place after the forty days and, in the eleventh century, the blessing of candles carried in solemn procession became part of the ceremony. On that day, Polish people brought candles decorated with either ribbons or liturgical symbols for blessing by the priest. In the evening, before a picture of the Blessed Mother, the people would burn one of the candles at home until sunrise. The candles were then used throughout the year for the ritual cleansing of a woman following childbirth as she was deemed unclean for about forty days after giving birth. The blessed candles were also lit near the bed of dying persons to protect them from Satan. Additionally, these candles were used along with special prayers to protect a house against lightning, and they were sometimes used in the sowing of seeds, during the storing of wheat or straw, and at the beginning and end of the harvest. The Church condemned the use of the candles for the casting of spells, but they were used nonetheless – for instance, to ward off evil spirits by burning crosses on door frames and windowsills (a practice that continued even in the late 1800s). Some also inhaled the candle's smoke when it was extinguished to prevent a sore throat. Similar to North American Groundhog Day, the weather on the feast day itself was used to foretell how long the winter would last and what the harvest would be like. The behaviour of animals on that day was also used to predict weather. (In one region, the bear was observed, to see whether he emerged to pull apart his hiding place because he expected that the winter would be short.) This day also was the official ending of Christmas celebrations, triggering the storing away of decorations and costumes.[162] I know that my mother as a child participated in traditional festivals at her local Catholic churches, as I inherited her Polish dance costume that I wore to a primary grade heritage "show and tell" day.

THE ARTS AND SCIENCES

Music was much a part of festivals and differed from one area to the next. For instance, in central Poland, the music and dance forms of the mazurkas, obereks, and polkas were well known; the Tatra Mountains and the lake district of north-west Poland had distinct styles of songs and instrumental music. In the Golden age of Poland in the 1500s and 1600s, between Poland and other European nations, there were cultural contacts reflected in the music and arts. And prominently, when Christianity was accepted in the tenth century, there was the music in the Roman Catholic churches in the form of liturgical chants, and religious music centred on the praise and worship of the Virgin Mary.[163]

With Poland not existing as a country in the nineteenth century, times were tough for Polish arts and sciences. However, one of the world's greatest composers, Fryderyk Chopin, emerged from this period. Many today do not realize that Chopin was Polish – he was born in 1810 in Zelazowa Wola and grew up in Warsaw. Though his father was born in France, he moved to Poland when he was sixteen and married a Polish woman, Justyna Krzyanowska, Chopin's mother. Fryderyk was a child prodigy who completed his musical

---

162 A summarization of the feast as set out in Knab, *Polish Customs,* pp. 65–69.

163 Taken from Maria Anna Harley (Maja Trochimchyk), "The Briefest History of Polish Music," *Polish Music Centre at the University of South California,* accessed February 8, 2024, www.polishmusic.usc.edu/research/publications/essays/briefest-history-of-polish-music/.

education and composed early works in Warsaw before the age of twenty. He left Warsaw just before the outbreak of the November 1830 uprising and settled in Paris where, at the age of 39, he died of aggravated tuberculosis. His major piano works include mazurkas, waltzes, nocturnes, preludes, and sonatas. He became "a national symbol of resistance and a source of cultural identity. His Polish audiences loved the Polonaises and Mazurkas."[164] When Chopin died, on his request, his heart was returned to Poland.

There are many other Polish composers, too numerous to list here, but a few to mention are Stanislaw Moniuszko, Henryk Wieniawski, Juliusz Zarebski, Maria Szymanowska, Zygmunt Noskowski and Wladyslaw Zelenski. One was a pianist as well as a prime minister – Igancy Jan Paderewski (1860-1941) born to Polish parents in Kurilovak in the Russian Partition. At the age of twelve, he was admitted to the Warsaw Conservatory to study music. A worldwide tour in 1888 triggered great public admiration. He was also an avid Polish nationalist and was made prime minister for a short time after the First World War but retired from politics and went back to his music.

Because the occupiers of the Polish-Lithuanian Commonwealth from 1795 onward had no interest in promoting Polish culture, Polish art and literature have often been unacknowledged.[165] Some artists are unknown as Poles because of an anglicized name such as Joseph Conrad, born Jozef Teodor Konrad Korzeniowski, or Marie Curie, born Marie Salomea Sklodowska. However, Polish artists, writers, and musicians forged on. An excellent compilation of

---

164   Harley, p. 2.

165   Jaroslaw K. Radomski, *The Magnificent 100* (New York: Blurb Incorporated, 2019),introduction. The book is available online at www.blurb.ca/b/9291815-the-magnificent-100.

biographies of 100 Polish artists and writers is set out in the book *The Magnificent 100* with the comment by the author that hundreds of additional names could easily be added.[166] I will offer just a few highlights from that compilation and from other sources of some better-known Polish artists and writers.

Among **Polish artists and writers,** one of the best-known works is *The Polish Tale Teller*, published in Vilnia in 1862, by A. J. Glinski (1817-66). Glinksi is regarded by some as a Polish equivalent of the Brothers Grimm. Some of his tales have been translated into English by M. A. Bigg in *Polish Fairy Tales*.[167] There is interesting controversy as to whether the folktales were actually of Polish origin or were remakes of Russian folktales. However, there is some indication that Glinski believed the tales he knew and heard had evolved over time from a common Slavic heritage.[168]

Joseph Conrad (Jozef Teodor Konrad Korzeniowski, 1857-1924), the most recognized Polish novelist writing in English, was born south of Minsk and west of Kviv, in Berdyczow, a town previously in the Polish-Lithuanian Commonwealth but, at that time, under Russian rule. He had a father who was a writer and one of the leading Russian Partition political activists who had been exiled and imprisoned in central Russia. Conrad had a fifteen-year-long merchant marine career and retired to married life in England. He is well-known for the writing of *Heart of Darkness*, a fictionalized account of Colonial Africa.[169]

---

166 Radomski, introduction.

167 A. J. Glinski, *Polish Fairy Tales*, trans. by Maude Ashurst Bigg, illus. by Cecile Walton (New York: John Lane, 1920: U.K. Registered Office: Sandycroft Publishing, 2015).

168 See Katia Vandenborre, "Antoni Jozef Glinski or the Making of a Polish Tale Teller," *Pegasus Oost-Europese Studies* 31 (2018): 79-103.

169 Radomski, pp. 19–20.

Mention must be made of Adam Mickiewicz (1798-1855), the famous Polish poet born near that part of the Polish-Lithuanian Commonwealth where the *Folwark* Rozpaszka farm was located. Poland has always been very multicultural, in some areas especially, with a mix of Poles, Lithuanians, Ukrainians, Belarusians, Jews, Armenians, Tatars, Germans, Czechs, Slovaks, Romanians, and Russians.[170] Mickiewicz comes from such a mix but identified with the Poles – he spent five years in exile in Russia for participating in Polish "patriotic" activity.[171] His works reflect the cultural and political upheavals in post-Napoleonic Europe; he is chiefly known for writing the poetic drama *Dziady* and the national epic poem *Pan Tadeusz*.[172] These and other works inspired uprisings against the three powers that partitioned and extinguished the Polish-Lithuanian Commonwealth. There were of course, many other outstanding writers during the 1800s and early 1900s, including Henryk Sienkiewicz (1846-1916), Janusz Korczak (1878-1942), Bruno Schulz (1892-1942) Wladyslaw Reymont (1867-1925), and Stefan Zeromski (1864-1925). Five Poles have won the Nobel Prize in Literature: Reymont, Sienkiewicz, Milosz, Szymborska, and Tokarczuk.

Not to be forgotten was the work and prominence of Bronisław Kasper Malinowski, born in the Austrian Partition of Poland in 1884, a Polish anthropologist whose writings on ethnography, social theory, and field research have exerted a lasting influence on the discipline of anthropology. His studies included Aboriginal

---

170 Mankowski, personal correspondence, May 11, 2022.

171 Roman Koropeckyj, *Adam Mickiewicz: The Life of a Romantic* (Ithaca, New York: Cornell University Press, 2008) is an extensive scholarly biography of Mickiewicz, the first of its kind in English.

172 Radomski, pp. 103–104.

Australia through ethnographic documents, and the Indigenous peoples on the Trobriand Islands and in other regions in New Guinea and Melanesia, where he resided for several years.

I previously highlighted the work of **scientist** Nicolaus Copernicus in Chapter 5. The discoveries of Madam Curie are used worldwide. Marie Sklodowska Curie (1867-1934) is a renowned Polish-born physicist for her work on radioactivity and for the isolation of radium and polonium (named after her country of birth). She jointly received the Nobel Prize for Physics in 1903 and was the sole winner of the Nobel Prize in Chemistry in 1911 (the first woman to win the Nobel Prize – twice). Her daughter, Irena Joliot-Curie, won a Nobel Prize in Chemistry in 1935.

It must be mentioned that it was Polish mathematicians who cracked the Enigma code – a sophisticated communication system created by the Germans at the end of the First World War that the British, French, and Americans had failed to break. The team of young mathematicians from the University of Poznan included Marian Rejewski (who cracked it in ten weeks), Jerzy Rozycki and Henryk Zygalski who deciphered the first messages in 1932. "The breaking of Enigma had a significant impact on the course of the Second World War. It is believed that it shortened the war by two years and saved countless lives."[173] This work has been, for the most part, overlooked, as has the work of Casimir Funk who was born in Warsaw in 1884. "He was the first scientist in the world to partially identify a substance essential for the health of animals in small quantities, which did not belong to any of the classes of essential

---

173 Magda Szkuta, "Polish Mathematicians and Cracking the Enigma," *European Studies Blog*, January 2, 2018, www.blogs.bl.uk/european/2018/01/polish-mathematicians-and-cracking-the-enigma.html.

nutrients known at that time. He called this substance a vitamines, and correctly predicted the existence of several different vitamines."[174]

Polish folk art would have been displayed in every household. Remains of the earliest painted eggs have been dated to the late 900s reflecting a Slavic belief that associated the eggs with the sun god, symbolizing new life and birth. The shells of eggs throughout this long tradition were coloured with natural dyes, including those derived from onion peels, walnut shells, oak and alder bark, shoots of young rye, mallow flower petals, and beet juice. Much decorative handicraft was made for all religious feasts, including decorations fashioned out of straw. Wood carving was popular (boxes and chests), as well as paper cut-outs, handmade and hand-decorated tableware, crochet and embroidery handiwork, the weaving and styling of flax and wool garments, and wall painting.[175] The extent to which folk art, along with festivals and traditions, were observed or created would have varied from village to village, but Poles under Russian rule would have known about them.

Polish painting during the time of the Partitions was dominated by those artists who were free to paint, acting as treasuries of the national memory or creating prophetic visions to sustain the people's spirit.[176] One of the great names of that period was Jan Matejko (1838-93), who lived in Krakow and painted portrayals of customs and significant events in Polish history. (Krakow had been a free city until 1846, when it became part of Austrian-administered

---

174 Paul F. Ostrowski, "Who Discovered Vitamins?", *The Polish Review*, Vol. XXXI, 1986, Nos. 2-3, p. 182-183.

175 Joanna Szymczak, "Polish Folk Art," *Reflective Journal*, May 20, 2014, www.joannaszymczak.wordpress.com/2014/05/20/polish-folk-art/.

176 Feliks Szyszko, "History's Impact on Polish Art: A Talk by Feliks Szyszko," *Info Poland, University of Buffalo*, accessed October 30, 2023, www.info-poland.icm.edu.pl/classroom/Szyszko.html.

Galicia as the result of an unsuccessful revolt.) One of Matejko's students was Jacek Malczewski (1854-1929), who came to Krakow from the Russian Partition and is regarded as a highly original visionary and Polish patriot. It must be mentioned, however, that during the Partitions, many Poles left for France, particularly Paris. Polish artists there were no doubt influenced by the artistic culture of France but also contributed to its evolution. In the opinion of the art historian Irena Piotrowska:

> Poland was developing a national style of her own, distinguished by its emotional content and its individual features of composition and colour. . . . In spite of their being saturated with the art culture of Paris, [Polish artists] differ from those painters who managed to lose their national individuality completely. . . . [O]f greatest importance is the fact that they were direct intermediaries between Poland and the West; that they maintained an intimate union between Polish art and the latest artistic developments in the world.[177]

Though my grandmother was busy working to support her children, she did pass down to me hand-embroidered table linens, a treadle sewing machine and a strong survivalist work ethic. Her businesses were well-run, and family members often assisted in her enterprises. I was brought up in a cultural milieu of self-sufficiency at home. Anything that needed to be fixed, repaired, built, or cooked, was done by someone in the house. Ours was a culture of inventiveness, handiness, and frugality, one that I'm sure came from ancestral necessity and tradition. My father and some

---

177   Irena Piotrowska, *The Art of Poland* (New York: Philosophical Library, 1947), p. 91.

brothers could fix most things (from cars to plugged drains). They remodelled rooms in various houses, took out walls, repapered, and painted them. My father took up oil painting in his retirement (the goose as mentioned earlier), and three more of us painted beautiful paintings on canvas as a hobby. My brother played the piano until his passing; another was a weekend woodworker and furniture maker; another at age fourteen built ham radios and communicated with the world with his own call letters and also made model ships and airplanes. Yet another brother established a chemistry lab in the house, a home for pigeons in the garage and, in his early teens, built a gasoline driven go-cart (shortly thereafter, he was prevented by the police from driving it on the streets). My sister and I knitted, crocheted, and sewed some of our own clothes. We were required to take piano lessons as children, and we learned to skate on our own skating rink in the backyard. I learned to ride a bicycle at age seven on an adult bike which, complete with rust and barnacles, my father and brothers pulled from the bottom of the Trent Canal – replacement tires made it sufficient for me. Our holidays were car rides to lakes for fishing and swimming and looking for the next beach. By today's standards, it was an unusual upbringing but one that I have come to appreciate. At first, I had no idea that I emerged from such a rich, vibrant culture that in recent centuries has been so oppressed and treated so poorly. However, the dignity, resourcefulness, and ingenuity of the Poles and their culture survived. It had been lost to me, but I have come to know the strength of my heritage.

CHAPTER TEN: WHY THEY LEFT

You get a strange feeling when you're about to leave a place... like you'll not only miss the people you love but you'll miss the person you are now at this time and this place, because you'll never be this way ever again.

> —Azar Nafisi, *Reading Lolita in Tehran*

The first recorded group of Poles coming to Canada were the Kashubians from northern Poland who left to escape the oppression in the Prussian Partition in 1858. They settled in the Barry's Bay region of Ontario (the town of Wilno). A little later, another group settled in the southern Ontario town of Berlin (Kitchener)[178] where my mother's family, from the Austrian-Hungarian Partition, settled. There were only about 600 Poles in Canada in the 1870s.[179] Between 1870 and 1914 most went to the United States; others went to German lands, more remote parts of Russia, other European countries, as well as to Canada and Brazil. Though few arrived in Canada before 1890, one exception was Sir Casimir Gzowski who emigrated in 1833 after the failed Polish protest of 1830. He lived for some time in the United States and acquired experience in construction methods and project management. In 1842, he was hired for projects in Canada and was responsible for many notable

---

178 Benedykt Heydenkorn, "Polish Canadians," *The Canadian Encyclopedia*, July 31, 2019, www.thecanadianencyclopedia.ca/en/article/poles.

179 D. H. Avery and J. K. Fedorowicz, *The Poles in Canada* (Ottawa: Canadian Historical Association, 1982), p.4.

works.[180] He later became the Lieutenant-Governor of Ontario and was appointed as a colonel in the Canadian militia.

A 1931 publication of the National Bureau of Economic Research[181] on Russian immigration and emigration pointed out that there were no actual accurate emigration statistics from Russia for this period because by law, no citizen could leave the country to become a citizen of another country without the government's permission. Violation of this law was punished by banishment and confiscation of the individual's property. However, emigrants found ways of leaving illegally, and they of course, were not documented. Between 1828 and 1915, the recorded total net outflow of Russian emigrants was 4,510,000, which included Poles in the Russian Partition, 90% of them going to the United States. Historians D. H. Avery and J. K. Fedorowicz indicated that between 1896 and 1914, 110,000 Poles entered Canada,[182] most from Galicia, the Austrian Partition. (Their estimations are that between 1870 and 1914, 1.2 million emigrated from the Prussian zone, 1.3 million from Russian zone, and 1.1 million from Galicia.)

The population of the Russian Partition in 1897, a predominantly agricultural land area, was about 9,402,000, with about 23% living in the cities.[183] There was intensive farming and rural overpopulation, although industry was starting to develop. Obolensky-Ossinsky

---

180 GZOWSKI, Sir CASIMIR STANISLAUS, *Dictionary of Canadian Biography*, accessed March 6, 2024, www.biographi.ca/en/bio/gzowski_casimir_stanislaus_12E.html.

181 V. V. Obolensky-Ossinsky, "Emigrations from and Immigration into Russia," in *International Migrations*, vol. 2, *Interpretations*, ed. Walter F. Willcox (Cambridge, Massachusetts: National Bureau of Economic Research, 1931), pp. 521–580. This extraordinary publication is a must-read for those interested in this topic. The author has done remarkable research and analysis on a complex issue.

182 Avery and Fedorowicz, p. 6.

183 Obolensky-Ossinsky, p. 533.

noted that serfdom had left behind a great mass of agricultural labourers who were bound to the land by a home, garden, or tiny allotments and oppressed economically and socially. Indeed, in 1901, he said that landless village inhabitants constituted 15.4% of the population.

> The landlords, if they did not carry on their own farms themselves, always preferred to let out their land as a whole to big lessees. The peasants were let only small parcels far from the buildings, or odd plots remaining after the division of the fields. These facts show that Poland, unlike Finland, was largely a country of landlord estates. . . . The average size of a nobleman's estate in 1887 was 1436 acres – a big farm, especially as agriculture was carried on intensively with complicated rotations. On the other hand, the average size of a peasant holding was about 19 acres. Three-fifths of the peasants in 1899 possessed holdings of less than 20 acres.[184]

In the "non-black earth" countryside, including Vilna and Minsk relatively near Rozpaszka, the soil was less fertile than in the other provinces and larger allotments were needed, particularly as families increased in size.[185] Obolensky-Ossinsky stated that in this context, emigration was a necessity, given the almost complete absence of peasant leaseholders, low agricultural wages, and industry unable to absorb surplus population. He wrote that the Finnish, Polish, Lithuanian, White Russian, and Ukrainian agricultural labourers and poor peasants emigrated because of low wages and a low

184 Obolensky-Ossinsky, p. 535.

185 Obolensky-Ossinsky, p. 550.

social position resulting from their deprivation of land in favour of the big landlords or their prosperous neighbours.[186] Since my grandmother Joanna was the youngest of twelve children on a farm, especially as a female, her entitlement to farm land was slim to nil; her husband Vincent (my grandfather) was one of two sons on a farm, and presumably his brother Casimir, married with a son, was the one chosen to inherit the farm rights.[187] So likely reasons that Joanna and Vincent and others emigrated were because of the lack of enough land to sustain them and/or the low agricultural wages described by Obolensky-Ossinsky.

Moreover, in the early 1900s there was general discontent among the Poles, reflected in a Polish uprising. At that time, worsening economic conditions in Russia, a prelude to the Russian Revolution of 1917, directly affected those in the Russian Partition and other Polish territories. In the aftermath of the Russo-Japanese War (late 1904), over 100,000 Poles lost their jobs; along with conscription to the Russian army and continued severe Russification policies,[188] it is not surprising that the Polish population was apprehensive. One Polish faction sought to regain independence through violent protests against the Russians; another faction thought it better to work with the Russian authorities to increase their representation in the Russian government. In 1905, there was a general strike over large areas of the Russian Partition,[189] and from 1905 to 1907, there were nearly 7,000 strikes and work stoppages across the country.

---

186   Obolensky-Ossinsky, p. 578.

187   Oldest sons were first in line to inherit the homestead. Vincent's father, Ignacy, still lived on the farm in 1935.

188   I have relied on material in Ascher, a very detailed and well-written book for my short summary herein. See pages 156- 157.

189   See Zamoyski, *The Last King of Poland*, pp. 230–232, for details.

The Russian government did agree to some concessions such as removing restrictions against the use of Polish in school classrooms, but many workers were still not satisfied; in some places, the school strikes lasted for up to three years. This time of general discontent and widespread protests resulted in the rise of Polish political parties, Polish nationalism, and significant emigration. Joanna had two older brothers, Janusz and Wladek, who immigrated to Canada in approximately 1905, a time when conscription to the Russian army was prevalent – probably a good incentive to leave the country and start anew elsewhere.

As I have no diaries or letters to refer to regarding how my grandmother felt about leaving her family, her village, and her Polish culture in April of 1914 with her husband and three children, I can only imagine that it must have been extremely heart-wrenching to say goodbye to her parents, her siblings, and her friends, and to her village and her homeland. As a mother, she also left behind the family members and farming community that on a daily basis would surely have helped her with her three children – Zygmunt aged three and half, Henry aged two, and Stephanie just nine-months-old. How do you pack for a trip like that? How do you prepare yourself for that "goodbye?" How do you care for small children on the train and ship? Such questions are daunting. It would be fifteen years before she again saw the family and home she left behind.

> From dealing with complicated paperwork to saying goodbye to loved ones, migration is an emotionally exhausting process, wrought with difficulty. Migrants face challenges such as acclimatizing themselves to a different cultural context, learning a new language, struggling with alienation, and

wrestling with feelings of remorse or guilt for leaving their home country, among others.[190]

On the other hand, Joanna was leaving a lost country that "regularly provided an arena for Europe's wars. In the nineteenth century, they supplied the armies of three martial empires with numberless recruits and conscripts. Yet no European nation has reaped fewer rewards for the sweat and blood expended."[191] Moreover Joanna, Vincent, and their three children left Rozpaszka, just months before the start of the First World War. With conflict on the horizon, Joanna and indeed her parents must have felt that for them emigration was the right decision, though Joanna might have been anxious, wondering if they would make it out in time or even if they would be allowed to leave. (And as Poland was still divided into the three partitions, Poles were recruited to fight for their governing authorities sometimes in combat against Poles from other Partitions.) In hindsight, it was a fortuitous time to emigrate as during the war about 450,000 Poles died, close to one million were injured, hundreds of thousands of civilians were moved to labour camps in Germany, and 800,000 were deported to the east by tsarist forces. I'm sure that by escaping the frightening reality of an imminent war, my grandparents would have felt excited by the promise of land, jobs, and refuge being offered by a far-off country.[192]

---

190 Robert T. Muller, "Trauma from Back Home Has Long-Lasting Effects on Migrants," *The Trauma and Mental Health Report* (blog), July 25, 2022, www.trauma. blog.yorku.ca/2022/07/trauma-from-back-home-has-long-lasting-effects-on-migrants.

191 Davies, *God's Playground*, vol. 2, p. 267.

192 Though the origins of the First World War were not related to Polish problems, the Polish lands were again turned into an international battleground.

CHAPTER ELEVEN: WHERE TO GO

Western Canada The New Eldorado / Homes for Everybody / Easy to Reach / Nothing to Fear / Protected by the Government / Wheat Land / Rich Virgin Soil / Land for Mixed Farming / Land for Cattle Raising / This is Your Opportunity / Why not embrace it?

"Western Canada: The New Eldorado," Poster 1908-1918, Library and Archives Canada

Daniel Francis in his book *Selling Canada*[193] described propaganda campaigns that shaped the nation. He begins with an 1899 quote from Clifford Sifton, Minister of the Interior for the Laurier government from 1896 to 1905:

I don't care what language a man speaks, or what religion he professes. If he is honest and law-abiding, if he will go on that land and make a living for himself and his family, he is a desirable settler.[194]

At another time, Sifton is quoted as saying:

When I speak of quality, I have in mind something that is quite different from what is in the mind of the average writer or speaker upon the question of immigration. I think that a stalwart peasant in a sheepskin coat, born to the soil, whose

---

193   Daniel Francis, *Selling Canada: Three Propaganda Campaigns that Shaped the Nation* (Vancouver: Stanton, Atkins and Dosil Publishers, 2011). This is an exceptional book—well illustrated and full of facts that I used regarding the selling of Canada.

194   Daniel Francis, p. 7.

forefathers have been farmers for ten generations, with a stout wife and half-dozen children, is good quality.[195]

Francis wrote that an aggressive advertising campaign to fill the "North-West" was commenced; this meant north and west of Ontario, out to the Rockies – Rupert's Land, which had been acquired from the Hudson's Bay Company in 1869. The government's purpose was to fill the area to prevent the Americans from taking ownership.[196] Canada had been granting land there to members of the North-West Mounted Police and public servants for their service, but settlers were needed. The area was rebranded as agricultural to attract immigrants away from the United States, Australia, and South America. The government particularly sought farmers, not city dwellers, and did not encourage Jewish or Italian immigrants, as they were deemed unsuitable for and uninterested in agriculture.[197] The immigration numbers reflect the success of such campaigns (both the government's and the Canadian Pacific Railway's): in 1896, 16,835 immigrants came to Canada, in 1901, 55,747 came, and in 1906, about 200,000 immigrants arrived.[198]

---

195 Knowles, Strangers, pp. 91–92.

196 The First Nations do not appear to have been given a voice in the development of the north-west at this time.

197 Facts are from Daniel Francis, pp. 7–52.

198 Daniel Francis, p. 7.

Figure 11: Canada West – the New Homeland

Francis described the campaign led by Sifton to sell Canada to immigrants as bold and focused. Early pamphlets targeted persons in Great Britain, and apparently at one time, the government had distributed a pamphlet to every farmer there. In August 1902 at the coronation of King Edward VII, Sifton advertised Canada as having "Free Homes for Millions,"[199] and there was a constant stream of promotional literature in the London immigration office. Francis told of "Canadian crackers" there who were primed to target those in the British Isles to venture to Canada.

199 Daniel Francis, p. 49.

Journalist Ralph Stock described being buttonholed by one of Canada's insistent sales representatives. "Unctuous gentlemen met you in the street with six page pamphlets," he wrote, "imploring you to come to such and such an address and hear of the fortunes in store for the man of initiatives who would take the plunge and emigrate to Canada."[200]

Later Francis detailed Sifton reaching out to other nationalities. Advertisements declared, "The North-west, the future destiny of which will be a great and glorious one, possesses all the true elements of future greatness and prosperity," and claimed the weather was as mild as England's, with less snow than fell in the settled parts of eastern America. It was a "climate of unrivalled salubrity… one of the healthiest in the world," an incubator of a more energetic and industrious race of people. The Canadian government published millions of posters and pamphlets in up to twelve languages, describing Canada as a "land of milk and honey." A 1903 pamphlet entitled "Evolution of the Prairie by the Plow" described the rise of "tall, red, hump-shouldered elevators, where settlements had clustered into villages," and "a fenceless, unbroken expanse of nothing but wheat, wheat, wheat" – all bountiful harvests and good living.[201] Yet while the government's stated goal was to attract farmers, many of the new settlers were actually recruited by railway companies, manufacturers, and resource extraction industries. For instance, in early 1912, the Russian American Line was "approached by several Canadian Firms who informed [it] that the Canadian Railroads were in want of about 60,000

---

200 Daniel Francis, p. 28.

201 Daniel Francis, p. 42.

labourers, *preferably Russians*, and [was] asked if [it] were possible to send over up to 1,000 per month by [its] steamers."[202] The Canadian Pacific Railway advertised in many languages in the late 1800s offering to some free land and rail transportation.[203] Advertisements also encouraged women to immigrate to provide household labour, though Francis commented that many such women actually became indentured servants.[204] To secure the immigration of Mennonites, Hutterites, and Doukhobors, the campaign promised a land free of religious persecution.

In 1905, Frank Oliver, who succeeded Clifford Sifton as Minister of the Interior, took a different approach to immigration – a selective one where origin was more important than occupation. He believed that certain "races" were not compatible with Canadian society and should be discouraged.[205] There is a surprising early opinion by Sifton noted in Knowles wherein "before he learned to temper his public criticism, the MP had even castigated Slav immigrants for being a 'millstone' around the necks of Western Canadians."[206] In 1906, the *Immigration Act* was changed to increase the number of prohibited immigrants and allow for easier deportation of "undesirables." The *Immigration Act* of 1910 further banned immigrants belonging to any race deemed unsuited to the climate

---

202　See Vadim Kukushkin, *From Peasants to Labourers: Ukrainian and Belarusian Immigration from the Russian Empire to Canada* (Montreal: McGill-Queen's University Press, 2007) p. 51, quoting (with Kukushkin emphasis) from RGIA, Fonds 104, delo 265, list 102. The Russian American Line to Lord Strathcona, August 22, 1912.

203　Daniel Francis, p. 28.

204　Daniel Francis, p. 44.

205　There is a good discussion of the policy differences between Clifford Sifton and Frank Oliver in Knowles, *Strangers at Our Gates*, pp. 84–126.

206　Knowles, *Strangers at Our Gates*, p. 107.

or requirements of Canada, which targeted Blacks and Asians. Ironically, the Canadian Pacific Railway had recruited thousands of labourers from China to build the railway, but these men, as well as the Japanese and South Asians, were resented. In 1885, a head tax of $50 was imposed upon every Chinese immigrant entering Canada, a sum that was increased gradually to $500. The Chinese were denied certain jobs and confined to specific neighbourhoods. In 1907, targeting the Chinese and Japanese neighbourhoods, the Asiatic Exclusion League organized a violent riot in Vancouver. In the interesting book, *Keeping Canada British: The Ku Klux Klan in 1920s Saskatchewan*,[207] James Pitsula detailed the challenges faced in that province during the 1920s by non-British immigrants and some Canadians who were attacked by the Ku Klux Klan.

Francis set out that Oliver increased efforts to attract British and American immigrants who were thought to share Anglo-Saxon values. In Oliver's opinion, the continuation of British heritage would make Canada one of the world's great civilizations. In 1907, government agents were paid a $2.00 bonus for every British agricultural worker they placed in Ontario or Quebec. At this point, fears were growing that other immigrants were "mongrelizing" Canada, reducing its British character.[208] Regarding this inconsistency, Francis noted that it was a paradox of the publicity campaign that at the same time "the government was abroad so aggressively selling Canada as a promised land for immigrants, Canadians there were making so many of them feel inferior and unwelcome."[209] An example given was that of Frank Oliver, speaking in the House of

---

207 James Pitsula, *Keeping Canada British: The Ku Klux Klan in 1920s Saskatchewan* (Vancouver: UBC Press, 2014).

208 Daniel Francis, p. 65.

209 Daniel Francis, p. 66.

Commons, who suggested that many immigrants were "of such class and character as would deteriorate rather than elevate the condition of our people and our country."[210]

By 1911, more than 80% of the inhabitants of the Prairie provinces had been born outside Canada; concern arose over how to ensure that the Prairies' populations were conditioned and assimilated with mainstream Protestant Anglo-Saxon values. There was no such concern for British and American immigrants. Francis concluded by saying that the openness that had attracted so many immigrants to the country began giving way to a very narrow interpretation of what constituted the Canadian nationality.[211] (For example, the change of policy after Sifton's departure required Doukhobor's to be naturalized, which they had opposed, and to occupy individual households rather than live communally.) Between 1896 and 1914, about three million newcomers settled in Canada. My grandparents, as well as their families and friends, were a few of those newcomers, but they arrived with a farming background as Eastern Europeans (Western Slavs), who had to learn new customs and a new language in a less-than-friendly milieu.

---

210   Daniel Francis, p. 66.

211   Daniel Francis, p. 66.

CHAPTER TWELVE: THE JOURNEY

What you leave behind is not what is engraved in stone monuments but what is woven into the lives of others.
　　—Pericles, Greek Politician (495–429 BC)

Life can only be understood backwards, but it must be lived forwards.
　　—Søren Kierkegaard

When my paternal family left the Russian Partition of Poland, emigrants leaving from rural areas often had to travel from their village by cart to catch a train to the coast to board a ship. The Polish village of Rozpaszka was located approximately ninety-sixty kilometres east of Vilnius. In the early 1900s, there was a network of trains in the western Russian provinces linking Vilnius, Grodno, and Lida on the Baltic coast. Shipping lines were becoming more competitive and sophisticated and ticket agencies in larger Eastern European cities offered tickets and packaged itineraries for trains, ships, and portside accommodations. Libau, its German name in 1914 but now named Liepaja, in Latvia, is a coastal seaport and was accessible from Vilnius (335 kilometres) or from Lida (425 kilometres) on the Libau-Romny rail line, built by the Russian Empire in 1871-74 to transport Ukrainian exports, especially grain, to the Baltic Sea for shipping. My grandmother and her family would have gone by horse and cart or wagon from Rozpaszka to Vilnius and then by train to Libau on the Libau-Romny Line to board a ship there.

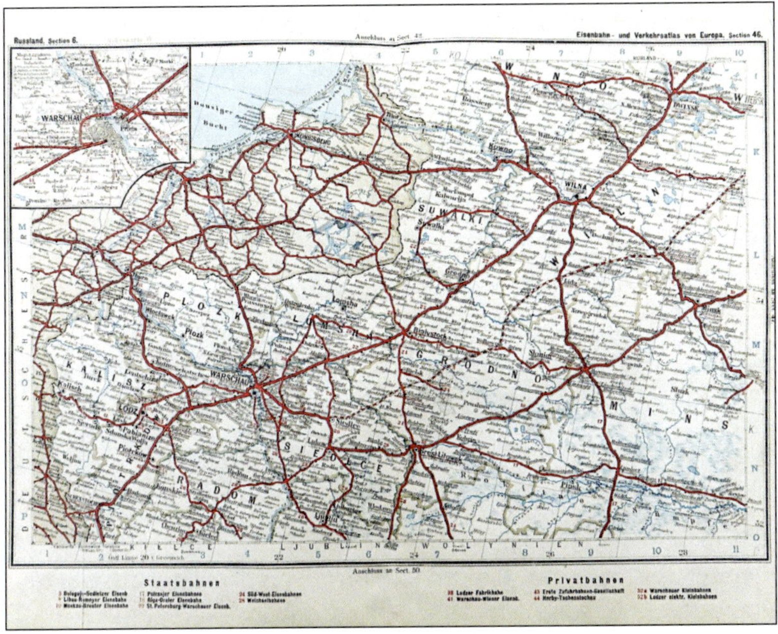

Figure 12: Map of Railway Lines in Eastern Europe and Russia, 1905

Figure 13: Emigrant Train Station in Libau (now Liepaja, Latvia), 1910

It took me some time to find documentation for the vessel that Joanna, Vincent, and their children boarded to emigrate. I sent away to the National Library of Canada in Ottawa to obtain microfiche films of manifests for ships leaving the Russian Partition in early 1914. After hours of looking at passenger lists on a screen at the Vancouver Public Library, to my delight I found a ship, the S.S. *Kursk*, whose manifest contained the names Vincent Ostrowsky (age 31) and Johanna (age 27), Sigismund (age 3½), Geurick (age 2), and Stefanie (age 9 months). On arrival at the port of entry and, indeed, even on the manifest, names were often simplified, anglicized, changed, or corrected by an immigration official. For instance, my father's name as we knew him was Henry, but on the manifest, it was Geurick, and Ostrowski was spelled in the Russian manner as Ostrowsky. Country of Birth was listed as Russia, Race of People – Polish, Destination – Truro, Occupation in [departure] Country – farmer and housewife, and Intended Occupation in Canada – farmer and housewife, Religious Denomination – Roman Catholic, and Travelled Inland on – ICR (Intercolonial Railway?).[212] Thus documented, my grandparents, my father, and his siblings boarded the S.S. *Kursk* from Libau[213] on April 14, 1914, just three and a half months before the outbreak of the First World War on July 28, 1914. Each ticket had cost them about $25.

As an interesting aside, how Polish surnames originated at this time is set out in Mikołaj Glinski's "A Foreigner's Guide to Polish

212   See Appendix A for a copy of the Manifest.

213   The first Atlantic crossing by a steamer was in 1818, the S.S. *Savannah*, an American hybrid sailing ship/steamer.

Surnames."[214] He explains that most surnames fall into three different categories:

1. Patronymic: usually derived from a person's given name and usually ending in a suffix suggesting a family relation, e.g., Piotrowicz (from a given name Peter).

2. Toponymic: derived from a place of residence, birth, or family origin, e.g., Tarnowski (from the town of Tarnow).

3. Cognominal: created from a nickname, usually based on an occupation, a physical description, or a character trait, e.g., Kowalczyk (from the Polish word for blacksmith); also Glowacz (from the word that describes someone with a big head).

Names ending in *ski* were originally used to indicate a topographic location or possessive relation and were used by Polish nobility. However, in the 1500s, *ski* names became popular with the middle class and peasants. Names ending in *kiewicz*, such as my grandmother's birth name of Pietkiewicz, were originally from the Belarus area; many families in the eastern region of the Commonwealth were originally Ruthenian and became Polonized over many centuries. Surnames of a woman differed from that of her husband or father, for example, Ostrowski for a male, Ostrowska for a female.

---

214 See Mikołaj Glinski, "A Foreigner's Guide to Polish Surnames," *Culture.Pl*, last updated February 18, 2021, www.culture.pl/en/article/a-foreigners-guide-to-polish-surnames.

Figure 14: Libau Osta Port Bridge

From about 1906 to 1914, Libau was an important (legal) emigration destination as it was the most direct route from western parts of the Russian Empire to North America; across the Atlantic, New York was an important destination starting in 1906, with Halifax added later. Western European ports were the departing place for illegal travellers.[215] The port of Libau had undergone a revitalization that included dredging and building infrastructure, and emigration companies were established to attract people in the poorest Russian provinces and ship them overseas. Early in this period, the emigrants arriving at the port often stayed in private homes, some of which were quite unsanitary. As there was a risk of infectious disease transmission, Libau city council in 1907 established a minimum level of hygiene for these homes, which included that the rooms be cleaned at least once per week, that the walls

---

215 Kukushkin, p. 51.

be painted at least twice per year, that fresh hay be used for beds and that water for the guests be drawn only from artesian wells.[216] Later, shipping companies built their own quarters for emigrants, one of which was the Great Emigrants House.

Figure 15: People carrying materials from the train to the ship at Libau

216 Geoff Chester, "Final Point of the Russian Empire: Liepāja's Half a Million Emigrants," *Deep Baltic*, December 2, 2015, www.deepbaltic.com/2015/12/02/final-point-of-the-russian-empire-the-story-of-liepajas-half-a-million-emigrants/. I have relied on the well-researched information provided in this article in my writing here.

Figure 16: The S.S. *Kursk*

The S.S. *Kursk*,[217] a twin-screw steamer, was one of thirteen ships on the Russian American Line, a subsidiary line of the East

217 The following is taken from "Kursk / Polonia 1910," The Ships List, accessed November 9, 2023, www.theshipslist.com/ships/descriptions/ShipsK.shtml. "The Kursk was built by Barclay, Curle & Co., Glasgow in 1910 for the Russian American Line. She was a 7,858 gross ton vessel, length 450 ft x beam 56.2 ft, with two funnels, two masts, and two screw propellors (hence, "twin screw"), able to travel 15 knots per hour. It could accommodate up to 120 in first class, 178 in second, and 1,288 in third and fourth. Launched on July 7, 1910, she sailed from Libau on her maiden voyage to New York on November 2 of that year. She commenced her last voyage from Libau to Copenhagen, Halifax, and New York on July 7, 1914 before being transferred to the Glasgow–New York service on November 5 of that year, sailing on her first voyage from New York to Archangel on November 20. In 1917, she came under the management of Cunard, a British company. In 1921, she went to the Baltic American Line, was renamed the Polonia, and began her first voyage between Glasgow, New York, Danzig and Libau on January 23. On March 8, she started her first voyage from Libau to Danzig, Boston and New York and in September of that year was refitted to carry 300 cabin and 500 third-class passengers. In October 1927, she was further altered to carry 120 cabin, 180 tourist, and 500 third-class passengers. On October 31, 1929, she commenced her last voyage from Danzig to Copenhagen, Halifax, and New York and in 1930 went to the Polish Gdynia America Line. They used her from April 11, 1930 on their Danzig–Copenhagen–Halifax–New York service and from May 28, 1930 on the Gdynia–Copenhagen–Halifax–New York run. She commenced her last voyage

Asiatic Company, in business from 1900 to 1917. The ship sailed on April 14 from Libau, bound for New York via Halifax, and arrived at Halifax on April 25 at 3 p.m. At the Halifax landing, seventeen persons from the second cabin and 210 in steerage disembarked. None was held in quarantine. The ship's Master was A. Kirschfeldt. Interestingly, the Certificate of the Ship's Surgeon (illegible signature) on the manifest indicated a detailed physical and mental examination had been conducted for each immigrant on board. He wrote as follows:

> I hereby certify that I have daily during the present passage made a general inspection of the passengers on this vessel and that I have at least once during the passage made a detailed individual examination of each immigrant on board and that I have seen no passenger thereon who I have reason to believe is, or is likely to become, insane, epileptic or consumptive, or who is idiotic, feeble-minded or afflicted with a contagious infectious or loathsome disease; or who is deaf, dumb or blind or otherwise physically defective or whose present appearance would lead me to believe that he or she might be debarred from entering Canada under [the] "Immigration Act" with the exception of persons whose names are enumerated on the Ship Surgeon's List for Medical Examining Officer which I have prepared for such officer giving my medical opinion on the cases therein dealt with; and that there were no deaths or births during the passage except those mentioned on the said list.

on this run on May 2, 1933 and was transferred to the Constanza–Haifa route until 1939, when she was scrapped in Italy."

However, the manifest shows that one person travelling in steerage for the Halifax port of entry and one for New York were detained by the medical examiner.

The Canadian Museum of Immigration at Pier 21 has good historical information that I have summarized below.[218] At the arrival port in Canada, legislation regulating entry into Canada began in 1869 with the *Immigration Act* of that year, brought in by John A. Macdonald's government to encourage settlement, especially in the west. The Act focused on the safety of immigrants coming to Canada, including protecting them from exploitation on arrival. Ships were overcrowded and lacked sufficient provisions, making passengers particularly vulnerable by the time they arrived, and businesses at ports of entry overcharged. It limited the number of passengers on board to one person for every two tons of the ship's weight and captains were required to provide customs officials with lists of the ship's passengers and the medical condition of each person. The federal cabinet had the right to prohibit paupers and destitute immigrants from entry which included refugees. Businesses offering lodging and transportation had to get a special licence. Immigration numbers were low for about thirty years after 1867.

In 1885, a Royal Commission on Chinese Immigration resulted in the *Chinese Immigration Act*, and after a 1904-05 Royal Commission on Italian Immigration, the more restrictive *Immigration Act* of 1906 expanded the categories of prohibited immigrants, formalized a deportation process, and assigned the government powers to make arbitrary judgments about admission. In 1908, a "Gentlemen's Agreement" restricted Japanese immigration to Canada and

---

218 See "Immigration Act, 1869," Canadian Museum of Immigration at Pier 21, accessed November 9, 2023, www.pier21.ca/research/immigration-history/immigration-act-1869.

introduced a Continuous Journey Regulation, requiring that immigrants travel to Canada by continuous journey from their home country (effectively blocking immigration from India). The *Immigration Act* of 1910 further expanded the list of prohibited immigrants and legislatively governed the passengers on the S.S. *Kursk*. Section 3 of that act stated:

> 3. No immigrant… shall be permitted to land in Canada… who belongs to any of the following classes… (a) idiots, imbeciles, feeble-minded persons, epileptics, insane persons, and persons who have been insane within five years previous; (b) persons afflicted with any loathsome disease, or with a disease which is contagious or infectious… (c) immigrants who are dumb, blind, or otherwise physically defective… unless they have sufficient money… (d) persons who have been convicted of a crime involving moral turpitude; (e) prostitutes and women and girls coming to Canada for any immoral purpose and pimps… (f) persons who procure or attempt to bring into Canada prostitutes or women or girls for the purpose of prostitution or other immoral purpose; (g) professional beggars or vagrants… (h) immigrants to whom money has been given or loaned by any charitable organization… unless it is shown that the authority in writing [from the appropriate Superintendent] has been obtained [this provision was included apparently due to an influx of impoverished British immigrants in 1907]… (i) [failure to comply with other conditions and requirements of any regulations].

Orders-in-Council in 1910 required immigrants of Asiatic origin to have $200 in their possession, and all other immigrants were required to have a minimum of $25 upon their arrival in Canada.

Most emigrants at the time would have travelled "steerage class." The name derives from the steering tackle running through a portion of the lower deck of a ship connecting the rudder to the tiller or helm, an area used to accommodate passengers – typically emigrants on their way to "the new land" – often in a single large hold. Back in the early 1900s, there was growing concern about the conditions in steerage class. Charged with the worst case of neglect of steerage passengers on record under the *Passenger Act* of 1882, the owners of the British steamer S.S. *Orteric* were fined $7,960 by Acting Secretary Cable of the U.S. Department of Commerce and Labor. Among her 1,242 passengers, there were in the eight weeks of her voyage 58 deaths, 57 being children; the births numbered 14; the sexes were not properly segregated during the larger part of the time; the ventilation of the ship was inadequate and greatly increased the mortality rate; the hospital facilities were ill-ventilated and without proper equipment, and the sanitary conditions of the vessel were almost beyond belief.[219]

In 1907, the United States Immigration Commission commenced a full inquiry, examination, and investigation into the subject of immigration. The result, published in 1911, was forty-one volumes of reports covering such subjects as Immigrants in Industries, Immigrants in Cities, and Changes in Bodily Form of Descendants of Immigrants.[220] In the commission's investigation on travel at sea, the members did an ingenious job, tasking their agents to travel in the guise of immigrants in the steerage of twelve

---

219 "Worst Case on Record," *The American Marine Engineer* 7, 1 (January 1912): 20, Gjenvick-Gjønvik Archives, accessed November 9, 2023, www.gjenvick.com/Immigration/Steerage/WorstCaseOfAbuse-SteeragePassengers-1912.html.

220 William Paul Dillingham, *Reports of the Immigration Commission*, 41 vols. (Washington, D.C.: Government Printing Office, 1911).

trans-Atlantic ships, which included all of the more important lines and every type of steerage. This was the subject of a very revealing report released in 1909. Though it focused on U.S. immigrant voyages, some ships crossing the Atlantic stopped at Canadian ports to offload immigrants, as the S.S. *Kursk* did on its way to New York.

Since the S.S. *Kursk* was built in 1910, I presume it is one of those described as the "new steerage" in the *Reports of the Immigration Commission*, which included liners carrying emigrants from the north of Europe. Generally, women travelling without a male escort went down one hatch to their part of the deck, men down another, and families down a third. (Some of the ships with new steerage facilities had enclosed berths or staterooms at higher prices.) The bedding was sometimes unsanitary, and floor space was used for hand baggage. There were hooks for clothes, a seat, a mirror, and maybe a washstand and towels. Open space above the partition walls allowed air circulation. Lights near the ceiling in the passageways lit the staterooms and berths. On larger steamers there were still some extensive compartments that lacked privacy, mostly occupied by men. Descriptions in the commission's report indicated that an ongoing problem in old and new steerage was air quality, and the lower the deck, the worse the air. For this reason, many passengers would escape to the open deck very early in the morning. The dining rooms, sometimes divided into one room for the men and one for women and families, were used as general recreation rooms between meals, sometimes with a piano. The general complaint regarding the food was that it was spoiled by poor preparation and lack of variety. Children received milk and beef tea, and those with eating problems were given gruel.

The report noted that inspections of the steerage quarters by customs officials at the ports of entry were quite perfunctory, and an inspector – who often was not familiar with the ship's plan – saw a steerage that had been prepared for his approval. The report's authors strongly recommended that a government official actually travel on the ship for the full journey so conditions throughout the journey would be continually open to inspection.

There appears to have been some variance in steerage conditions from ship to ship. Although the American investigator, disguised as an immigrant, rode on twelve different ships, her reports did not name them. Her summary of one steamer she rode from London, England, reads as follows:

> To sum up, let me make some general statements that will give an idea of the awfulness of steerage conditions on the steamer in question. During the twelve days in the steerage, I lived in disorder and in surroundings that offended every sense. Only the fresh breeze from the sea overcame the sickening odors. The vile language of the men, the screams of the women defending themselves, the crying of children, wretched because of their surroundings, and practically every sound that reached the ear, irritated beyond endurance. There was no sight before which the eye did not prefer to close. Everything was dirty, sticky, and disagreeable to the touch. Every impression was offensive. Worse than this was the general air of immorality. For fifteen hours each day I witnessed all around me the improper, indecent, and forced mingling of men and women who were total strangers and often did not understand one word of the same language. People cannot live in such surroundings and not be influenced. . . . All that has been said of the mingling of the crew with the women of the steerage is also true of the association of the men steerage passengers with the women. Several times, when the sight of what was occurring about me was no longer endurable,

I interfered and asked the men if they knew they might be deported were their actions reported on land! Most of them had been in America before, and the answer generally given me was: "Immorality is permitted in America if it is anywhere. Everyone can do as he chooses; no one investigates his mode of life, and no account is made or kept of his doings."[221]

The investigator also wrote a report on old and new-type steerages in the same ship on which she travelled:

The nearly 300 passengers were a mixed lot from fairly well-to-do Americans, German artisans, clerks, etc. coming to America to try their fortune to servants returning from a visit to their native lands, labourers returning after the crisis, peasant women going to their husbands in the mining section, and sheep herders, clothed in crude garments made by themselves from the skins of the sheep; from those who understood the use of the fork to those who ate with their fingers. Nor was this mingling of extremes delightful to either side. Those who came from comfortable circumstances found accommodations somewhat too plain and simple and the presence of "them people awful" meaning the immigrants. The latter, again being made to feel their inferiority, held themselves in the background and hesitated to enjoy the comforts for which they had paid. Some who had been obliged to pay the difference with their last money and go third class

221   Dillingham, *Reports of the Immigration Commission*, vol. 37, "S. Doc.No.753, 61st Congress 3d Session," p. 23. (The title of vol. 37 is "Steerage Conditions – Importation and Harbouring of Women for Immoral Purposes – Immigrant Homes and Aid Societies – Immigrant Banks" and makes fascinating reading.)

worried about their admittance at Ellis Island, and so did not enjoy the added comforts. Others were glad that they had escaped the steerage, though it took their last or all but their last.[222]

. . . . [The] entire lack of privacy accounts for more than one of the filthy or indecent habits of the immigrants on board. People, both men and women, who were ordinarily cleanly about their person complained that it was totally impossible to keep clean with the given accommodations. A self-respecting person couldn't wash properly in a room that was being used at the same time by several others, and there was no avoiding becoming dirty. Some very nice German girls, seeking to change their linen in private, waited until long after midnight, when all were asleep, and even then stood as guard and screen for each other against the steward on duty in the compartment.

The floors in all the steerage quarters except on the main or open deck were made of large sheets of iron. In the sleeping compartments, though the floors, even under the berths, must be kept free of baggage, they were never washed. They were swept in the morning in preparation for the daily inspection by the captain and his officers. And whenever the waste accumulated it was again swept. But this sweeping by no means kept the floor clean. No sick cans or receptacles for waste of any kind were provided. The sea was rough much of the time and there were many sick. That alone kept the

---

222 Dillingham, *Reports of the Immigration Commission*, vol. 37, p. 33.

floor wet and in an awful condition, and since it was never washed the smell from it was dreadful.[223]

It was intriguing to piece together what my grandparents, my father, and his brother and sister may have experienced! I imagine their emotions would have been intense: fear and surprise at the poor living conditions on the ship, fear of the dark nights and turbulence on the ocean, fear of sickness and theft, and anxiety of what awaited them on landing. My father recalled seeing a horned cow on the ship as they crossed the Atlantic; such cows were used to supply fresh milk for the infants on board. But how sanitary was the food and drink? How many passengers got seasick? From the report above, many would have become sick.

Not only was physical wherewithal needed to arrive in sufficient health to start a new life, but special attributes were needed to *emotionally* survive the trip – courage, vision, steadfastness, and resourcefulness.

---

223 Dillingham, *Reports of the Immigration Commission*, vol. 37, pp. 34–35.

CHAPTER THIRTEEN: HALIFAX

Just after the war, I remember an incident in which a soldier was arrested for stealing a bar of soap from Woolworths in Halifax. He was jailed. Other soldiers came to his rescue, and a riot broke out. All of the police and firemen were called to hose the rioters. I saw a fire truck being pushed off a wharf into the harbour. All the stores were closed, and many windows were smashed.

—Henry J. Ostrowski, *My Life and Work*

The S.S. *Kursk* landed (it arrived at 3:00 pm) in Canada at Halifax, Nova Scotia at 7:30 pm on April 25, 1914. The passengers disembarked in Halifax at Pier 2, Canada's east-coast immigration shed from 1895 to 1915; during that time, 2.7 million immigrants arrived through this pier. A historian at the Canadian Museum of Immigration at Pier 21[224] has described the immigration service in Halifax in 1914 as in transition: the department had a new building in progress in 1912, but to erect it, the old one needed to be torn down, so the temporary quarters were in a nearby building that had been operated by a steamship company.

---

224 Steven Schwinghamer at Canadian Museum of Immigration, personal communication with the author, 2021.

Figure 17: Ships docked at Pier 2, the Deep Water Halifax Terminals

As mentioned, the ship's manifest indicates that the destination of my grandmother and her family was Truro, Nova Scotia. Having arrived in 1905, my grandmother's brothers, John and Wladek, were already in the province. They had worked for a few years as labourers in the Sydney coal mines for Nova Scotia Steel and Coal Company Ltd., then had lived for a short time in Truro, a farming community. I don't recall my father ever mentioning Truro, only his life as a small boy in Halifax, so I presume my grandparents did not actually go to Truro. John and Wladek moved to Halifax from Truro sometime later to start their own businesses.

My grandmother and her family lived in Halifax from 1914 to 1920. Those were tough times for them. She bore three additional children during those years – Casimir, Felix and Peter. All died, possibly due to the Spanish flu of 1918[225] and/or malnutrition in a nursing home where one or two were placed. I have yet to find birth and death records for any of the three.

My grandfather Vincent, after initially working at Moirs Chocolates for a short time, ran a candy store on Gottingen Street in Halifax, and the family lived behind it, with a small vegetable garden and chickens. The candy store made little money, and food was scarce. As my father did not eat regularly, he remembers being hungry and stealing three eggs from a hen house; upon confessing to his teacher, he was punished by having to save up and pay seven cents for them. At age six, making half a cent per paper (which sold at two cents), my father and his older brother started selling the *Halifax Herald* newspaper on the street. By the time they left Halifax in 1920, my father had saved $6.00. My father's sister Stephanie did not walk until she was three years old because of rickets brought on by a lack of vitamin D that led to calcium and phosphorus deficiencies. Later on Joanna worked part-time for her brother John in a restaurant he opened, but because she could not speak English, she found the work was difficult. My father went to St. Patrick's School[226] in Halifax, next to St. Patrick's Church,

---

225 "Remembering the Forgotten Dead: Nova Scotia and the Great Influenza Pandemic of 1918–1920," Nova Scotia Museum, accessed November 14, 2023, www.museum.novascotia.ca/collections-research/virtual-exhibits/remembering-forgotten-dead.

226 St. Patrick's School was opened on April 8, 1872, a brick building with ten classrooms and 786 pupils. Overcrowding led to a girls' school being built in 1888. Due to a fire in 1898, renovations were made to the boys' school, which again became overcrowded. Construction of a new school building on Brunswick Street was contemplated, but the start of the First World War put this on hold. In the Halifax explosion of 1917, St. Patrick's Girls High School, St. Patrick's Girls School and St. Patrick's Boys School were all damaged. The boys' school was repaired but not replaced until 1920. See "St. Patrick's High School, Halifax, Nova Scotia," Wikipedia, accessed November 14, 2023, www.en.wikipedia.org/wiki/St._Patrick%27s_High_School_(Halifax,_Nova_Scotia).

and was held back in kindergarten for three years because he could not speak English.

For immigrants like my grandmother and family, life was clearly very hard. They spoke little or no English; there were no government medical plans; they had very little money, and they lost three children. Things could have gotten worse, though – and they did. The Halifax explosion occurred at 9:15 am on December 6, 2017. My father was in his school room, and below are the notes he wrote about the event:

At the time, I was attending St. Patrick's school, next to St. Patrick's Church on Barrington Street when two ships, the *Mont Blanc* and the *Imo* collided. The Mont Blanc, which was loaded with dynamite and ammunition, burst into flames and exploded. The school shook, followed by a large bang, and the school windows imploded while our teacher Miss White[227] was walking to the window to see what was happening. The flying glass killed her. All the school children who remained seated ran out. One side of the school collapsed. I ran out of the school and walked around the town for a few hours picking up caps. I saw many of the dead being hauled away in coal wagons with all kinds of store merchandise strewn on the streets. A flowerpot fell on Zig's head, causing some minor injuries. On reaching home, I found that mother had been injured by flying glass. About 2,000 people were killed and thousands were blinded. The next day we had a record snowfall. The houses in Bedford basin were all

227 Susie White, age thirty-two, is listed as having died on December 6, 1917. See "Halifax Explosion: A List of Those that Died," Nova Scotia Archives, accessed November 14, 2023, www.novascotia.ca/archives/remembrance/results/.

flattened and a piece of plate steel from one of the ships was found in Windsor, forty miles away. While houses were being repaired, the Red Cross set up tents and provided emergency food and shelter on Citadel Hill. After a week some children were still found alive buried in the ruins.[228]

Figure 18: Campbell River Road after the Halifax Explosion

I did not find any further information about my grandmother's wounds caused by flying glass, but I'm sure this explosion caused lasting trauma to all who were there.

The "Spanish Flu" followed, killing close to 2,000 people in Nova Scotia from 1918 to 1920. It is speculated that the flu could

228   Henry Ostrowski, *My Life and Work* (Mississauga, Ontario: Self-Published, 1987), p. 4.

have arrived via ships carrying sick troops returning from war, or on fishing boats from New England that docked in Nova Scotia ports. The first reported death was on September 1, 1918. It is probable that one or more of my grandparents' three young children who passed away died from this flu, as mortality was high in children younger than five years old.

My father reported additional personal incidents from these times in Halifax that could have been fatal for him. Once, he was alone on a raft in Halifax harbour and the raft disintegrated. He couldn't swim and was left holding onto a small log until he was rescued by someone in the harbour. On another occasion, he was in the waters in the Northwest Arm – an Atlantic inlet immediately south of Halifax – and slipped into a hole. He still hadn't learned to swim, and after he had gone down six or more times while shouting for help, a stranger dove in and pulled him out. A further narrow escape occurred when the family were living in the basement of a dry-goods store on Gottingen Street where my grandparents worked from 1917 to 1919. On a cold winter night, he was awakened by a burning sensation in his lungs. He first covered himself with a blanket but finally realized he had to get up and out when he saw his clothes burning on a chair. He was the last person out of the house. He was six or seven years old.

My grandfather Vincent left the family in about 1919 and, at that time, the family was struggling financially. I am not aware of the particular circumstances that brought about this departure, but it could be that he was looking for a new place for the family to settle as it had been so rough for them since their arrival. He went to Buenos Aires, Argentina. In the 1800s, especially after various failed insurrections, a number of Poles immigrated to Argentina – some joined the Argentinian armed forces; others obtained professional positions in government or civil society. However, in 1897,

Poles migrated for agricultural opportunities, generally to an area in Misiones Province where the government gave new families 25-50 hectares of land along with a financial loan to build a home and purchase supplies. The area took on a distinctly Polish look, with small homes, roadside chapels, churches, and schools. The number of Poles who actually settled there is difficult to ascertain, as the immigrants from the partitioned homeland were identified as Austrian, German, or Russian rather than Polish.[229] In 1901, Misiones Governor Juan Jose Lanusse wrote to a friend:

> I've seen 500 of these immigrants arrive in Posadas in a steamer barely able to take half of them… Eminently Catholic, the first thing they do upon arrival in Posadas is go to church…. In agriculture they only have rudimentary skills…. [T]here are Poles who have resown three or four times in a season, fields destroyed by ants with a patience and persistence inconceivable in Italian, Spanish or any other farmers. . . . Their crime rate is very low; they are very moral and marry very young and their women are most fecund.[230]

Vincent's absence was hard on the family he left behind, especially on my father. He later learned from his cousin Adela, who came from Poland and joined them in Timmins several years later, that Vincent had returned to Poland and later died there after an unknown time in Argentina. My father later vowed that he would

---

229 I have relied on Bernarda Zubrzycki, "Polish Immigrants in Argentina," *Polish American Studies* 69, 1 (Spring 2012): 75–98, for the information presented here on this issue.

230 Michael Soltys, "A Different Kind of Multinational: Immigrants to Argentina from Eastern Europe," *Buenos Aires Herald*, September 1988, as quoted in Zubrzycki, p. 82.

never leave his family as his father had, even though Vincent's departure could have been to search for a better place to settle. Now as a parent on her own, Joanna must have been distressed at her predicament. However, I wonder about the real personal loss to her, as I understand hers had been an arranged marriage and Vincent certainly had not done well as an entrepreneur in the candy business. Family innuendo suggests he became a gambler to try to make money for the family. The lure of free land in Argentina and a loan to build a home might have been another gamble, one he counted on that unfortunately did not work out. Since Canada's early ads for immigrants as a "land of milk and honey" did not describe the reality that many immigrants experienced, Argentina's economic promises to settlers also might not have been accurate. But I feel that like many other Poles, Joanna was used to loss – the loss of her homeland, her parents, siblings, and three children. She was a strong woman. Her two brothers, who were now in Halifax, and a Polish family, the Seniuks, gave her assistance at this time. In true Polish fashion, she moved on in her life.

In fact, her brother John was credited with being a big help and support. Her brother Wladek, now married to a "sophisticated English lady who had little use for her poor in-laws," from 1919 to 1920 owned a restaurant business on Barrington Street across from the City Hall. When my father and my brother were eight and ten years old respectively, Wladek employed them to wash dishes and crank the ice cream machine for which they received a free meal as payment. For unknown reasons, he sold the restaurant and then bought into the Waverly Hotel at 1266 Barrington Street. (Joanna and the children then moved in there.) The hotel was not profitable and unfortunately left him with little money. (Whatever its difficulties back then, the Waverley is still operating as a hotel in

Halifax.)[231] In 1920, the family moved to Montreal, prompted by the six difficult years in Halifax and the report of new opportunities in that city with a population of over 600,000.

Figure 19: Waverley Hotel, Barrington St., Halifax

231   "The Waverly Inn," BB Nova Scotia, accessed November 14, 2023, www.bbnovascotia.com/content/waverly-inn.

CHAPTER FOURTEEN: MONTREAL AND TIMMINS – THE MINING TOWN

Remaining silent about the past does little to immunize the next generation.

  —Mark Wolynn, *It Didn't Start with You*

My grandmother Joanna, two of her three children, and one of her brothers took the train to Montreal; only her son, Zigmund, and my grandmother's brother Wladek stayed in Halifax. Zigmund continued to attend St. Patrick's School for a while and helped Wladek with the hotel. In Montreal, my grandmother's brother John had opened a dry goods store on the corner of St. Philippe and Notre Dame, near the St. Henri railway station, and Joanna and her two children were able to live in the back and side of the store.

My father went to school in Montreal for only a few weeks. Once, five or six French boys attacked him for being an immigrant and stuck pins in his neck, but his brother (who had by that time also arrived in Montreal) came to his rescue, and they ran away. Another time, my father was lost and was knocked out by a girl who came up from behind and hit him over the head with a stick. While all the family was out one day on a picnic at the Lachine Rapids, the dry goods store burned down. After that, Joanna's brother John went to Detroit to join brother Wladek who had opened a confectionary and ice cream parlour there. John later started a similar business but was robbed twice and injured.

My grandmother and her three children then moved to Timmins, Ontario, on their own in 1921 to join the Seniuks, the Polish family she knew from Halifax.[232] The population of Timmins at that time was just 3,843 persons. The Seniuks had obtained work at the McIntyre Mine, an underground gold and copper mine in Schumacher, Ontario. Initially, grandmother and the children lived with the Seniuks in their home. They then moved to 31 Main Avenue, where on borrowed money my grandmother started a small grocery store, she and her children living above the store. The premises were very basic – no indoor plumbing, water from a well, and a couple of wood stoves for heating. My ten-year-old father did most of the wood chopping for the stove. A few years later, the house was connected to water and sewer pipes.

Children growing up in Timmins had lots to do, though schooling was somewhat in disarray. The English Catholic School was closed shortly after they arrived in Timmins. At the French Catholic School where the nuns taught in English about one hour per day, my father was strapped by the janitor for causing damage which my father denied having done; after the strapping he quit that school and did not go to school for the rest of the year. He then went to the Mattagami Public School, a one-room rural schoolhouse, but it closed after one year. He then was sent to Central Public School and did well there, and on finishing, went to a Timmins high school. Outside of school, the students created their own hockey rink in the winters by hauling water from a ditch; they worked at part-time jobs, and they generally explored the area.

In 1925 when he was fourteen, my father came down with typhoid fever, followed by pleurisy and pneumonia. He believed

---

232 There is an article in *The Porcupine Advance*, Timmins, Ontario, dated April 15, 1925, describing unusual circumstances around the death of Mrs. Seniuk. Her body was found near a Hollinger fence with rocks placed on her clothing, and she had been dead since the evening before. An inquest was held.

he contracted the typhoid fever when drinking water from a stream that drained nearby swamps where a cow was pastured. He was delirious and then in a coma for ten days. Put on a starvation diet, he went from 120 pounds to seventy-five. My grandmother hired a young girl from Cobalt to help in the house, and a nurse came by daily, but for a while, there was little hope of him surviving, and at one point, he received the last rites from a Catholic priest. As he finally began to improve, friends and his teacher came by to see him as he had missed many months of school. In his recuperative period, he apparently was fed a lot of eggnog with brandy. He said what pulled him through this illness was his Catholic faith and his concern for his pets – his pigeons, rabbits, and chickens.

Around 1923, my grandmother met Joseph Pluto, a Polish fellow who operated a grocery store nearby on Wilson Avenue in Timmins. He had previously been a prospector for gold, worked in mines, and before opening the store was employed as a mucker boss in the Hollinger Mines. He and my grandmother married, combined their grocery businesses, hired a reliable French butcher, Edgar Lemaire, and successfully attracted Polish, French, and English customers. They had a thriving enterprise until 1929 when Mr. Pluto became ill with silicosis from his work in the mines, whereupon they sold the business fortuitously, just before the stock market crash. Leaving my father to board with the Talaska family and Zigmund in a boarding house, Joseph and Joanna took a three-month trip to Poland with daughter Stephanie – a trip that reunited Joanna with her family that she had not seen for fifteen years. After many initial years of hardship in Canada, my grandmother had finally started a life for herself and her family in Timmins, a town that had a Polish community and attracted many other immigrants, as the mines and the usual ancillary businesses offered plenty of employment.

In 2016, my husband and I visited Timmins and did some searching for family history. The reference librarian at the local library,[233] Karina Douglas, was a great help, showing me books on early Timmins and old phone books. In the 1926-27 phone book, I found an address for "Joanna Ostrowsky (widow Vincent; meats and groc)" listed at 31 Main Street, and in the 1928 phone book a "Mrs. J. Ostrowsky, grocer," still at 31 Main Street. In the 1936 phone book was "Johanna Pluta" (that being, in Polish, the feminine form of the surname Pluto); at "160 Spruce north, Zigmund Ostroski [*sic*] (my uncle), Goldfields Dry Goods, 70 1/2 Tamarack," as well as Adela Orpel (my grandmother's niece) at 162 Elm Street, Henry Ostrowski at 160 Spruce North and "Stephanie Ostrowski, stenographer at Gauthier & Platus, 160 Spruce north." In the early 1930s, the family moved to 77 Wilson Avenue. Joanna's dry goods store, Goldfield's Dry Goods, which she opened after Joseph Pluto's death, was at the corner of Algonquin Boulevard and Pine Street.

---

233   Next to the Timmins library and museum was a walk-in display of a Hollinger home, one of the 250 alternating green and red tarpaper row houses built by the company and rented to the miners. The house was quite small (probably about 20' x 25' inside) but warmly done up, with crocheted doilies on an armchair; a home suitable for a small family.

Figure 20: 160–162 Spruce St. N., Timmins, 1935

The Timmins area is renowned for mining – gold, zinc, copper, nickel and silver. How did Timmins get its name? How did Noah Timmins acquire his first bonanza? It was silver found by two workers – McKinley and Darragh – near Long Lake (later called Cobalt Lake about 230 kilometres southeast of Timmins) during the construction of the Temiskaming & Northern Ontario Railway (T&NO) in August 1903; it was a big find at that time. A great interest in mineral exploration in northern Ontario was beginning. A month later, a blacksmith named Fred La Rose, who was also working at the time on the T&NO railway and living out of his small cabin in the area (near mile 103 from North Bay), according to legend, threw a hammer at a pesky fox, missed the fox but hit a rock revealing silver. At that time, Noah Timmins, born in Mattawa, Ontario, was working in his father's shop that sold supplies to travellers to and from the north. La Rose came to the shop for supplies and told Noah about his find. Noah was very interested and soon after bought into the claim and later fully bought the claim with others. Later, Noah then asked his nephew, Alphonse Paré, a geology student, to investigate further prospects. He, then, in partnership with others bought out stakes from Benny Hollinger, Alec Gillies, and others with adjacent claims in the Porcupine area. A new community was developing near the mining claims, and it was Noah's nephew who suggested that it should be named after his uncle Noah. The community grew swiftly and was incorporated as a town in 1912. Noah Timmins is considered one of the founding fathers of Canada's mining industry.[234] He died in January 1936 at the age of sixty-nine while vacationing in Palm Beach, Florida.[235]

It was gold though, that triggered the Porcupine Gold Rush in 1909 near Timmins. Gold in quartz veins was first found by geologists in 1896 near Porcupine Lake, a lake about twelve kilometers from Timmins. In 1909, a prospector named Jack Wilson in the Harry Preston prospecting crew found a hill of quartz full of gold, later to be referred to as the Golden Staircase, not far from Porcupine Lake. It was this huge find that set off the Porcupine Gold Rush of 1909 to the Timmins area. It was developed initially using open-pit mining and was later known as the Dome Mine. Also that year, Benny Hollinger, a barber from Cobalt, struck gold south of Gilles Lake, located in the heart of present-day Timmins. The Timmins brothers created a syndicate with Hollinger and others and incorporated the Hollinger Mine in 1910, which at one point in time, was the largest gold mine in the world. More

---

234 Information from "Founding Fathers," *Timmins.ca*, accessed June 19, 2016, www.timmins.ca/visitors/explore-timmins/founding-fathers (site discontinued).

235 This is a very simple rendition of the origin of the Timmins name. Many interesting facts have been omitted—for example, the need to defend their claim from the T&NO Railway Commissioner, Noah Timmins's various partnerships, etc. that are well worth reading about elsewhere.

gold deposits were found that year by Sandy McIntyre. By 1912, there were three large mining companies in the area:[236] Hollinger, McIntyre, and Dome.[237] In 1934, U.S. President Franklin Roosevelt raised the price of gold from $20.67 an ounce to $41.34 to counteract bank failures and a depressed economy. This facilitated the development of Ontario mining properties at a time when the Depression was dominating the economy.

In our 2016 trip to Timmins, my husband and I drove to Porcupine and South Porcupine, two former towns now within the municipality of Timmins. South Porcupine was founded in 1907 as a townsite for gold prospectors and miners. Unfortunately, as the result of hot, dry summer conditions and wind, on July 11, 1911, two days after the first train arrived, a fire tore through the area, killing at least seventy persons. It was devastating.

When all was said and done, the Great Porcupine Fire of 1911 pretty well flattened the Porcupine Goldfields. Eleven mines were completely destroyed. Not one business or home was left standing. The telegraph service was gone; the new railway that, just days before had been a source of pride, was now a series of twisted metal beams. By October 1911, the towns were well on their way to recovery. New businesses opened

236 Information from "History of the Gold Rush," *Timmins.ca*, accessed June 19, 2016, www.timmins.ca/visitors/explore-timmins/founding-fathers (site discontinued).

237 My father, Henry, worked at the Dome Mine—Canada's second all-time producer of gold—for the summers of 1932 and 1933. While lifting a heavy drill machine up a ladder, he strained his back which affected him for many years.

up, homes were rebuilt and Porcupine, like the legendary phoenix, had risen from its ashes.[238]

Needless to say, the fire set Porcupine back, while the area that Noah Timmins was developing as a new company town (Timmins) grew.

Our one stop in South Porcupine was at the hardware store, which was amazingly well stocked with everything you could imagine. We then had a pleasant two-hour walk around a scenic part of Porcupine Lake, followed by a drive to the Goldcorp mine nearby, which looked in excellent shape. Though no tours were offered, the receptionist told us that 350 persons worked there and went as far as 1,800 feet underground. They worked long shifts, five days on, four off, and quite a few came from neighbouring homes as well as from further afield. Because a several-day mining expo was starting in Timmins the next day, accommodation in Timmins was full. After many phone calls, we found availability to stay in a yurt at Wild Exodus on Lake Kenogamissi. However, there was no yurt that I could identify there, just a cabin which, on questioning the owners, we were informed was a moveable cabin and therefore qualified as a yurt. (Could have fooled me.) The thirty-kilometre drive to get there had taken longer than we'd anticipated and it was too late to go back into town for food, so we had one granola bar each for dinner. That night, the black flies were vicious, requiring us to stay indoors. We got up early the next morning and were out of there in no time flat.

---

238 Karen Bachmann, "Survivors Offered First-Hand Account of Great Porcupine Fire of 1911," *The Daily Press* [Timmins], July 14, 2023, opinion column.

As of 2023, Timmins had an estimated population of 39,934,[239] which is slowly decreasing even though the city covers a huge area and has amalgamated many small towns, including Schumacher, Dome, Porcupine, South Porcupine, and Hoyle. Timmins is set alongside the Mattagami River, which flows north into James Bay. The surrounding area contains over 500 lakes and rivers, and fishing and hunting are popular pastimes. Goldcorp, the parent company for the Dome Mine, is now the main mining corporation, reworking its old claims as the price of gold has increased. During its 100-year history, the Timmins area has been the home to more than 100 working mines, yielding gold, copper, lead, and zinc.[240] The Timmins Mining Hall of Fame 2010 write-up marking the 100th anniversary of the start of gold production from Timmins's historic mines states that ironically, Hollinger, McIntyre, and Wilson never made great fortunes from their discoveries. Records show that McIntyre sold his interest for $65,325, of which $60,000 was never collected. However, he received a pension for the use of his name. This could reflect the cut-throat tactics employed at that time to gain ownership of rich deposits.[241]

---

239 In 1931, Timmins had a population of 14,200.

240 Timmins's newest mine was opened in 2011.

241 See "2010 Inductee Timmins Mine Finders/Builders," *Canadian Mining Hall of Fame*, accessed November 14, 2023, www.mininghalloffame.ca/timmins-mine-finders-builders.

CHAPTER FIFTEEN: FINDING GOLD – THE TRUE DISCOVERERS

The alchemists in their search for gold discovered many other things of greater value.

—Arthur Schopenhauer

My grandmother Joanna's second husband, Joseph Pluto, was one of the three discoverers of the ore that became the Siscoe Gold Mines, named after another Polish immigrant, Stanley Siscoe (previously spelled Szyszko) from the Prussian Partition. Szyszko arrived in Canada as a seventeen-year-old in 1908.[242]

Figure 21: Photo of Joseph Pluto, 1933

242 Mankowski, personal correspondence, October 28, 2020.

The mine was located on Siscoe Island, near the east shore of Lake Dubuisson, about eight kilometres west of Val D'Or, Quebec, 340 kilometres or so east of Timmins. The veins of gold ore were found around 1908 by three "illiterate foreigners" from Poland, Felix Bijakowski, Joseph Hoffman, and Joseph Pluto, though this fact has been overlooked for many decades.[243] They had very little understanding of English. Stanley Siscoe – who spoke fluent English and had familiarity with business transactions – has been regarded as the discoverer, but actually, he was the developer of the mine, having apparently convinced the three discoverers to let him develop it in exchange for dubious compensation. He staked claims in the area in 1913 with three others,[244] but not with the discoverers. In the case of *Siscoe Gold Mines Ltd. v. Bijakowski*,[245] the Supreme Court of Canada's (SCC) five justices who had access to extensive testimony by witnesses at the lower court level, stated definitively: "The respondent and his two associates Pluto and Hoffman were the original discoverers of the Siscoe Gold Mines."[246]

---

243 See, for instance, "Quebec: 150 years of Mining," *Canadian Mining Life and Exploration News* (1992), p. 43: "Jim Sullivan and Stanley Siscoe have been credited with the first discoveries of gold in the Val D'Or area. . . . Stanley Siscoe discovered gold-bearing quartz veins on an island that became the foundation for the Siscoe mine."

244 Reported in the newspaper *L'Abitibi* on February 12, 1920.

245 Joseph Pluto and Joseph Hoffman assigned their rights in the court action to Felix Bijakowski.

246 *Siscoe Gold Mines Ltd. v. Bijakowski*, [1935] S.C.R. 195, at 193, www.decisions.scc-csc.ca/scc-csc/scc-csc/en/item/8658/index.do. See also Appendix B.

Figure 22: The Siscoe Gold Mines, May 1930

The transcript of the testimony from the trial level of that court case[247] presents pieces of the story. Testimony given under oath by Joseph Pluto sets out how Joseph and his two associates found the gold:

> Question [by Siscoe Gold Mines lawyer]: Have you had much mining experience?

> Answer (in translation): I have experience in mining by labouring, picking and shoveling, and doing some prospecting.

> Question: Do you know the Siscoe Mine was a gold mine?

> Answer: Yes, I know it, because we dug there and looked for the gold, and it was ourselves discovered the gold.

247 *Felix Bijakowski v. Siscoe Gold Mines Ltd.*, Kings Bench (Montreal) April 29, 1933, No. 1-96425.

Question: And you knew when it produced it would produce gold?

Answer: Yes.[248]

The counsel for the Siscoe Gold Mines did not object to this assertion; notably, the transcript shows elsewhere that they had no hesitation in objecting to evidence with which they disagreed.

There are a couple of indications in the transcript that the three discoverers were not properly compensated for their discovery. Joseph Hoffman testified that they each had received 20,000 shares for their work of the past ten years. The trial transcript sets out Joseph's comment on his work for the shares: Counsel: Q. How hard did you work to obtain the 20,000 shares? A. by Joseph Hoffman: I am afraid I should bring you gentlemen to tears if you heard how much and how hard I worked to obtain those 20,000 shares. He also received 42,813 shares as 1/11 members of the Siscoe Mines Syndicate[249] when Siscoe Island was sold to Siscoe Gold Mines Ltd. Hoffman added that "as for the property itself we have not obtained anything yet."[250] The interpreter indicated that the word for property could also be translated as "earth or soil." Additionally, the three discoverers were known to be very unhappy with Stanley Siscoe. On page 224 of the transcript, Mr. Tebutt, the president of Siscoe Mines Ltd., stated that he was asked by Stanley Siscoe to request that Bijakowski, Hoffman, and Pluto each

---

248 *Bijakowski v. Siscoe* [1933], transcript, p. 325.

249 *Bijakowski v. Siscoe* [1933], transcript, p. 119. The eleven members were Stanley Siscoe, Andrew Bowers, Stanley Standick, A. Janiec, Walter Glod, Anthony Dregas, Stanley Hadish, Peter Siscoe, Felix Bijakowski, Joseph Pluto, and Joseph Hoffman. The syndicate was formed on June 25, 1918.

250 *Bijakowski v. Siscoe* [1933], transcript, p. 119.

donate 10,000 shares to liquidate a debt that Siscoe owed to a Mr. Baillie. (The debt had not been authorized by the company). When counsel asked why Mr. Siscoe didn't make the request himself, he answered that "they would not give him [Siscoe] one share of stock." Furthermore, Mr. Siscoe's business practices were questionable in that the three discoverers had very little comprehension of English and had been asked by Siscoe to sign quantities of papers, some that contained writing while others were blank pages.[251]

Production at the mine started on January 19, 1929, and from the ore, gold and silver were extracted. The Siscoe mine property produced 883,000 ounces of gold between 1929 and 1949. This was Val d'Or's first and richest mine. At its close, Siscoe had only been mined to a depth of 600 metres.[252]

Besides denying them the honour of being the true finders of the gold in the Siscoe area, an attempt to further take advantage of the three discoverers was the subject of the SCC case mentioned above – *Siscoe Gold Mines Ltd. v. Bijakowski* – which dealt with the admissibility of oral testimony regarding the transfer of shares, verbal conditions as to their return, and whether the transfer was a loan or a gift.[253] At issue in this case were the 20,000 shares that Bijakowski, Hoffman, and Pluto had each received purportedly in lieu of wages for a ten-year period and that the men had subsequently been asked, on January 21, 1927, to transfer 10,000 shares each back to the company. Siscoe Gold Mines Ltd. executives

---

251 *Bijakowski v. Siscoe* [1933], transcript, p. 379.

252 Deep drilling in 1997 returned high gold grades as deep as 800 metres below the surface, suggesting more mineralization at greater depths.

253 The lower court decisions are at Superior Court, April 27, 1934, which is the appeal of the Kings Bench (Montreal) April 29, 1933, No. 1-96425 trial decision. The appeal was summarily dismissed, and costs were ordered against Siscoe Gold Mines.

alleged that the shares were donated to the company. The company lost its case at both the trial and appeal levels; so as not to be outdone, it appealed to the Supreme Court of Canada. In that decision, the Justices stated:

> The President, Mr. Tebbutt, went to Timmins and gathered together the three illiterate associates and, according to their version, which was unanimously accepted by the courts below, disclosed to them that the company needed funds, and that, in order to carry out a plan which would bring production and profit, other members of the syndicate and officers, including Mr. Tebbutt and Mr. Siscoe, the president and the vice-president of the company, had already loaned to the company a certain number of shares. These foreigners agreed to the demand of the president and took his word that this was a loan and signed a document which he had prepared.[254]

The Respondent's (Bijakowski) SCC Factum on page 4 sets out a few more details of the background and evidence from the lower courts for the three founders, including the plying of the three with liquor at the time of the signing over of the shares.

> The Plaintiff Bijakowski and his two associates, Pluto and Hoffman, the original discoverers of the Siscoe Gold Mines formed part of a group that was known as the Siscoe Gold Mine Syndicate. A Company was incorporated and promoted, and for their interests they were supposed to have obtained a certain number of shares. While the Company

---

254 *Siscoe Gold Mines Ltd. v. Bijakowski*, p. 195, or see Appendix B, p. 3.

was in operation, it apparently needed funds to bring the property into operation. The three members of the Syndicate had already received part of their shares. They expected more shares but did not know how many. It must be remembered that were dealing with three foreigners, originating from Poland. They were illiterate and did not understand English very well. One of them received a telegram from the Vice President of the Company, Mr. Siscoe, telling him to meet Mr. Tebbutt, the President at Timmins. The wire did not give the reasons for Mr. Tebbutt's visit. . . .

Before discussing the question of shares, Mr. Tebbutt supplied Mr. Bijakowski with $10.00 with which to buy four bottles of brandy. Apparently, after the brandy was consumed, or while it was being consumed, the question of lending the Company 10,000 shares each was taken up, and to these foreigners, a president of a company represented someone of importance, and someone in whom one could place implicit confidence. They took him at his word that this was a loan and when he prepared the document which merely is an authorization to split up three certificates of 20,000 shares. . . . they were satisfied that their interests were fully protected. They could neither read nor understand this document.

The company officers took the position that the shares had been donated by the three unconditionally; alternatively, they said that the agreement had not been authorized.

The trial Judge Loranger in his judgment stated that:

This entire business seems to me to have been deliberately prepared by Siscoe, Tebbutt and Herbert. Siscoe conceived the idea, but knowing that he would be unable to accomplish it, he dispatches Tebbutt to Timmins to obtain the 30,000 shares he needed to complete his transaction with Billy [Baillie].[255]

In their judgment dismissing the action, the SCC justices set out that the president had taken advantage of the fact that the plaintiff and his two companions were illiterate foreigners and deliberately drafted the document in indefinite terms, leading them into error and making them believe that they, in concert with other large shareholders (there were no other such shareholders), were lending to the company a large amount of stock, which would be returned immediately after the company began producing.

The SCC found that parol (oral) evidence could be adduced to determine whether the transfer was conditional or unconditional. The company officers then said that only $9,750 should be returned, the amount for which the shares had been sold. The court disagreed and awarded the current value (around $50,000 at that time) on December 21, 1934. Costs were also awarded against the company, and it was ordered to give the three founders either the shares or the current value, whichever each of them preferred.[256] This was a great win for the three.

It is remarkable that the three "illiterate foreigners" were able to obtain skilled counsel to represent them and to use our justice system at that time to attempt recompense from a large corporation. Well done. However, I'm sure that there were many other such

---

255 *Bijakowski v. Siscoe* [1933], transcript, p. 217, translated by Emeric de Traversay.

256 One of the legal representatives for the three was an esteemed constitutional lawyer, Louis Félix Aimé Geoffrion KC. There are streets named for his father in various cities in Quebec.

immigrants who were duped and did not or were unable to access the courts. It was a cut-throat time. Though the corporation lost the case at both the first instance and the appeal, it did not take the loss lightly and again appealed, a decision to their detriment. Obviously, the SCC regarded the issue on the use of oral evidence an important one that needed to be reaffirmed and took the case on, a step which is taken only in certain instances. In denying the company's case, the court also awarded "costs" against Siscoe Gold Mines Limited. This awarding of costs to be paid by the loser is often interpreted as a deterrent by the court to discourage parties from bringing forward baseless claims.

Stanley Siscoe died on March 25, 1935, just a few months after the Siscoe Gold Mines lost its appeal to the SCC. Siscoe had pressured a pilot with limited flying experience to fly in inclement weather to Siscoe Island on March 19. The plane was forced to land on a frozen lake, and Siscoe and the pilot took refuge in an abandoned cabin to wait out the storm. After four days, Siscoe became impatient and left on foot by himself, wearing his city clothes and street shoes. The pilot was rescued a day later. Siscoe was found frozen to death shortly thereafter.[257] His passing was highlighted in national and international news.

Unfortunately, Joseph Pluto's grave marker in Timmins indicates his date of death as January 12, 1934, almost a year before the SCC's decision in his and his co-founders' favour. He died from silicosis, a disease characterized by progressive fibrosis of the lungs, as a result of inhaling dust containing crystalline silica, contracted in the mines (Siscoe and Hollinger) where he had worked before

---

257 "Finds Frozen Body of Stanley Siscoe," *The New York Times*, March 27, 1935, p. 3.

starting up his grocery store.[258] Joseph's health actually started failing in 1928, and he and Joanna made a decision to sell their prosperous joint grocery business and go for a three month visit to relatives in Poland. On their return, they opened a dry-goods store; Joanna managed it as well as cared for her children and for Joseph. The store developed into a profitable business. At the trial in 1932, in the transcript at page 104, Joseph stated:

Q. Did you keep a store in Timmins?

A. Yes.

Q. Still keeping it?

A. Yes, my wife is carrying it on; before it was a groceries and now it is dry-goods.

Q. You are still acting in the store?

A. It is my wife who is in charge as because I am too weak to carry on…

Q. You are a sick man?

A. Yes, it is too much of an effort to follow your English.

Joseph was not particularly fortunate in business dealings as he had sold some of his Siscoe stock in the late 1920s or early 1930s at ten cents a share; in 1934, a share was valued at $1.67. Additionally

---

258 Symptoms include persistent cough, shortness of breath and difficulty breathing, and also weakness, fatigue, fever, night sweats, leg swelling and bluish discoloration of the lips.

in 1930, he had transferred his share interest of the 10,000 shares to Felix Bijakowski in repayment of a $1,000 loan.[259] Perhaps these premature sales/transfers were prompted by his failing health. It therefore appears that Joseph Pluto would have received no funds from the SCC win, as his interest had been transferred to Felix Bijakowski. Joanna received a small payment from the death of her husband, presumably from one of the companies he had worked for in the mines, a payment which she used to expand their store now called Goldfield's Dry Goods. There was sufficient money to buy an extra-large monument for Joseph in the Timmins cemetery.[260] (Adela Orpel, Joanna's niece who died of consumption in 1943, is also buried in that same plot.)

It was sad to learn that Joseph had been denied his true place as one of the three founders of the Siscoe Gold Mines, but I am glad to have corrected that fact here. Though he was not a businessman, he was a hard worker. It must have been a tough life to prospect with Bijakowski and Hoffman in the Val D'Or region – very cold with lots of snow in the winter and lots of biting insects in the summer. In the mining season, prospectors set out with their pick and shovel in the morning and generally put in twelve to sixteen repetitive and backbreaking hours per day, digging, scraping, hauling, and washing dirt and gravel. They returned to a camp tent at night to eat beans with hot fat and molasses or dried meat and rice,

---

259 *Bijakowski v. Siscoe* [1933], transcript, p. 109: "Q. Supposing the Plaintiff [Felix Bijakowski] collects $2,000 out of these shares, would you be entitled to keep $1,000 and give him $1,000? A. . . .In the event of recovering more than $1,000 on the share claim, the understanding is that the Plaintiff could keep the balance of the surplus. Q. And the cancellation of that $1,000 debt was all the Plaintiff gave you for the transfer, is that right? A. By Joseph Pluto: Yes, it is really so."

260 For one summer after finishing high school, my father worked at the Siscoe Gold Mines, where Polish friends of the family were employed. He slept on the beach until he started the job.

---

potatoes, and onions.[261] Working in a mine itself was dangerous.[262] Death from silicosis was not unusual. Joseph must have worked at least fifteen years in prospecting and mining.

My step-grandfather did well to marry Joanna – they were good partners as both were hard workers, and Joanna cared for him for years after he became sick. She showed her business acumen in starting her own grocery business in Timmins before meeting Joseph Pluto and combining their stores, a decision that reflected her business experience acquired over the years as a working mother in the candy store in Halifax, in her brother's restaurant and hotel businesses there, and later in her brother's dry-goods store in Montreal. Meanwhile her brothers were continuing their own entrepreneurial ventures. Wladek had gone broke in North Bay and Detroit, moved in with Joanna and Joseph, bought the remains of a burnt-out drug store including its showcases in Timmins, held a fire sale in another location, packed the remains into a freight car, moved to Sudbury, and opened Radek's[263] Patent Medicines. Brother John started a patent medicine store in Moneta, a suburb of Timmins and later moved with his wife to Rouyn in Quebec. Using her own and Vincent's joint funds, while managing Goldfield's Dry Goods store, Joanna branched out in the early 1930s to property development – the

---

261 *Life as a Miner: A Day in the Life* (Charlotte, North Carolina: Discovery Education, Social Studies Techbook, n.d.), www.joliet86.org/assets/1/6/Life_as_a_Miner.pdf.

262 In the year 1928, in Ontario there were 2,558 employee accidents and 85 deaths, from T. F. SUTHERLAND Toronto, J. G. MCMILLAN, Cobalt; D. G. SINCLAIR, Sudbury; GEO. E. COLE, Timmins; A. R. WEBSTER. See Province of Ontario, Department of Mines, *Report on the Mining Accidents in Ontario in 1928, Bulletin No. 67* (Toronto: Printed by Order of the Legislative Assembly of Ontario, 1929), www.geologyontario.mndmf.gov.on.ca/mndmfiles/pub/data/imaging/B067/B067.pdf.

263 Wladek Pietkievicz had changed his name at this time to Richard Radek.

building of homes on Main Avenue, Commercial Avenue, and Spruce Street in Timmins.[264] With the gold fields booming, property development obviously was a very good investment strategy.

264 Henry Ostrowski, p. 16.

CHAPTER SIXTEEN: REMARRIAGE TO VINCENT DUDEK

...having one veil lifted from our vision does not necessarily mean that we have fully recovered our sight. Even as we lament the collapse of biological diversity, we pay too little heed to a parallel process of loss, the demise of cultural diversity, the erosion of what might be termed the ethnosphere, the full complexity and complement of human potential as brought into being by culture and adaption since the dawn of consciousness.

—Wade Davis, *Light at the Edge of the World*

Joseph Pluto had died in January 1934, so it would have been later that year or in 1935 that during a visit to Montreal where Joanna occasionally travelled to visit Polish friends, she was introduced by John Michalek[265] to Vincent Dudek. Vincent had come to Canada with the assistance of an uncle in 1905 when he was fourteen to avoid compulsory service in the Russian army, since the family had been living in the Russian Partition of Poland. As mentioned in an earlier chapter, Russification was very prevalent in the partition at that time, so Vincent had had to learn Polish secretly by candlelight from his grandfather.[266] Vincent had worked at several jobs in Montreal, including teaching Polish for a short time at the Montreal Catholic School Commission and working as a fireman for the St. Henri district of Montreal. After the birth of his first child, he worked as a tailor for a clothing manufacturer and drove a truck for a brewery.

---

265   John Michalek had also introduced Joanna's brother John to his wife-to-be, Janina.

266   This and other facts are described in the biography by Stromberg-Stein, p. 3, and elsewhere. Stromberg-Stein's book is particularly noteworthy as she interviewed Louis Dudek extensively for the book.

Figure 23: Photo of Joanna Dudek and Vincent Dudek, Florida

Vincent Dudek[267] was a widower when he met Joanna. His first wife, Stanislawa Rozynska Dudek, had died in 1926 when she was thirty-one,[268] leaving three children: Lillian, eight-year-old Louis, and Irene. Vincent brought his sister, Walerya, from Poland to

---

267 There is some information that the Dudek name could have been adopted around the middle of the 1800s when a great-great-grandfather who was a Polish patriot-revolutionary took the name and identification papers from a dead Czech soldier. Apparently the original family name was something like Sierakowski. This was not uncommon in those days. See Shannon Selin, "How Were Napoleonic Battlefields Cleaned Up?," www.shannonselin.com>napoleonic-battlefield-cleanup.

268 Unfortunately, from surgery.

care for them. Joanna and Vincent were married sometime in 1935 or 1936.

Vincent had few funds for his children's education. In his autobiography, Louis described his family's financial situation during his teen years:

> Money pressures at home nearly made me drop out of high school before finishing, but advice from a YMCA counsellor sent me back to school and I completed the course – Grade Thirteen, at that time equivalent to first year of college. I then went to work in a warehouse, on St. Helen Street, in the old part of Montreal, an area of brick, dust, and grime, devoted to tight-fisted business operations.[269]

In a poem he wrote ten years later about his view of working life and working men, Louis expressed the view that they should be celebrated more than millionaires. That said, he regarded his work in the warehouse as a "dead end" but had no hope of an alternative. Then came life-changing support from my grandmother Joanna who was newly married to Vincent: "suddenly my father was able to send me to college, I think by persuading his wife, since he had remarried, to help finance my education; and I registered as a sophomore at McGill University."[270]

Louis started writing for the campus newspaper, The McGill Daily, and saw his articles reprinted in other college papers in Canada. He became very entrenched in college life, and the

---

269 Endre Farkas and Carolyn Marie Souaid, eds., "Louis Dudek: Autobiography," *Poetry Quebec Biographies*, no. 1 (July 2010), p. 4, www.web.archive.org/web/20120507121606/, www.poetry-quebec.com/pq/biography/printer_6.shtml.

270 Farkas and Souaid, p. 4.

groundwork was laid for his lengthy career as a celebrated Canadian poet, academic, and publisher.

Louis had a Polish upbringing, and he wrote that his aunt Walerya, "a literate person," recited many Polish poems from memory that were deeply moving. He said that

> [h]er only punishment for me was to make me memorize poems, which was actually a kind of reward I thought, and through her I came to like Slowacki [a Polish poet] and Mickiewicz [perhaps Pan Tadeusz, a Polish classic by Adam Mickiewicz], Polish Romantics, before I ever knew Byron, Keats, or Shelley.[271]

He had been part of a Polish community and would have been immersed in Polish culture, including theatre performances, music, traditional holidays, and the Roman Catholic religion. He spoke both Polish and English. He wrote:

> At home in our Polish family, or later with my in-laws and relatives after my marriage, there was a custom at Christmastime and on other holidays, to do some old-fashioned group singing at table. The great songs of the Ukraine, of Lithuania, of Russia, and of Poland would be sounded in chorus, and repeated to one's heart content, while glasses klinked and drinks were poured out. . . . This music, too, is part of my inheritance, though there is no way perhaps to recognize its plangent melodies and vigorous rhythms in my poetry.

---

271 Farkas and Souaid, p. 2.

Somewhere it must be there, since nothing is lost that moves us deeply and is part of our continuing memory.[272]

However, in later life, Louis considered himself a citizen of the world and played a leading role in promoting the development of modern Canadian literature as well as acquiring a reputation as an activist. In his autobiographical writings he said:

I say the Protestant School Board, though I and my two sisters were Roman Catholics. We were actually "illegals" in the Protestant system at that time, just as recently there have been many "illegals" in the English-language school system in Montreal, students whom the law wants to propel into the French school system.[273]

As the son of Polish parents, he valued direct feelings; he also exhibited the reflection and religious interests common in those of Polish heritage. He was known, however, to keep his personal life very private.[274]

Louis and his first wife divorced but they continued to keep in contact. Her 2020 obituary notes that she "almost single-handedly raised a son Gregory" and that she helped launch Louis on his literary and professional career.[275] He remarried Aileen Collins. He was

---

272 Farkas and Souaid, p. 6.

273 Farkas and Souaid, p. 2.

274 Aileen Collins, Michael Gnarowski, and Sonja A. Skarstedt, eds., *Eternal Conversations: Remembering Louis Dudek* (Montreal: DC Books, 2003), chapter by Gregory Dudek, p. 91.

275 "Obituary: Stephanie Dudek," *Dignity*, accessed November 14, 2023, www.dignitymemorial.com/obituaries/montreal-qc/stephanie-dudek-9050980.

the author of over two dozen books, an editor of eight, a teacher and a publisher. In an afterword by Frank Davey, he described Louis's particular contribution:

> He engaged but did not assimilate to the acknowledged poetries of mid-twentieth-century Canada, instead returning again and again – poetically and literally – to Europe for ways of fashioning a more public, discursive, and idea-oriented Canadian poetry than ever became acceptable to Canada's literary gatekeepers during his lifetime.[276]

In 1984, he was invested with the Order of Canada, and in that same year, Susan Stromberg-Stein wrote his biography with many references to conversations with him. He was honoured with a special Canadian Writers Award in 1990, and a German translation of his selected poetry was published posthumously in 2006. Louis Dudek: Essays on His Works appeared in 2001,[277] the year he passed away. His eighty-three years of life had undoubtedly been set on their richly varied, highly intellectual course by Joanna's early gift of financial support for his education.

I was able to contact a long-time friend and colleague of Louis, Michael Gnarowski, who referred me to a Tribute Anthology entitled Eternal Conversations: Remembering Louis Dudek.[278] Published in 2003, it contains contributions from thirty-one

---

276 Louis Dudek, *All These Roads: The Poetry of Louis Dudek.* Selected with an introduction by Karis Shearer and an afterword by Frank Davey (Waterloo, Ontario: Wilfrid Laurier University Press, 2008), p. 61.

277 George Hildebrand, ed., *Louis Dudek: Essays on His Works* (Montreal: Guernica Editions, 2001).

278 Collins, Gnarowski, and Skarstedt. This collection includes articles by a variety of authors, including Michael Gnarowski.

authors, family members and friends, who wrote remembrances and highlights from knowing Louis. Among these is an article by his second wife, Aileen Collins, who referred to him as a brilliant and provocative teacher. She shared that hundreds of Louis's students at McGill University had talked and written about their powerful and stimulating experiences in Louis's classes. She said that like many other children of immigrants from disadvantaged homelands, such as my family, Louis believed strongly that education had a transformative power, and he applied this in his life. About his start in higher education, she wrote the following:

> Dudek recalls by sheer luck he was able to leave the menial job in a warehouse where he had worked since completing Grade 13 at the High School of Montreal, and to register at McGill University. "For me, a new life began in the university, a life without parental supervision, a life of freedom and exploration." In later years, he often contemplated this twist of fate that had made possible his subsequent career in teaching and his accomplishments as a poet, professor, publisher, critic, and man of letters.[279]

That "twist of fate," was the funding made available through the kind generosity of my grandmother who provided financial support not only for her own children but also for her new stepson.

Joanna and Vincent wanted to be in a more southerly climate, so with her funds they bought a summer cabin business just south of Orillia and worked at this for about five years. They then sold it and bought the Armory Hotel in Hamilton but finding the

---

279 Collins, Gnarowski, and Skarstedt, p. 245.

city too hot in the summer, sold the hotel after two years. They then bought Lakeside Cabins, a resort business on Blake Street in Barrie where they lived for many years. During the winters, they holidayed in Florida.

Figure 24: Photo of Lakeside Cabins

Vincent Dudek was very much part of our Ostrowski family, and I recall many wonderful meals at their home in Barrie when I was a child, as well as dinners at our home. My sister Mary remembered him as a soft-spoken, kind gentleman. During some of our family moves, we would temporarily live at their cabin resort. My brothers Henry, John, and Paul each spent summers living there and helping out with the resort business – mowing lawns and working in the small store. Paul recalls working for at least three summers there when he was in his teens and has very pleasant memories. He told me that Mr. Dudek would order supplies for the store and was very good with the customers and cabin patrons, many of whom were return visitors. Mr. Dudek would often read the newspaper on the porch. Mary remembered that he had an extensive collection of tools and looked after the repairs to the resort cabins. As my step-grandfather, I remember Mr. Dudek as always gentle, kind, and welcoming. He and my grandmother were very happy together.

Vincent died suddenly in 1959 from a heart attack; my father was there and drove him to the hospital, but he could not be saved. Paul had noticed that for a few days before Vincent passed away, he was complaining of chest pains and holding his hand over his heart. Our family attended Vincent's funeral and met his family's relatives.

Joanna was very distressed by the loss of her husband and began to slow down. In the 1960s, she made another trip back to Poland to visit "home" with her daughter, Stephanie. She died prematurely in August 1967 at the age of seventy-eight in a less-than-elegant nursing home in Brampton, Ontario, due to long-term complications arising from injuries sustained when hit by a car several years earlier and a subsequent stroke. She had been in several nursing homes during those years – it was sad for me to see her in such surroundings, distraught and disoriented, probably due to medications for her various conditions and having lost her ability to speak any English. Perhaps she was, in her own way, returning home. Her death was a great loss!

Joanna's generosity in financing the university education of Louis Dudek deserves recognition and gratitude. She was a woman of dignity and her accomplishments reflected intelligence, resourcefulness, kindness, and an ability to fit into a new culture where she not only survived but also thrived. She has served as a role model for me and her other grandchildren.

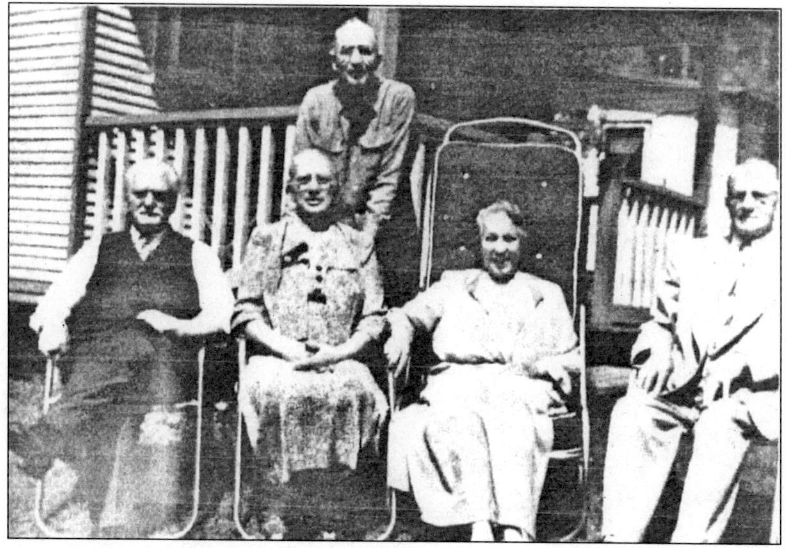

Figure 25: Photo of John Pietkiewicz, Joanna and Vincent Dudek, Rose and Wladek Radek (Pietkiewicz)

CHAPTER SEVENTEEN: LEGACIES

*I'm one of the millions of immigrant children, children of loneliness,
wandering between worlds that are at once too old and too new to
live in.*
>—Anzia Yezierska, "Children of Loneliness"

The past is never lost, not completely; we carry it with us.
>—Carolyn Abraham, *The Juggler's Children*

Why is this story of my grandmother's life important? Well, I have
been truly and profoundly moved by what I have learned about
her; it has been remarkably enriching and grounding to recover
my heritage. All of us have ancestors like her whose stories have
been lost. I regard her, her family, and others like them as just a
few of the many tough, resilient early immigrants, encouraged by
our country to come and settle but having to do it all on their own,
sometimes with tragic results along the way.

To recap, I found out that all of Joanna's formative years were
in a Polish agricultural village recovering from serfdom but where
the Russian culture was forcibly imposed and where the Polish
culture was denigrated. All education was in Russian, and young
men who failed Russian high school exams were liable for conscription into the Russian army; law courts and administration were
in Russian. The youngest of twelve children, Joanna was married
off at a young age to a neighbour's son and soon after bore three
children. With economic prospects looking poor in the village of
Rozpaszka, a policy of Russification and conscription in force, and
a world war about to start, the young family departed to join two
of her brothers in the "new country." Canada in 1914 provided little
to newcomers other than low wages in difficult resource jobs like

coal mining and the opportunity for self-start entrepreneurships, all without language instruction or skills training, and with no provision of medical care for low-income immigrants who had left supportive communities and villages behind. I am sure the tragedy of the Halifax explosion did not endear their newly found land to them, nor did the "Spanish flu" that killed many in Nova Scotia. Joanna endured the devastating deaths of three further children born to her in Halifax, and her husband's mistake of leaving the family to search unsuccessfully for a new homeland in Argentina where there were again grandiose promises to lure immigrants to settle rough lands. She had to make a new life for her family and to provide for her children in arduous circumstances. I am grateful to have known her in her later years as the owner and operator of a tourist business, happily married to a kindly gentleman who shared her Polish culture – a woman with a thoughtful and serene presence and a dignity that I am sure reflected her inherent nobility and that I still hold in my heart. Her early years in the agricultural village, though culturally and politically repressive, must have given her cultural mileposts, a good grounding in communal living and, above all, the quality of resourcefulness which I know my family inherited.

Some of the stories of others that I previously shared – the Vietnamese boat immigrant hung on a hook by pirates on his journey to Canada, the Irish escaping famine, the Doukhobors wanting peace and non-violence – could also ignite a deep appreciation by the friends or descendants of those immigrants who left home behind but in one way or another passed on some solid values. Their history is important in the context of our multi-national country.[280]

Immigration stories open doors to understanding ourselves, our communities, and our country. For me, my grandmother's story is an example of the importance of the rediscovery of a lost ancestral history. But immigration is bigger than just ourselves finding some noble blood and selfless deeds and experiencing delight in new found descriptions of the Golden Age of a country that had been *terra incognita* for over a century and, in my lifetime, the brunt of cruel jokes. Rarely set out under one cover, there are legacies, impacts, and consequences of immigration for both the immigrant and the host country that others have studied across a variety of fields (e.g., psychology, economics, politics, and the environment). I am setting some of them out here. These further consequences are substantial. Almost daily, our newspapers describe immigration issues invariably controversial and happening across the world. Recently, over seventy-nine migrants, including women and children, drowned in the Mediterranean Sea when their overloaded boat sank off the coast of Greece. Having been a social psychologist, I find it important in these last few chapters, at least to introduce some consequences that I have found interesting and that I label "legacies" – impacts, both positive and negative, which make each immigrant's "story" and circumstances valuable for policy considerations.

---

280 In 1982, multiculturalism was recognized by section 27 of the Canadian Charter of Rights and Freedoms (www.en.wikipedia.org/wiki/Section_27_of_the_Canadian_Charter_of_Rights_and_Freedoms), and the *Canadian Multiculturalism Act* was subsequently enacted by Prime Minister Brian Mulroney (www.en.wikipedia.org/wiki/Brian_Mulroney). The policy envisages a mutual respect between ethnicities. Official bilingualism was set out in our Canadian Constitution to, *inter alia*, protect the English- and French-speaking minorities in the provinces.

GRATITUDE FOR A CONNECTION TO THE PAST

My grandmother left an extraordinary legacy – a single life story otherwise lost that has changed my world view to one of awe at the resiliency and wisdom of my ancestor as she confronted challenges, and after much struggle, won a decent life. Finding that legacy has returned to me my Polish heritage and connected me to a rich history known only to a small community of Poles in our Canadian society, a society where I and others like me seem to exist as a virtually invisible minority and where a tragic, impactful departure or escape from our homeland is often unrecognized.

I now know that I am of Western Slavic heritage,[281] a classification demarcating the many various tribes who lived since Paleolithic times in the area that is now Poland. The Golden Age of Poland was second to none in the Early Modern Era in Europe when my paternal ancestors were most likely part of the nobility. I am proud to know about the outstanding victories of King Sobieski in protecting Christianity in Europe, the genius of Copernicus in understanding that the earth is not the centre of the universe, the many artists and composers, the enlightened constitution of May 3, 1791, Poland's openness to cultural diversity, and the emphasis on the importance of religion and education. Also, I now understand the complicated factors that led to the loss of that great country – including King Poniatowski's naive idealism and trust in the Empress of Russia and the unfortunate location of Poland surrounded on three sides by aggressive territorial entities. My parents' emphasis on education, religion, and resourcefulness are now well appreciated, and I see that I have in turn followed those values in raising my children. Above all, connection to the past has

---

281 My mother's family came from the Austrian Partition of Poland.

granted me an appreciation and gratitude for the struggles, fears, and challenges that our forebearers endured in their lifetimes.

EXPANSION OF OUR VIEW OF REALITY

Over the years, I have somewhat understood but never fully appreciated how tenuous our view of reality is. A simple example: a rainy day is bemoaned by some as depressing and praised by others for garden rainwater, respite from a hot day, a day for quiet reading on a couch. According to the American psychologist and philosopher William James, thoughts become perception and perception becomes our reality, a reality not necessarily constant or unchangeable. The world we live in, its quality and character, is nothing but a reflection of our own minds. And importantly, the differences that immigrants bring can expand or even change our view of reality, ushering in a new understanding of our challenges that can be more comforting or wise.

One who has studied and written extensively on this topic is Wade Davis, an anthropologist, ethnobotanist, filmmaker, photographer, and internationally renowned explorer, who has lived among many different peoples of the world. He maintains that ancient wisdom matters and that "different beliefs create different realities."[282] He says that every culture is a unique answer to a fundamental question: What does it mean to be human and alive? He has presented the very interesting view that we presume modernity[283] to be a relentless force of history but, in fact, it is not; the culture of modernity is just another ideology, and the domination of consumerism and anxiety now prevalent in our lives thrusts us

---

282 Davis, *Light at the Edge of the World*, p. 12.

283 Modernity, in very simple terms, can be regarded as a period marked by a questioning or rejection of tradition.

into the politics of hysteria. In his book *The Wayfinders* (a CBC Massey Lecture) he writes:

> But whether we travel with the nomadic Penan in the forests of Borneo, a Vodoun acolyte in Haiti, a *curandero* in the high Andes of Peru, a Tamashek *caravanseri* in the red sands of the Sahara, or a yak herder on the slopes of Chomolungma, all these peoples teach us that there are other options, other possibilities, other ways of thinking and interacting with the earth. This is an idea that can only fill us with hope.[284]

He describes the Barasana people of the Amazon, who say that white people only see with their eyes, whereas Barasana see with their mind. They journey back and forward in time, "visiting every sacred site, paying homage to every creature," with the profound cultural insight that "animals and plants are only people in another dimension of reality." This tradition is based on knowledge gathered over time and on intense priestly study and initiation. Importantly, "status accrues to the man of wisdom, not the warrior."[285]

Later in his book,[286] Davis highlights the fear of anthropologist Margaret Mead, that we are laying the foundations of a blandly amorphous and singularly generic modern culture that will have no rivals. Our imaginations could become limited to a single intellectual and spiritual modality. Mead's nightmare was the possibility that we might wake up one day and not even remember what has been lost. Davis notes that although our species has been around

---

284 Wade Davis, *The Wayfinders: Why Ancient Wisdom Matters in the Modern World*, CBC Massey Lectures Series (Toronto: House of Anansi Press, 2009), p. 2.

285 Davis, *The Wayfinders*, p. 114.

286 Davis, *The Wayfinders*, p. 192.

---

for some 200,000 years, our modern industrial society is barely 300 years old. He states that this shallow history should not suggest to any of us that we have all the answers for the challenges that confront us; indeed, we should realize that we are culturally myopic.

> Our way of life, inspired in so many ways, is not the paragon of humanity's potential. Once we look through the anthropological lens and see, perhaps for the first time, that all cultures have unique attributes that reflect choices made over generations, it becomes absolutely clear that there is no universal progression in the lives and destiny of human beings.[287]

In his semi-autobiographical book *Light at the Edge of the World*, Davis describes in words and photographs many of his travels in places such as Borneo, the Andes, Colombia, the Brazilian Amazon, and Haiti. Marvelling at how it was to experience a diversity of world views, he laments their loss:

> The ultimate tragedy is not that archaic societies are disappearing but rather that vibrant, dynamic, living cultures and languages are being forced out of existence. At risk is a vast archive of knowledge and expertise, a catalogue of the imagination, an oral and written literature composed of the memories of countless elders and healers, warriors, farmers, fishermen, midwives, poets, and saints. In short, the artistic and spiritual expression of the full complexity and diversity of the human experience.[288]

---

287 Davis, *The Wayfinders*, p. 195.

288 Davis, *Light at the Edge*, p. 14.

He describes our current way of life as we know, with its stunning technological wizardry and cities dense with intrigue; it is one alternative rooted in a particular intellectual lineage.

That being the case, Poland's Golden Age, renowned for its excellence in education, science, and art, for defending Christianity and welcoming diversity (Jews were allowed to settle there; country leadership was chosen from an international slate), unfortunately was then transformed into a country which had to endure centuries of oppression and cultural suffocation. Over these centuries emerged a revised reality – a survival mode encompassing resilience and fortitude evolved to deal with that oppression, encompassing as well very practical ways of living and beliefs, including religious beliefs, supportive under such circumstances, as evidenced in my own family.

GENERATIONAL INHERITANCES

Recent research has also highlighted a different sort of legacy that we might receive from our ancestors: traits and memories inherited from one generation to the next. Studies done by Brian Dias at the Emory University School of Medicine, in Atlanta, Georgia, support the idea of a biological mechanism that passes traits from one generation to another, a process called "epigenetic inheritance."[289] In his experiment, the fathers and grandfathers of mice were taught to associate the smell of cherry blossoms with an electric shock. Some of their pups and grandpups responded fearfully to lower concentrations of cherry blossom smell than normal mice. Experimentation

---

289 Brian G. Dias and Kerry J. Ressler, "Parental Olfactory Experience Influences Behavior and Neural Structure in Subsequent Generations," *Nature Neuroscience* 17, 1 (2014): 89–96, www.doi.org/10.1038/nn.3594.

in this area has continued. Geneticist Dr. Moshe Szyf[290] says that some behavioural inheritances are clear – for example, coming from a poor family may make it harder for a person to break out of the poverty cycle. He also suggests that experiences might program sperm, as has been clearly found in animal studies; very particular, specific, and organized transgenerational transfer of information could occur. However, researchers have not yet discovered what exactly is transmitted. I find this all very intriguing, as it suggests that those of us who are descendants of ancestors who escaped from war-torn areas of the world, or from situations of poverty, illness, or oppression, may have inherited both behaviourally and genetically some associated memories or traits, such as fear, which could affect our daily lives.

That idea has been taken up in research by Mark Wolynn,[291] author as well as founder and director of The Family Constellation Institute, which offers therapeutic assistance to individuals and groups who have not been helped with their long-standing difficulties by traditional therapy and drugs. He contends that traumatic legacies play a far greater role in our health than has previously been understood, stating, "[w]hen our family members have suffered, perished, or perpetrated violence in a war, we can inherit a virtual minefield of trauma,"[292] and he believes we share an unconscious

---

290 Moshe Szyf is also a professor of pharmacology and therapeutics at McGill University, where he holds a GlaxoSmithKline-CIHR Chair in Pharmacology. Szyf's main research interests are epigenetics, including behavioural epigenetics, as well as cancer research. He speaks on this topic in a YouTube presentation titled "Epigenetics with Dr. Moshe Szyf, Part 1" (January 11, 2020), www.youtube.com/watch?v=OEAJmDPJz_I.

291 Mark Wolynn, *It Didn't Start with You: How Inherited Family Trauma Shapes Who We Are and How to End the Cycle* (New York: Penguin Random House, 2016).

292 Wolynn, p. 216.

obligation to resolve past family tragedies. In his treatment model, he uses diagnostic self-inventories to uncover and work through inherited family trauma with his clients and has found in many cases that realizing the fear (or whatever you are suffering from) does not belong to you, can alleviate it. He himself regained his eyesight through this process, even though his ophthalmologist had said he would no longer be able to see. This is an interesting concept for those of us whose ancestors may have experienced trauma or hardship (as many did), as it may shine a light on vulnerabilities and handicaps we wish we didn't have.[293] This postulation of generational transmission is also mentioned in the writing of Ken McGoogan,[294] who refers to Richard Dawkins's argument that memes, or ideas and values, are transmitted from one person to another through time and across space. He writes about cultural genealogy and states:

> More than nine million Canadians claim Scottish or Irish heritage. . . .Did the ancestors of more than one-quarter of our population arrive without cultural baggage? No shared attitudes and beliefs, no common vision? Impossible. They gleaned their values from their leaders and heroes. And they bought them across the Atlantic to Canada.[295]

---

293 See also Claire Sicherman, *Imprint: A Memoir of Trauma in the Third Generation* (Halfmoon Bay, British Columbia: Caitlin Press, 2017), who describes her inherited intergenerational trauma from the suffering of her maternal grandparent in the Holocaust.

294 Ken McGoogan, "En-lightening Genealogy," *Vancouver Sun*, September 26, 2015, p. E7, reviewing his book *Celtic Lightning*.

295 McGoogan, "En-lightening Genealogy," p. E7.

I have no recollection nor do my siblings of my grandmother being an anxious person. Remarkably, she was organized, calm, dignified, and intelligent, and she helped others. She was hard working and resilient. In her earlier days, having lost her home, three children and a husband, she just carried on, working to support her three older children. How did she do it? Many I know in Western culture would have been completely devastated and scarred for life. As time went on, she crafted a better life for herself. When a husband left, she worked with her brothers; when their store burned in Montreal and her brother left to join their brother in Detroit, she was in touch with Polish friends and moved to the boom town of Timmins to start her own store. Her life got better and better. In the world view of the Poles I know, many did not dwell on losses – they just moved on. Through necessity, they had learned to cope with the loss of their country and with the tyranny of Russification imposed by a government to be feared. With those challenges, particularly in the 1800s, their Catholic faith grew stronger and their Polishness grew more important.

Understandably, the everyday reality of Poles in my family included little reliance on the state for help. I went to my first real doctor's appointment when I was in university. During our childhood, my mother was our doctor using various liniments and other home remedies that kept us all well. Cod liver oil was a winter must. Politicians, government resources, and the media were particularly mistrusted. My brother recalls that Vincent Dudek once remarked while reading the newspaper on the veranda that when it came to most of what you read in the paper, the opposite is more likely the truth. That viewpoint is not uncommonly heard in my family, many of whom maintain a critical and sceptical view of state-operated entities, often precipitated from failed results.[296] Reliance is placed on family and close friends, on personal research and educational resources.

CULTURAL DIFFERENCES

Drawing upon a ten-year study of children of immigrants coming of age in New York City, sociologist Philip Kasinitz and his colleagues argued that cultural differences made it possible for the immigrant children to select the best traits from their parents and their American peers, giving them a creative advantage by providing a wider range of options and strategies to pursue in life.[297] This opinion is supported by Simon Fraser University ethicist Mark Wexler, who postulates that having multiple cultural loyalties helps us grow, stretches our boundaries, and makes life adventurous.

Cultural differences have become an increasingly studied aspect of international negotiations. The authors of the text *Essentials of Negotiation*[298] report on many research programs and present various study results. For example, Geert Hofstede conducted research on cultural dimensions in international business by examining data on values, gathered from over 100,000 IBM employees worldwide, which drew upon fifty cultures. His statistical analysis suggested four dimensions that could be used to describe the

---

296 One family member died tragically when given an experimental drug by a medical professional and without proper consent. The drug was contraindicated in medical texts for the age range and symptoms.

297 Philip Kasinitz, et al., *Inheriting the City: The Children of Immigrants Come of Age* (New Haven, Connecticut: Russell Sage Foundation Books at Harvard University Press, 2009).

298 Roy J. Lewicki, et al., *Essentials of Negotiation*, 6th ed. (Toronto: McGraw-Hill, 2016), especially ch. 11, "International and Cross-Cultural Negotiations," which sets out a comprehensive description and analysis of this topic.

important differences among the cultures in the study: individualism/collectivism, power distance, career success/quality of life, and uncertainty avoidance. Canada ranked fourth in the world on individualism.[299] This dimension describes the extent to which societies encourage their young to be independent and look after themselves, whereas collectivist societies integrate individuals into cohesive groups that take responsibility for the welfare of each individual. This could imply that negotiators from collectivist cultures will strongly depend on a cultivated and sustained long-term relationship, whereas negotiators from individualistic cultures may be more likely to swap negotiators. The authors of *Essentials of Negotiation* write that negotiating across borders is complex.

The fact that there are differences in cultural realities and personal traits among societies was researched intensively by psychologists Joseph Henrich and Steven Heine and anthropologist Ara Norenzayan, who in 2010 found that most of what is known about human psychology was based on studies using undergraduates from Western societies. They found that 96% of the study subjects came from Western countries (i.e., North America, Australia) with only 12% of the world's population and 70% of those studies used American undergraduates as subjects. They found that in many domains[300] there was a much greater variation than had been represented in psychological and behavioural economic textbooks and journals and the results are often generalized with the implicit assumption that there is little variation across human populations. The research found, among other things, that Westerners

---

299 Lewicki, et al., p. 232.

300 The experimental domains included visual perception, fairness, cooperation, spatial reasoning, categorization and inferential induction, moral reasoning, reasoning styles, self-concepts and related motivations, and the heritability of IQ.

are highly individualistic, self-obsessed, control-oriented, non-conformist, and analytical.[301] Here's an example: the authors asked U.S. undergraduates to respond to the question "Who am I?" They also asked that question of several groups in Africa. At one end of the spectrum, the U.S. undergraduates focused almost exclusively on their individual attributes, aspirations, and achievements while the Nairobi labourers, Maasai, and Samburu (two rural tribal groups) focused on their roles and relationships.

From their research work, the authors concluded there is an inherent bias – that is, the results of Western psychology and behavioural studies are not generalizable beyond a limited sampling. They did experiments in decision-making, cooperation, self-concept, and visual perception on diverse population samples (both adults and children) from various social groups and locations, such as San foragers in Botswana; the Songe, Fang, Suku, Toro, Yuendumu and Zulu people; as well as in Senegal, South Africa, Europe, and Evanston (U.S.). They found that members of Western societies were among the least representative populations for generalizing about humans.[302] These results cast serious doubt on our oft relied upon presumption that certain facets of human nature are universal.

> Many of these findings involve domains that are associated with fundamental aspects of psychology, motivation, and behaviour – hence, there are no obvious *a priori* grounds for claiming that a particular behavioural phenomenon is

301 Joseph Henrich, *The WEIRDest People in the World: How the West Became Psychologically Peculiar and Particularly Prosperous* (New York: Farrar, Strauss and Giroux, 2020), p. 21.

302 Joseph Henrich, Steven J. Heine, and Ara Norenzayan, "The Weirdest People in the World?" *Behavioral and Brain Sciences* 33, 2–3 (2010): 61–83, www.doi.org/10.1017/S0140525X0999152X.

universal based on sampling from a single subpopulation. Overall, these empirical patterns suggests that we need to be less cavalier in addressing questions of human nature on the basis of data drawn from this particularly thin, and rather unusual slice of humanity.[303]

Did my grandmother bring to Canada psychological domains unique to her part of Eastern Europe as her life suggests? I think so. She was not a Westerner, but her resilience and resourcefulness certainly shone through. Growing up on a farm complex with only a little education was not enough to give her skills to become a businesswoman and entrepreneur, but she learned those skills out of necessity and by hard work. First there was the candy store in Halifax with her husband, later the restaurant and hotel there with her brothers, then the dry goods store in Montreal with a brother, and then her own grocery store on borrowed money in Timmins, followed by a joint grocery business with Joseph Pluto, property acquisitions and development in Timmins, a cabin resort in Orillia, then the Armory Hotel in Hamilton, followed by the Lakeside Cabin business in Barrie, Ontario. For a woman who spoke little English, hers is an amazing record of hard work and ability to adapt to the circumstances. She kept her Polish language, her Polish friends, and her strong family focus. But she managed to see that education opened doors in Canada and funded the university education for my father and Louis Dudek. And the value of education is one thing that has undoubtedly been passed on to us.

Maybe my generation (second-generation immigrants) has become "Westernized" in that we are educated, relatively "rich,"

---

303 Henrich, Heine, and Norenzayan, p. 61.

industrialized, live in an apparently democratic country (despite misgivings), but still hold onto family and close friends. Some of us though, do not run with the flow. I myself resisted changing my Polish surname in 1973. I wanted to be who I was and not take a British last name. My decision came naturally. Naming is indeed an important part of cultural differentiation. In Polish tradition, often in remembrance, the name of a deceased relative is given to a newborn. Each of my sons carries the name of a grandparent; my sister and I have a grandmother's name for our second name; my brother has the name of my father's deceased brother. Newborns also often carry a saint's name. I myself and all of my siblings have a saint's name as our first name. It feels special.

THE LOSS OF CONNECTEDNESS

During the past few decades, various writers have observed an epidemic of people feeling unconnected. Leaving aside the isolation mandated by our government during the COVID-19 pandemic, some of this loss of connectedness may be because many immigrants left strong family networks behind and ended up in crowded urban settings with few replacements for these networks. In Professor Blum's chapter titled "The Village and the Family,"[304] he describes the forces driving communal cooperation to ensure the survival of all. Small villages and settlements engendered a familial quality, even more so when there was intermarriage within the community (as was the case with my grandfather and grandmother who both lived in the same area). The villagers knew each other very well and were all part of the same day-to-day joys and sorrows,

---

304 Blum, *Our Forgotten Past*, pp. 9–24.

seasonal celebrations, and religious observances. They would meet to decide matters of importance to the community, and they all had to deal with the lord of the manor and his delegates who often made their lives more difficult.

> Each household in the village depended upon every other household for mutual assistance. When a new dwelling had to be built or an old one repaired, when a roof needed thatching, when help was needed in an emergency, when a disaster befell a household, the villagers could count on their neighbours for help.[305]

However, as Professor Blum points out, the villages were not free of discord, and this same closeness could and did lead to gossiping and prying, so privacy was impossible, and there were family feuds and physical assaults. But the villagers managed such discord within their community, as many had learned from experience that complaints to outside authorities often resulted in anger and annoyance from those in power. Most of our immigrant parents, grandparents, or great-grandparents probably left similar supportive cocoon-like existences behind, or at least a familial support system of communal cooperation, if they emigrated from a society dominated by collectivism (as my grandparents did). Currently, many feel that the "virtual communities" formed through Zoom connections, Skype, iPhones, and the like are not a sufficient replacement.

Johann Hari, in his book *Lost Connections,* discusses the dilemma of feeling homesick while actually being "at home":

---

305 Blum, *Our Forgotten Past,* p. 12.

When we talk about home today, we mean just our four walls and (if we're lucky) our nuclear family. But that's never been what home has meant to any humans before us. To them, it meant community – a dense web of people all around us, a tribe. But that is largely gone. Our sense of home has shrivelled so far and so fast that it no longer meets our need for a sense of belonging. So we are homesick even when we are at home.[306]

He cites social psychologist and loneliness expert John Cacioppo, who commented that we are the first humans to dismantle our tribe, leaving us alone on a savanna we do not understand and puzzled by our own sadness.[307] That can be a challenging legacy of our ancestors' migration. Could that be the root of some of the discontent in our society – obesity, out-of-control consumerism, addictions, and depression? Hari insightfully postulates that perhaps, comparable to the way junk food distorts our bodies, junk values resulting from disconnection distort our minds.[308] After much research and self-examination, his conclusions are that the problem doesn't necessarily originate with an individual – rather, it is a cultural unhappiness that cannot be remedied alone. He recommends that the solution is getting together and working with others. He gives an example of a situation he observed while in Berlin, when members of a group demanding a rent freeze formed wonderful personal connections that they had been missing. He tells of a woman he met in that group who had grown up in

---

306 Johann Hari, *Lost Connections: Uncovering the Real Causes of Depression—and the Unexpected Solutions* (New York: Bloomsbury Publishing, 2018), p. 81.

307 Hari, p. 90.

308 Hari, pp. 96–97.

Turkey. There, she had thought of the whole village as her home, but when she came to live in Europe, she soon learned that you are supposed to think of your home as just the apartment you live in, and she felt very alone. When she joined the rent freeze group, she experienced a sense of community she had been missing. She then realized that she had felt homeless for more than thirty years, but now she had a replacement home.[309]

This feeling of disconnectedness and homesickness is also discussed in the book *Urban Tribes*,[310] by journalist Ethan Watters who speculates, based on his personal experience, that "urban tribes" – communities formed by bands of friends – might to some extent be the replacements for the household and village communities of our grandparents' generation. However, as the book progresses and after much "tribe" time, he finds a marital partner; his wife and literary life take over as the more important priorities, and his life in the "tribe" becomes a distant third.[311] Western culture could benefit from understanding and appreciating that values such as connectedness have the potential to substantially decrease the pervasive malaise in our societies.

I'm sure coming from a large family and a small village collective Joanna felt the loss of connectedness. But in my review of her life, she compensated by keeping as close as she could to her two brothers in Canada and then teaming up with Polish friends like the Semiuks she met in Halifax and later followed to Timmins. My grandmother made the effort to continue a connection to the Catholic Church and to Polish organizations where possible. In

---

309 Hari, pp. 260–261.

310 Ethan Watters, *Urban Tribes: Are Friends the New Family?* (London: Bloomsbury Press, 2004).

311 Watters, *Urban Tribes*, p. 213.

Halifax and Timmins, my father and his siblings went to Roman Catholic schools when available. In Timmins, a Polish priest was added to the Church of the Nativity, and he shortly thereafter formed the Polish White Eagle Society. Joseph Pluto was the second president of that society.

CHAPTER EIGHTEEN: DIVERSE VIEWS OF IMMIGRATION

For here [in Canada], I want the marble to remain the marble; the granite to remain the granite; the oak to remain the oak; and out of these elements, I would build a nation great among the nations of the world.

> —Sir Wilfrid Laurier, 7th Prime Minister of Canada, July 11, 1896–
> October 6, 1911

Reality has changed chameleonlike before my eyes so many times that I have learned, or am learning, to trust almost anything except what appears to be so.

> —Maya Angelou, "Shades and Slashes of Light"

Today immigration is a very poignant issue around the world, causing political turmoil among countries. One regularly reads in newspapers of the loss of lives in overturned emigrant boats, attacks on political leaders who are regarded as too lenient about safeguarding their borders or too stringent about allowing others into their country, community reaction to a dominance of one immigrant group and dramatic court appeals of immigrants ordered deported.

My grandparents, my father and his siblings came to Canada from the Russian Partition of Poland during a time of Canadian government campaigns to populate and settle the new land, which often enticed many by using misrepresentations about the bounty they could expect in Canada. Immigrants at that time, some with an inbred resilience and a strong will to survive, had a tough journey, were given little on arrival, yet somehow contributed greatly to this country and nurtured families to carry on in a place relatively safe from violence and war, disease and famine.

Their life stories are tremendous resources – legacies – for which we ought to thank them. But their efforts are often forgotten and the lack of support they received on arrival and thereafter is over-looked.[312] Is history repeating itself in not properly accommodating our immigrants? Are the current targets of close to 500,000 immigrants to Canada per year realistic when our medical system, housing and environmental footprint are all very challenged? And why are many immigrants leaving the country?[313] Consider the diverse discussions on the impacts of present-day immigration on our society, consequences which can be considered legacies, both positive and negative.

Economic consultant Patrick Grady and Professor Emeritus of Economics Herbert Grubel stated in 2011 that "to all but the blind there is mounting evidence that immigration [to Canada] is not working as well as it did in the past."[314] Martin Collacott (formerly of the Centre for Immigrant Policy Reform) has opined that immigrants should come in "reasonable numbers." Stephen Hume talks about a prevalent societal attitude: "I'm in the lifeboat. Pull up the ladder"; he notes ironically that most of us are immigrants or

---

312   "I'd wonder why nobody talked about the land that had been taken from my parent and grandmother by the Russians, and why nobody cared and nobody asked that the Polish people be compensated, too." Apolonja Maria Kojder and Barbara Glogowska, *Marynia, Don't Cry: Memoirs of Two Polish-Canadian Families* (Toronto: Multicultural History Society of Ontario, 1995), p. 136.

313   Gagandeep Kaur Sekhhon, "Reverse Migration from Canada: Here Are the Top 5 Reasons," *Immigration News Canada*, June 12, 2023, www.immigrationnewscanada. ca/know-about-reverse-migration-from-canada/. Among the reasons mentioned are the following: rising cost of living, urban congestion, wish to return to cultural origins, increasing housing expense, and a very competitive job market.

314   Patrick Grady and Herbert Grubel, "A Mawkish View of Immigration Overlooks the Facts," *Vancouver Sun*, June 6, 2011, p. A2, www.fraserinstitute.org/article/mawkish-view-immigration-overlooks-facts.

descendants of immigrants and urges that we instead embrace the concept of "hybrid vigour."[315] A guest editorial from the *Ottawa Citizen* published in the *Vancouver Sun*[316] stated that "one in every seven human beings on the planet is a migrant." Douglas Todd, a journalist for the *Vancouver Sun*, wrote in 2014:

> The United Nations Global Commission on International Migration… details how the migration story today is generally not the traditional one of arrival, settlement and integration. Instead, migration, especially for the affluent, has turned into a globalized trend of unprecedented mobility, porous national borders, weak loyalties, opportunism and fragmented families.[317]

Catherine Dauvergne, former Dean of the University of British Columbia Law School, in an interview for the *Vancouver Sun* on May 3, 2016, stated that there is a moral and ethical imperative to take refugees[318] and that we must think beyond borders. Charles Foran in the *Globe and Mail* remarked:

---

315 Stephen Hume, "Canada's Bigots Grant Themselves Permission to Vent," *Vancouver Sun*, March 28, 2015, www.vancouversun.com/opinion/columnists/stephen-hume-canadas-bigots-grant-themselves-permission-to-vent.

316 Guest Editorial from the Ottawa Citizen, "The Merits of Migration," *Vancouver Sun*, October 20, 2009, p. A10.

317 Douglas Todd, "The Floating Life of Affluent 'Transnational' Migrants," *Vancouver Sun*, August 2, 2014, www.vancouversun.com/news/metro/douglas-todd-the-floating-life-of-affluent-transnational-migrants.

318 I find no evidence in our Canadian records that persons now described as refugees were historically treated differently from immigrants, as they are now. For instance, many Jewish people arrived in Canada as immigrants between 1900 and 1921, but they were actually "refugees" by today's standards, fleeing from the pogroms in Eastern Europe and Czarist Russia. In 2019, 29,950 persons came to Canada as refugees, most

> …our family ancestors…were once immigrants, and most arrived in distress, and without much welcome or legal sanction, never mind language skills or professional qualifications or the right religion or skin colour. . . . [A]ny country can fall apart. When it does, any one of us may end up recast as the illegal alien, the queue jumper, the hostile invader… there are no real differences between humans.[319]

There are many more views and opinions on this topic, but the few I have selected provide some idea of the scope. Below is a brief consideration of some factors that influence and are influenced by immigration. Immigration is a complex issue, but from my grandmother's story it is apparent to me that unless we learn from history and from such life stories, we will repeat the mistakes made in the past.

ECONOMICS

Economics has traditionally been one of the forces driving countries to admit immigrants. In the early 1900s, this was particularly evident in Canada when strong men and their families were needed to plough fields, to settle the land, and to work in coal mines as my great uncles did in Nova Scotia. Economics is still a driving force, but not without controversy. Take, for instance, a column by Gabriel Friedman, reviewing the 2019 Conference Board of Canada's report titled *Canada 2040: No Immigration Versus More*

---

sponsored under the Private Sponsorship of Refugees Program; 313,580 persons came into Canada as immigrants. In 1914, 150,500 persons immigrated to Canada.

319 Charles Foran, "Tales of Our Shared Exodus Narrative May Just Be How Democracy Fights Back," *Globe and Mail*, December 29, 2018, www.theglobeandmail.com/arts/books/article-tales-of-our-shared-exodus-narrative-may-just-be-how-democracy-fights/.

Immigration.[320] The report concluded that immigration has a net positive effect on the economy because workers are needed, and workers pay taxes, contribute to the Canada Pension Plan, and support GDP growth. The following are some of the facts and views set out in Friedman's column:

> Canada hasn't had a replacement rate fertility level – defined as 2.1 children per woman – since 1971. At the same time, the number of centenarians has tripled since 2001 to more than 10,000 people due to increased life expectancy, and they all collect rather than pay for benefits.
>
> . . . . But the big challenge for Canada is that its labour force is out of balance. During the next two decades, 13.4 million people are projected to exit the workforce, but only 11.8 million people will finish school and join the workforce.

Friedman's column also reports that, according to Parisa Mahboubi, a senior analyst at the C.D. Howe Institute, a non-profit policy thinktank, "[this imbalance] will create labour shortages, and it's going to affect economic growth." Friedman points out that economists say each class has different labour outcomes in that some immigrants integrate more easily into the economy than others. Because so many factors affect immigration outcomes, Peter Dungan, a professor at the University of Toronto's Rotman School of Management, built a complex computer model to examine the macroeconomic effects of immigration in Canada, in which the computer processed more than 700 variables. Summarizing his

---

320 Gabriel Friedman, "All the Reasons Why Canada Needs Immigration—and More of It," *Financial Post,* October 8, 2019, www.financialpost.com/news/economy/all-the-reasons-why-canada-needs-immigration-and-more-of-it.

findings, he said that "[it] found generally positive impacts of immigration on the economy" but noted that these effects were higher when the immigrants were better integrated.[321] My question here is: Are immigrants truly aware that there could be an expectation that they give up their ancestral history and their culture and beliefs in coming here? Many Poles left the Russian Partition because Russification was forced on them. We are aware of how the loss of one's culture and language impacts families for generations. With that realization, aren't we now attempting to compensate for the damage to First Nations peoples when integration was forced on them?

In 2019, Douglas Todd wrote about his interview with UBC economist David Green. To summarize, David Green and others listed economic "discoveries" relating to immigrants in Canada:

1. New immigrants aren't doing as well in Canada as in the 1980s.
2. Language matters a lot.
3. Source country also makes a difference.
4. Foreign degrees are not quite as valuable as Canadian degrees.
5. Offshore work experience doesn't pay off as expected.
6. There are winners and losers in migration.
7. Immigrants tend to pay less in taxes.
8. Immigrants lean toward self-employment and small business.[322]

---

321 As reported in Friedman's article.

322 Douglas Todd, "10 Surprising Lessons about Migration from Economists," *Vancouver Sun*, May 11, 2019, www.vancouversun.com/opinion/columnists/douglas-todd-immigration-may-lift-economy-but-not-peoples-wages-plus-other-economists-lessons.

Douglas Todd concluded his column with the opinion that many people make sweeping generalizations for and against immigration, but instead of going with high-sounding verbiage, economists show that truth is in the details. These differing opinions again show the complexity of the issues involved.

CONSEQUENCES OF AMALGAMATING DIVERSE CULTURES

Issues arise when diverse cultures come together.[323] In 1972, under the government of Prime Minister Pierre Trudeau, Canada allowed peoples from non-European countries to settle in significant numbers.[324] Questions then arose: Are we a multicultural mosaic or a "melting pot," and which is better? Do differences in religion and cultural heritage pose challenges to social cohesion? Is assimilation the target? How do diverse cultures affect a society? One opinion was that of George Jonas in a *Vancouver Sun* article in 2011 (also published in the *National Post*), who commented that Mr. Trudeau's multiculturalism hinted of a "founding nations" snobbery: "[T]he reluctance of the British and French to share the country with the riff-raff of the world on a completely equal footing, in contrast to

---

323   Gira Bhatt, "Home Away from Home," *Vancouver Sun*, March 23, 2010, p. A11: "Whereas it seems somehow easy to be critical of ethnic minorities in Canada who appear to stay tied to their homeland politics and traditions, there is a tendency to overlook the thousands of immigrants from Anglo-European countries who may be just as reluctant to make Canada their true home—like my elderly parents-in-law."

324   See the *Canadian Multiculturalism Act*, R.S.C. 1986. Also: "There is no such thing as a model or ideal Canadian. What could be more absurd than the concept of an 'all-Canadian' boy or girl? A society which emphasizes uniformity is one which creates intolerance and hate." Pierre Elliott Trudeau, Remarks at the Ukrainian-Canadian Congress, October 9, 1971.

'the American 'melting pot' with its gung-ho patriotism and crude pressures of assimilation."[325]

In a 2011 *Vancouver Sun* column,[326] Douglas Todd presented data indicating that Metro Vancouver neighbourhoods are increasingly defined by ethnicity; at that time, there were 110 ethnic enclaves in Metro Vancouver. In a later column, Todd described this as being hyperdiverse, not cosmopolitan.[327] In a column from 2014, he cited the findings of Harvard sociologist Robert Putnam, who surveyed 30,000 Americans and found that people who live in ethnic enclaves generally tend to be more distrusting of those around them.[328] In another 2014 column, Todd quoted Farid Rohani of the Laurier Institution as saying, "celebration of our diversity has turned into a policy allowing for divisions."[329]

Three years later, on January 21, 2017, Todd wrote on the pros and cons of diversity through an interview with UBC social psychologist Ara Norenzayan. In that column, Todd starts off with the fact that we are often told it is morally good to celebrate diversity.

---

325 George Jonas, "Trudeau's 'Cultural Mosaic' a Failed Cultural Experiment," *Vancouver Sun*, September 21, 2011, www.pressreader.com/canada/vancouver-sun/20110921/288535904413710.

326 Douglas Todd, "Ethnic Mapping Conclusion: As Enclaves Grow, Will Metro Residents' Trust Fade?" *Vancouver Sun*, October 20, 2011, www.vancouversun.com/news/staff-blogs/ethnic-mapping-conclusion-as-enclaves-grow-will-metro-residents-trust-fade.

327 Douglas Todd, "Vancouver Ranks Fourth for Foreign-Born Residents, but Is It 'Cosmopolitan?'" *Vancouver Sun*, July 21, 2013, www.vancouversun.com/opinion/columnists/vancouver-ranks-fourth-for-foreign-born-residents-but-is-it-cosmopolitan.

328 Douglas Todd, "Ethnic Diversity's 'Inconvenient Truths,'" Vancouver Sun, February 9, 2014, www.vancouversun.com/news/staff-blogs/ethnic-diversitys-inconvenient-truths.

329 Douglas Todd, "We Must Stand on Guard for Canada," *Vancouver Sun*, July 10, 2014, www.vancouversun.com/opinion/columnists/douglas-todd-we-must-stand-on-guard-for-canada.

Norenzayan, however, notes that many in North America mistakenly think respecting diversity means holding the belief that everyone is essentially the same, but he points out that this is a lazy, ethnocentric approach; the real way to learn about difference, he says, is to cultivate curiosity. He goes on to describe the benefits of diversity: that it concentrates talent, that diverse groups are more creative in problem solving (lab experiments show groups of varied people can imagine many more novel uses for an object than a more homogeneous group), and that people in diverse contexts learn the skill of interacting without polarizing (giving the example of young Jews and Palestinians at summer camp who became friends).[330]

The downsides of diversity include self-segregation, diminished contact, reduced likelihood of diverse neighbours knowing each other, and importantly, as sociologist Robert Putnam noted in the study discussed in Todd's article above, "the more ethnically diverse the people we live around, the less we trust them."[331] Diversity benefits can unravel very fast. Ara Norenzayan has suggested that to avoid conflict, we should accept differences (e.g., that Asians value group cohesion and obedience to authority), but that limits must be set. For example, if polygamy were legalized, Canada would be a magnet for polygamous immigrants, which is not a value that would fit in with our current culture. In the short personal interview I had with Ara Norenzayan, he smilingly suggested that

---

330 Douglas Todd, "The Pros and Cons of Diversity," *Vancouver Sun*, January 21, 2017, www.vancouversun.com/opinion/columnists/douglas-todd-canada-needs-strong-dose-of-cultural-curiosity.

331 Todd, "Ethnic Diversity's 'Inconvenient Truths.'"

the best way to get to know another culture is to marry someone from that culture (as he did).[332]

In his book *The WEIRDest People*, Joseph Henrich speculated as to why the West became peculiar and prosperous. He makes a case that it is linked to immigration. Noting there was massive proliferation of innovations after the Industrial Revolution, Henrich argues that because some societies had broad-based trust, there was a flow of individuals between occupations and between higher and lower social strata which led to recombination and the spread of ideas. On investigating the effects of immigration on innovation, he found that immigrants bring ideas and recombine these with the local protocols of their new surroundings, a process resulting in novel inventions.[333]

Opinions differ regarding the advantages of a multicultural versus a melting pot approach. My grandmother's story has the answer: we should learn from and respect each other. She learned entrepreneurship here, and we should learn from her and others like her about the strengths her culture espoused (such as religion and education) and what her story tells us about the nefariousness of totalitarianism in the regime that she left. Perhaps a more descriptive way of describing this model is neither as a melting pot nor as a multicultural mosaic. The metaphor of a tapestry has been referred to by various visionaries such as V. Seymour Wilson in 1993 where he endorses policies in a tapestry framework which reflect democratic ideals of procedural justice, human equality, and mutual respect.[334] In my view, the tapestry image goes beyond a

---

332   Ara Norenzayan, personal interview with author, 2021.

333   In Henrich, *The WEIRDest People*.

334   V. Seymour Wilson, "The Tapestry Vision of Canadian Multiculturalism," *Canadian Journal of Political Science* 26, 4 (1993): 645–669.

multicultural mosaic of ethnic enclaves and goes beyond a melting pot where distinctions disappear into the soup. As defined in the *Gage Canadian Dictionary*, a tapestry is "a heavy, thick handwoven fabric having designs or pictures woven into it, used to hang on walls, cover furniture, etc."[335] Individual (cultural) threads require the interdependence of the other threads and all contribute to the whole of the design (or identity). I have found that my grandmother had lots to offer Canada as Canada had lots to offer her — all such exchanges result in a sum greater than its parts to create a distinct Canadian culture and surely "hybrid vigour" as suggested by Stephen Hume.[336]

IMPACT OF LARGE NUMBERS AND SELECT PROFESSIONAL GROUPS

There is a further consequence of current immigration that some have highlighted: the impact on the environment. Take for instance, the opinion of renowned scientist and environmental activist David Suzuki, founder of the Suzuki Foundation. He has been quoted as saying that because most immigrants go to a few large cities in Canada, "Canada is full."[337]

The Global Footprint Network provides an interesting calculation for policy analysts and decision-makers: "overshoot day." Earth Overshoot Day is the date on which humanity has exhausted the natural world's budget for the year. A country's "overshoot day"

335 *Gage Canadian Dictionary*, s.v. "tapestry" (Toronto: Gage Educational Publishing Company, 1983).

336 Hume, "Canada's Bigots Grant Themselves Permission to Vent."

337 Douglas Todd, "Radical Environmentalists Have Strong Views on Immigration," *Vancouver Sun*, October 22, 2018, www.vancouversun.com/opinion/columnists/doug-las-todd-how-radical-environmentalists-view-immigration.

is the date on which Earth Overshoot Day would fall if all of humanity consumed like the people in that country; Canada's Earth Overshoot Day in 2023 was March 13, indicating that we are high consumers.[338] (Is high consumerism a value that we need to rethink? Could resourcefulness that many immigrants have shown us trump consumerism by finding second uses for our many possessions?)

David Suzuki further points out that we also are poaching professionals from developing nations that need their own doctors, scholars, teachers, and skilled workers to stay. Our health system is in crisis to such an extent that in British Columbia cancer patients are being sent to Washington State for treatment. In a recent commentary, Diane Francis expressed the view that we need to have a responsible and ethical federal immigration policy such that there are enough family physicians, ICUs, hospital beds, and health care services in place both for those already in Canada and those we invite in.[339] My grandparents lost three children in their first years here. These children should have had medical care, and they should have not suffered from lack of food when they had been encouraged to come to Canada. They were poor, but hard working and had no help in learning English. Are our current invitees experiencing similar challenges?

A complex and extraordinary situation currently exists in our health care system. We are short of doctors here as the number of doctors trained in Canada was purposely limited to keep the cost of health care at a certain level. Now foreign medical students

---

338 For more information on overshoot days, see Earth Overshoot Day, www.overshootday.org.

339 Diane Francis, "Health System Can't Support Immigrant Influx," *Financial Post*, November 30, 2022, www.financialpost.com/diane-francis/canada-health-system-cant-support-immigrant-influx.

and professionals are preferred over Canadian citizens who have obtained medical degrees abroad in some of the best medical schools in the world, presumably for the reasons that these foreigners can afford to pay high tuition fees and agree to "return of service" contracts once they graduate. We seem to be filling our high schools, colleges, and universities with rich international students, and our Canadian students lose out.[340] Perhaps we should take care of our Canadian students and graduates first?

CHANGING A BELIEF SYSTEM

There is an additional element to consider regarding the inter-joining of cultures which is set out in the book *Crazy Like Us: The Globalization of the American Psyche*, by Ethan Watters.[341] Watters makes the compelling argument that Western concepts of wellness and healing, including notions of mental health, threaten to homogenize the current cultural differences in these areas of human existence. Here are two extraordinary examples of this cross-cultural migration.

In his first chapter, Watters discusses the rise of anorexia in Hong Kong, where it had previously been quite unknown. He interviewed Dr. Sing Lee, a pre-eminent researcher on eating disorders in China. Dr. Lee conducted a thorough search of one hospital's database that recorded medical information for thousands of patients and found only ten possible cases of anorexia from 1983 to 1988, leading him to conclude it was an exceedingly rare disorder. He decided to find out why it was rare as Hong Kong had been under Western

---

340 See the website of the Society of Canadians Studying Medicine Abroad (SOCASMA.com) for more information on this matter, including their legal action.

341 Ethan Watters, *Crazy Like Us: The Globalization of the American Psyche* (New York: Free Press, 2010).

influence via British rule for some time, when Western and Chinese celebrities were admired and fast-food restaurants were in vogue. He suggested that perhaps Chinese cultural beliefs or practices contained protective mechanisms. He knew, for instance, that historically there was little Chinese stigma surrounding larger body shapes. In fact, popular Chinese sayings suggested that "being about to eat is to have luck;" "gaining weight means good fortune," and "fat people have more luck."[342]

In one particular case, Dr. Lee noticed the doctor's notes reflected that "the patient still denied having a fear of fatness or dieting," and so the patient did not conform to the DSM criteria. Dr. Lee worried that these doctors were adhering to a foreign diagnostic manual, the DSM, at the expense of understanding both the patient's subjective experience and the cultural meaning specific to Hong Kong at that time.[343] He also noted there had been no Chinese celebrities with anorexia and little mention of it in newspapers and magazines.

Dr. Lee speculated that this very lack of public awareness about anorexia might be key to the rarity of the disorder, reducing the likelihood that distressed individuals would, as he put it, choose "anorexia as a convenient form of illness." This was postulated as another way of saying that anorexia remained outside the symptom pool for much of the population. Dr. Lee feared, however, that an "epidemiogenic trigger" might occur, with an explosive effect. Five years later, that fear was realized as the diagnosis of anorexia was becoming accepted across the globe. Watters suggests that as evidenced by anorexia in Hong Kong, we are engaged in "globalizing

---

342 Watters, *Crazy Like Us*, p. 14.

343 Watters, *Crazy Like Us*, p. 36.

our understanding, treatments, and categories of mental illness. As of now there is no acknowledgement that in doing so we may be changing the symptom pool by which people in other cultures [and from other cultures] find expression for their distress."[344]

Watters offers another example of differences in belief systems leading to mistaken conclusions about cultures. In December 2004, an Indian Ocean tsunami reached Sri Lanka as well as other neighbouring countries and left about 200,000 people dead or missing. Watters describes how Western medical health systems responded in Sri Lanka, spearheaded by individuals such as Debra Wentz, executive director of the New Jersey Association of Mental Health Agencies: "I knew that the mental health needs after the tsunami would be unlike anything the world has ever seen," she recounted, but without a sophisticated mental health system or trained counsellors, she surmised that the survivors had nowhere to turn. They had almost no psychiatrists, and most primary care doctors were not trained in psychiatry or mental health education. They didn't have a system in place to care for these people.[345]

What resulted was fundraising in the U.S. to send American trauma experts to Sri Lanka to train local counsellors to spot and treat PTSD. Trauma counsellors and researchers came from the United States, Britain, France, Australia, and New Zealand. Watters writes that Wentz's efforts "were clearly motivated by a set of assumptions and beliefs about the nature of psychological trauma and its appropriate treatments. Wentz assumed, as do many Western mental health specialists who focus on trauma, that the psychological reaction to horrible events is fundamentally the same

---

344 Watters, *Crazy Like Us*, p. 61.

345 Watters, *Crazy Like Us*, p. 68.

around the world."[346] Some experts were warning that without professional counselling, as many as 16% of the PTSD sufferers might commit suicide.[347]

What clinicians found when they arrived in the disaster areas was unexpected – the clinicians were confused and concerned that the local population weren't behaving as they had predicted. For example, children were more interested in returning to school than discussing their experience of the tsunami; they were then labelled as in denial.[348] Reporters were amazed that thousands of Sri Lankans wanted to leave the refugee camps to go back to their devastated villages or to depend on friends or family.[349] It was found that most Sri Lankans wanted medicines, food, and their homes rebuilt, not counselling, not unlike my grandmother's resourcefulness that propelled her to just move forward when confronted with tragedies. Apparently, a memo sent just after the disaster from faculty members at the University of Columbo in Sri Lanka was ignored. "The professors acknowledged that 'disaster zones attract "trauma" and "counselling projects,"' but they pleaded with the arriving army of counselors not to reduce survivors' experiences 'to a question of mental trauma' and the survivors themselves to 'psychological casualties.'" They presented argument that Western ideas about trauma are not universal.[350]John Mahoney, the director of the World Health Organization's mental health initiative in Sri Lanka, told a reporter, "We found one organization just handing out anti-depressants to

---

346 Watters, *Crazy Like Us*, p. 68.

347 Watters, *Crazy Like Us*, p. 69.

348 Watters, *Crazy Like Us*, p. 77.

349 Watters, *Crazy Like Us*, p. 77.

350 Watters, *Crazy Like Us*, pp. 76–77.

---

people."[351] Hopefully the Sri Lankans were not too distracted from their own way to recover by the Western nations' faulty conclusions as to how people should react to a disaster.

CANADA'S INDIGENOUS LEGACY

In his book *A Fair Country: Telling Truths about Canada*, John Ralston Saul[352] gives our early era of settlement an interesting contextual overlay that is both insightful and persuasive. He sets out that the Canada we know today is an amalgam of Indigenous and European ideas and values,[353] and he argues that in fact, "what we are today has been inspired as much by four centuries of life with the indigenous civilization as by four centuries of immigration."[354] Further,

> our leaders endlessly mull over our institutional and cultural inheritance from British parliamentary democracy, British and French justice, the Enlightenment, British liberalism, Western individualism with its important variations, U.S. populism, Judeo-Christian moral questioning, Athenian

---

351 Watters, *Crazy Like Us*, p. 81.

352 John Ralston Saul, *A Fair Country: Telling Truths about Canada* (Toronto: Penguin Canada, 2008), pp. 3–7.

353 In his essay "The Three Lies Canada Tells about Itself," Doug Saunders highlights the research findings of David Verbeeten. See "The Three Lies Canada Tells about Itself" July 1, 2009, www.dougsaunders.net/2009/07/canada-multiculturalism-immigration-lies/. David Verbeeten of Cambridge University sets out that most people in Canada are descended from non-British immigrants who arrived during and after the years of 1896–1911 (the Laurier years). Many went to Australia and the United States (he found that one-half to three quarters of immigrants in the nineteenth century went to the U.S.). He postulates that it was the "second wave" of immigrants who formed the fundamental core culture.

354 Saul, p. 1.

> principles of citizenship and democracy, Western European philosophy, Western social democracy, Western capitalism, in particular its U.S. form.

Yet, he observes, many of our ethical principles originated from Indigenous values. For instance,

> on the single issue of immigration and citizenship diversity, we seem unable to notice the obvious – that it is a non-racial idea of civilization, and nonlinear, even nonrational. It is based on the idea of an inclusive circle that expands and gradually adapts as new people join us. This is not a Western or European concept. It comes straight from Aboriginal culture.[355]

We should not overlook the violent inter-tribal warfare in the Indigenous past; nevertheless, it is useful to consider Saul's thoughts about the artificial Europeanization of Canada – "colonial elites pretend[ing] they weren't where they were" [356] – and its destructiveness to Indigenous peoples and certain groups of immigrants. Ironically, this backfired on some of the early British and U.S. explorers, who died because of their refusal to dress, act, or eat like "savages." However, they finally came to realize in the late 1800s that their own inferiority and tragic-comic self-absorption was not working. All it took was one naval officer breaking ranks to spend the winter with the Inuit, then coming back to the ship in the spring – healthy, happy, well fed – to find the usual collection of

---

355 Saul, pp. 3–4.

356 Saul, p. 9.

sick shipmates and lists of those who died.[357] Saul presents Susanna Moodie as an example of someone who resisted adapting and consequently endured much hardship after she and her husband naively decided to settle in Canada in the early to mid-1800s. For instance, she learned that possessing a servant was very different in Canada. They are "persons of no small consequence, for the dread of starving no longer frightens them into servile obedience," as was the case in England. If they are scolded "for any slight omission or offence, you rouse into active operation all their new-found spirit of freedom and opposition," and they threaten to quit. Delicate porcelain and tea sets were completely incongruous in her rustic backwoods log cabin.[358]

There is a very interesting article by Hayden King that points out that Indigenous cultures had accomplishments that rivalled many civilizations around the world in many ways, including living sustainably and having extraordinary ecological knowledge. ("Indigenous peoples were adept farmers, originally cultivating two-thirds of the foodstuffs the world consumes today.") He gave some specific examples:

> The Wet'suwet'en practised a matriarchal society, while on the other side of the Atlantic, women were the property of men. While Christians were burning "heretics" at the stake for suggesting the Earth wasn't the centre of the universe, the

---

357 Saul, p. 12.

358 See Susanna Moodie, *Roughing It in the Bush*, ed. by Carl Ballstadt (Ottawa: Carlton University Press, 1995).

Mayans were charting the movement of the stars, creating a calendar within seconds of modern day atomic clocks.[359]

While immigrant societies had endless stories of poverty and hard times until well into the nineteenth century, Saul notes that many found a place of comfort and belonging when it was much needed, including those who built the nation of Canada: working-class people, farmers, and refugee immigrants. In his view, such people are extraordinary, as they would have shown themselves to be highly conscious and to have a certain courage, often facing impossible situations. He concludes that such consciousness and courage was the reason that Canada has prospered, and this is the "real source of our renewable energy."[360] My grandmother's story exemplifies that proposition.

A SUGGESTION

John Meyer, president of Canadians for a Sustainable Society, wrote an article entitled "International Migration: A Disaster Coming Soon…to a Neighbourhood Near You."[361] He makes an interesting and convincing argument that most people migrate only under extreme duress — when circumstances in their homeland are so dire that they choose to abandon their culture, family, friends, and social capital to take an often perilous journey to a foreign land. He talks about uncontrolled population growth, high-consumption

---

359 Hayden King, "Indigenous Cultures Rivalled Those of Many Other Civilizations," *Globe and Mail*, October 29, 2008, www.theglobeandmail.com/opinion/indigenous-cultures-rivalled-those-of-many-other-civilizations/article716632/.

360 Saul, p. 317.

361 John Meyer, "International Migration: A Disaster Coming Soon…to a Neighbourhood Near You," *Humanist Perspectives* 204 (Spring 2018): 17–24.

societies, high greenhouse gas emissions, and large-footprint societies as very concerning issues. He points out that Africa's population is forecast to increase to four billion this century from the current three billion. In Canada, he states, immigrants now cost the government $30 billion more in services than they pay in taxes, and immigration constitutes 80% of the demand for additional housing units. He concludes:

> The solution to migration lies not in accommodating it but eliminating the reasons for it. It is necessary to address the root causes of migration by drastically reducing consumption levels in more developed countries via very strong conservation measures and lifestyle changes and by providing the high population growth nations with the tools they need to rapidly stabilize their populations. . . . So far, the international community spend far more money on accommodating migrants than on solving the problems which create the migrant stream.[362]

I recently viewed on YouTube an interesting documentary[363] describing the Great Green Wall, an initiative sponsored by more than twenty countries in Africa to combat the desertification in the Sahara and the Sahel in order to give their people the chance for a livelihood and food security in their own country. Launched in 2007 by the African Union, the project aims to restore the continent's degraded landscapes and to transform millions of lives. I found this initiative well worth learning about.

---

362 Meyer, p. 23.

363 There are several YouTube videos on this topic.

I know that my grandmother and in fact all my grandparents would much rather have stayed home in a free Poland (if it had existed).[364] Her story and the other stories of the Irish, the Doukhobors, the African slaves escaping the U.S. clearly indicate to me that many of our immigrants left homes sorrowfully, some forcibly, others out of necessity. I have learned from her story that our efforts firstly should be to help those in their homelands remain there. However, if that is not feasible, we must ensure we have sufficient capacity and that those whom we have invited here are welcomed, supported, and respected.

364 I have been told that my maternal grandmother from the Austrian-Hungarian Partition who came to Canada at the age of seventeen was sad all her life because she missed her homeland.

CHAPTER NINETEEN: FINAL THOUGHTS

We learn from history that we do not learn from history.
—Georg Wilhelm Friedrich Hegel (1770–1831)

Ancestral history and life stories provide valuable groundwork to establish a context for who we are – connections to the past that enhance understanding of our current place. It also fosters gratitude and admiration and uncovers forgotten generosities and unacknowledged discoveries. My grandmother's life story has been extraordinarily inspiring and energizing, and my study of the history of Poland has revealed a fascinating but unappreciated country that once dominated Europe. Every society, and indeed every person, has something to offer to help define our reality if we choose to consider it. Understanding why our families came to be in Canada is helpful for sorting out current dilemmas, as many of our ancestors came out of desperation and longed for their homes for the rest of their lifetimes here. Those of us in subsequent generations may be carrying some of that desperation and loss. And then there are the less personal consequences of immigration, about which some have expressed consternation – for example, that immigrants provide a new pool of labourers but also draw upon social support systems, that they introduce new ideas but are treated with distrust in some communities, that they contribute to a larger environmental footprint and "disrupt" established belief systems.

So what do the stories, my research about Polish homelands, and my study of views and opinions about immigrants' legacies contribute to my journey of learning from the life of my grandmother? To me, they underscore that our life is a continuum – that the present contains the past, and the past supplies the context for the present and the future. The "old ways" had truth and solidity in them, reflecting a past culture and often an alternate approach to how we deal with day-to-day matters now. This knowledge renders my personal life easier to understand and makes me proud of their achievements and of mine. It helps me frame my attitude toward immigration and better grasp the consequences immigrants to our country's experience when they leave their home and culture.

Where do we go from here? I conclude that we need to explore our own family stories of immigration and the countries they came from to gain a personal context and appreciate the legacies there for us, both wonderful and challenging. We also must be cognizant of the consequences of immigration at a global level and determine what we can do to reduce people's need to flee their home countries. And we should ask how we can better assist those we have chosen to accept into our country – welcome them, learn from them, and provide for them as needed, inviting them to be part of the Canadian cultural tapestry. I was led to this exploration by listening to stories.

APPENDIX A

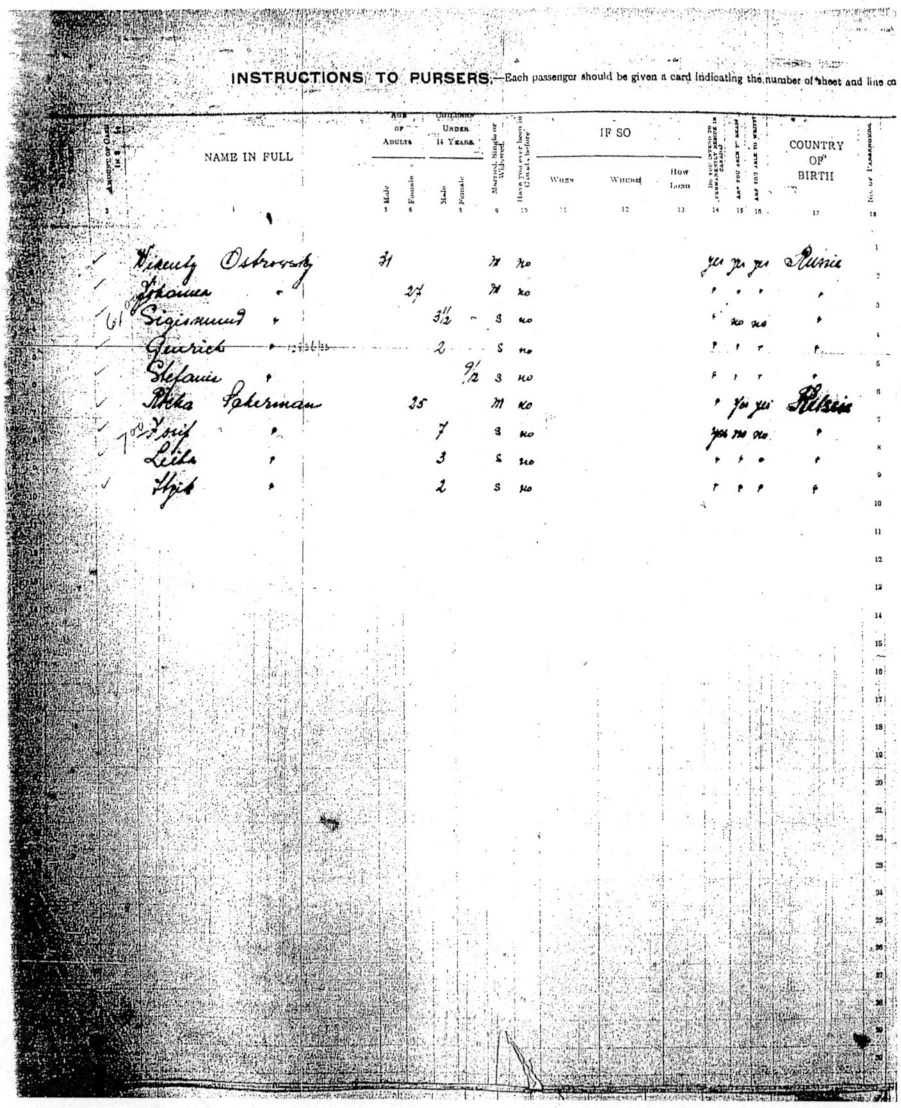

Page No. 1 Canada

sheet on which name is to be found. Columns 3, 29 and 30 are to be filled in by the Immigration Agent at the Port of Landing.

This sheet is to be used for "INTERMEDIATE" passengers only.

RACE OF PEOPLE	DESTINATION		WHAT WAS YOUR OCCUPATION IN COUNTRY FROM WHICH	WHAT IS YOUR INTENDED OCCUPATION IN CANADA?		IF NO.			RELIGIOUS DENOMINATION.	TRAVELLED INLAND ON	INITIALS OF CIVIC EXAMINER.	No. OF PASSENGER.
	Post Office.					When	How Lost	When				
19	20			23	24	25	26	27	28	29	30	31
Polish	Truro	H.	farmer	farmer	yes	farmer			Rom. Catholic			1
"	"	"	housewife	housewife	"	no				I.C.R.		2
"	"	"	child	child	no	no				I.C.R.		3
"	"	"		"	no	no				I.C.R.		4
"	"	"	infant	infant	no	no				I.C.R.		5
Hebrew	Winnipeg	Male	housewife	housewife	no	no			Hebrew	C.C.R.R.		6
"	"	"	child	child	no	no				C.C.R.R.		7
"	"	"	"	"	no	no				C.C.R.R.		8
"	"	"	"	"	no	no				I.C.&G.T.		9
										C.P.R.		10

MANIF

INSTRUCTIONS TO PURSERS. Each passenger should be given a card indicating the number of sheet and is on s

VESSEL'S NAME	MASTER'S NAME	TONNAGE	Total number of superficial feet, in the several compartments set apart for passengers, other than Cabin Passengers	Total num of Adult Passengers, exclusive of aster Crew and bind Passengers which the vessel ca egally carry
F. S. S. "Kursk"	A. Kirschfeldt	7869 Brutt 4637 Nett	22175	147

SUMMARY

		Number of Souls	Number of Adults to which they are equal under the Immigration Act
Adults	Canada	152	Canada 116
	U. S. via Halifax	51	U. S. via Halifax 100
Children under 14 years of age	New York	222	New York 239
	Canada	7	
	U. S. via Halifax	51	
Total		483	455

I Hereby Certify that the above is a correct description of the ___Twinscrew steamer___
(Description of Vessel as Ship, Brig, &c.)

___Kursk___ ____and correct list of all the Passengers on board the same at the time of her departure from
(Name of Vessel)

___Libau___ ____and that all the particulars therein mentioned are true.
(Made from whence she comes)

A. Kirschfeldt
Signature of Master.

Dated this ___25th___ day of ___April___ 19 14

Certificate of Ship's Surgeon

I Hereby Certify that I have daily during the present passage made a general inspection of the passengers on this vessel, and that I have at least once during the passage made a detailed individual examination of each immigrant on board and that I have seen no passenger thereon who I have reason to believe is, or is likely to become, insane, epileptic or consumptive, or who is idiotic, feeble-minded or afflicted with a contagious, infectious or loathsome disease; or who is deaf, dumb or blind or otherwise physically defective or whose present appearance would lead me to believe that he or she might be debarred from entering Canada under the "Immigration Act" with the exception of the ____ persons whose names are enumerated on the "Ship Surgeons's List for Medical Examining Officer" which I have prepared for such officer giving my medical opinion on the cases therein dealt with; and that there were no deaths or births during the passage except those mentioned on the said list.

Signature of Ship's Surgeon.

Dated this ___25th___ day of ___April___ 19 14

EST

heet on which name is to be found. Columns 3, 20 and 30 are to be filled in by the Immigration Agent at the Port of Landing.

PORT OF EMBARKATION	DATE OF SAILING	WHERE BOUND
Libau	April the 14th 1914	New York via Halifax

This space to be filled in by Immigration Agent at Port of Landing

S.S. _Kursk_ Line _Russian – American_

Sailed from _Libau_ on _April 14th_ 1914

Arrived at _Halifax_ on _April 25th_ 1914 at _3_ o'clock _p_ m.

Landed at 7 30 o'clock _p_ m. Saloon _✓_ 2nd Cabin _17_ Steerage _210_ Total _227_

Bill of Health _Clean_ No. held at Quarantine _None_

2ND CABIN INSPECTION

Medical Examiners _Gow_ began at 9 05 pm completed at 9 10 pm

No. detained by Medical Examiners for Canada _✓_ for United States _✓_ Total

Civil Examiners _Esther_ began at 9 05 pm completed at 9 pm

No. detained by Civil Examiners for Canada _✓_ for United States _2_ Total _2_

STEERAGE INSPECTION

Medical Examiners _Douglas (&) Rankine_ began at 9 10 pm completed at 9 30 pm

No. detained by Medical Examiners for Canada _1_ for United States _1_ Total _2_

Civil Examiners _Heskerighn Esther_ began at 9 pm completed at 9 pm

No. detained by Civil Examiners for Canada _✓_ for United States _13_ Total _13_

C. P. R. passengers left by _Special_ train at _7 am (1st)_

G. T. R. passengers left by _✓_ train at

I. C. R. passengers left by _✓_ train at

APPENDIX B

<table>
<tr><td>S.C.R.]</td><td>SUPREME COURT OF CANADA</td><td>193</td></tr>
</table>

SISCOE GOLD MINES LIMITED (DEFENDANT) .... APPELLANT;

AND

FELIX BIJAKOWSKI (PLAINTIFF).......RESPONDENT.

1934
*Nov. 8
*Dec. 21

ON APPEAL FROM THE COURT OF KING'S BENCH, APPEAL SIDE, PROVINCE OF QUEBEC

Evidence—Contract—Admissibility of oral testimony—Transfer of shares —Verbal condition as to their return—Whether a loan or a gift.

The respondent, by virtue of a transfer of their rights by two associates to himself, claimed to be the owner and demanded the delivery to him of 30,000 shares of the Siscoe Gold Mines Limited, which he alleged had been lent by way of a transfer by himself and his associates to the appellant company, on the condition that a like number of shares would be returned by the appellate company upon its mining properties being brought into production. The appellant company pleaded that the above transaction was carried out by the president of the company without authority expressed or implied and was never ratified by it, and, in the alternative, that in any event the above shares were not lent as alleged by the respondent, but were given or donated without condition as to their return. On the first point raised by the appellant company, after hearing its counsel, this Court decided that the findings of fact of the trial judge in favour of the respondent, unanimously affirmed by the appellate court, should not be disturbed; but this Court decided to hear the respondent on the question of law, raised by the appellant company in support of its second point, concerning the admissibility of oral evidence to prove the loan of the shares.

Held that, under the circumstances of this case, oral testimony was admissible. As both parties were admitting the existence of some contract for the transfer of the shares, parol evidence could be adduced to determine whether the transfer was conditional or unconditional and whether the shares were to be returned to the respondent and his associates as having been merely loaned. *Campbell* v. *Young* (32 Can. S.C.R. 547) foll.

APPEAL from the judgment of the Court of King's Bench, appeal side, province of Quebec, affirming the judgment of the Superior Court, Loranger J. and maintaining the respondent's action and condemning the appellant to deliver to respondent 30,000 shares of appellant's capital stock and to pay to the respondent the sum of $4,200.00 the amount of dividends declared on a like number of shares, or in the event of the appellant failing to deliver the said shares, to pay to the respondent the sum of $51,600.00, being the market value of the said shares with the dividends aforesaid.

*PRESENT:—Duff C.J. and Rinfret, Cannon, Crocket and Hughes JJ.

93259—4½

1934

Siscoe Gold
Mines Ltd.
v.
Bijakowski.

The material facts of the case and the questions at issue are stated in the above headnote and in the judgment now reported.

Henry N. Chauvin K.C. and *E. S. McDougall K.C.* for the appellant.

Aimé Geoffrion K.C. and *B. Robinson* for the respondent.

The judgment of the Court was delivered by

Cannon J.—This appeal is asserted from the unanimous judgment of the Court of King's Bench confirming the judgment of the Superior Court (Loranger J.), which maintained respondent's action and condemned appellant to deliver to respondent 30,000 shares of appellant's capital stock and to pay to respondent $4,200, the amount of dividends declared on a like number of shares; or, in the event of the appellant failing to deliver the said shares, to pay to the respondent the sum of $51,600, being the market value of the said shares, reserving also a recourse to be discussed later.

The respondent claims to be the owner and demands the delivery to him of 30,000 shares of the Siscoe Gold Mines Limited which, he alleged, had been lent by himself and his associates, Joseph Hoffman and Joseph Pluto, to appellant on the 21st day of January, 1927, on the condition that a like number of shares would be returned by the appellant upon its mining properties being brought into production. Artifice, fraud and error were also alleged as vitiating the transaction.

The respondent sues in the right of himself and his associates by virtue of a transfer by Pluto and Hoffman to respondent.

The appellant says in defence that the transactions in connection with the above-mentioned shares were carried out by one J. T. Tebbutt, the president of the appellant company, without authority, expressed or implied, and that whatever contract was entered into or understanding arrived at between him and other persons associated with him is not binding upon appellant, who, moreover, never ratified the action of its president.

Under reserve of the foregoing plea, the appellant pleaded, in the alternative, that in any event the said shares which were transferred to the Eastern Trust Company as trustee of certain shares of the capital stock of the appellant were not lent, as alleged by respondent, but were given or donated without condition as to their return.

The respondent and his two associates Pluto and Hoffman were the original discoverers of the Siscoe Gold Mines and obtained for their interest a certain number of shares in the appellant company. The president, Mr. Tebbutt, went to Timmins and gathered together the three illiterate associates and, according to their version, which was unanimously accepted by the courts below, disclosed to them that the company needed funds, and that, in order to carry out a plan which would bring production and profit, other members of the syndicate and officers, including Mr. Tebbutt and Mr. Siscoe, the president and the vice-president of the company, had already loaned to the company a certain number of shares. These foreigners agreed to the demand of the president and took his word that this was a loan, and signed the document which he prepared, i.e. an authorization to split up three certificates of 20,000 shares each so that half would go the company and the other half back to each of them. Eventually the division took place and each received back a certificate of 10,000 shares; and the other shares were placed in the company's treasury account with the Eastern Trust Company. In reply to a demand for a return of these shares, the appellant contended that it never received them, that it had nothing to do with them, or, in the alternative, that they were donated unconditionally.

It was proven that the company actually received the shares and disposed of them in order to reimburse itself of a commission of 10 per cent in cash and 15 per cent in stock payable to W. R. Baillie through whom one G. N. Coyle had agreed to invest $75,000 with the company, under the express condition that no commission was to be paid out of the funds of the company. Whatever may have been the promise made by Siscoe to Coyle, the fact is abundantly established that the commission was paid by the appellant and that the proceeds of the sale of the 30,000 shares were deposited to the credit of the respondent. After these shares were transferred to the treasury in the hands of the Eastern Trust Company, they lost their identity and could not be further traced.

1934
Siscoe Gold
Mines Ltd.
v.
Bijakowski.

Cannon J.

After hearing the appellant, this Court decided that the findings of fact of the trial judge, unanimously confirmed by the Court of King's Bench, should not be disturbed; and, we, therefore, in view of the character of the evidence given, say that the shares were not donated to Tebbutt, nor to the company, by the respondent; that they were loaned to the company, who received them and placed them in its treasury, in the care of the Eastern Trust Company.

If respondent agreed to deliver, and did deliver, their shares to appellant, what that company or its officers did after is more or less irrelevant, except to show that it benefited from them. If they are not in the treasury, they must have been disposed of for the purposes of that company. In either case, the company's liability towards the respondent would not disappear.

The company was in operation when the action was taken and the time had then arrived when the loan had to be repaid. If, as pleaded, the company never authorized this agreement nor the receipt of these shares, there seems to be no good reason why it should not return them. There can be no question of a donation to the company, because the latter has expressly pleaded that never, at any time, through its board of directors or by officers duly authorized, were these shares accepted. Moreover, the evidence and the findings of the courts below disprove this contention. Both courts below reached the conclusion that the only witness heard on this point on behalf of the appellant is unreliable, and on this question of credibility, great consideration must necessarily be given to the findings of the trial judge who heard and saw the witness. Moreover, it is more than doubtful that such a gift could be legally made in the form of a verbal agreement. Art. 776 C.C.

This Court, therefore, decided to hear the respondent only on the question of law raised by the appellant concerning the admissibility of oral evidence to prove the loan of these shares.

In view of the rejection by the trial judge of Tebbutt's version of what took place when the respondent and his associates signed the authorization to transfer the 30,000 shares to the appellant and the adoption below and by this Court of respondent's evidence, the only possibility for the appellant to succeed was to have this verbal evidence set aside as illegal. Our attention was drawn to the following part of respondent's testimony:

1934

SISCOE GOLD MINES LTD. *v.* BIJAKOWSKI.

Cannon J.

Q. Before you brought Hoffman, Pluto and Steinslick, did Mr. Tebbutt tell you what he wanted?

By defendant's counsel: I make a preliminary objection to anything said by Mr. Tebbutt, to the witness prior to the signing of these documents, in view of the fact we have not only this document referred to by Mr. Genest, but we have a transfer signed by the plaintiff and the other parties, of the shares in question.

And I make formal objection to any evidence as to what was said, which was preliminary to the signing of these documents.

By the Court: It explains the circumstances under which the deed was signed. Reserved.

Tebbutt was subsequently brought forward by the appellant to prove the alleged donation or gift of the shares, after he had explained to them that he had to have this stock to liquidate the alleged personal debt of vice-president Siscoe to Baillie. The trial judge gave his decision in the final judgment:

Objection est faite à toute preuve verbale comme tendant à contredire l'écrit. En remarquant que le document P. 1 ne définit aucunement la nature de la convention, pour l'interpréter il faut donc connaître les circonstances dans lesquelles l'écrit a été signé afin de se rendre compte de l'intention des parties et de lui donner effet; sans cela, il est impossible de décider le bien ou mal fondé de la réclamation. Qu'est-ce que l'écrit comporte? Est-ce un don manuel? Est-ce un prêt? Pour répondre à ces trois questions, il faut nécessairement savoir ce qui s'est passé; et seule la preuve peut nous le révéler. L'objection est rejetée.

Exhibit P. 1 reads in part as follows:

We the undersigned owners of 20,000 shares each of the Siscoe Gold Mines Company stock do hereby authorize the secretary of the Siscoe Gold Mines Company or the Eastern Trust Company of Montreal to split each 20,000 shares of stock into two certificates, one certificate for ten thousand shares to be made out to the Siscoe Gold Mines Company, and one certificate for ten thousand shares to the undersigned.

Joseph Pluto.
Joseph Hossman.
Felix Bijakowski.

The declaration alleges that the above document was signed at the request of Tebbutt, the president of the company appellant, who represented that a group of shareholders were lending a portion of their holdings to the company in order to bring it into production sooner; that the president took advantage of the fact that the plaintiff and his two companions were illiterate foreigners and

1934

SISCOE GOLD
MINES LTD.
v.
BIJAKOWSKI.

Cannon J.

deliberately drafted the document in indefinite terms, leading them into error and making them believe that they, in consort with other large shareholders, were lending to the company a large amount of stock which would be returned immediately after the company would begin producing; and that the plaintiff, Pluto and Hoffman were induced to sign the said document through artifice and fraud.

Plaintiff's allegation that the whole transaction was tainted with fraud and false representation, might have supported the trial judge's decision to admit parol testimony, although his judgment does not mention that ground and he did not find fraud against Tebbutt. In support of the admissibility of the evidence, it might also have been considered whether or not the writings, the books of the company, the attitude of some of the appellant's witnesses in the box, which was severely criticized by the trial judge, were not sufficient to constitute a "commencement de preuve par écrit" which would make probable the loan alleged by the respondent. In fact, some of the learned judges below adopted the view that such a foundation for oral testimony existed and quoted this Court's decision *re Campbell* v. *Young* (1). Under that precedent, both parties admitting the existence of some contract, parol evidence could be adduced to determine whether the transfer was conditional or unconditional, whether the shares were to be returned or not.

Moreover, even if the verbal evidence of what took place at Timmins, when exhibit P. 1 was prepared by Tebbutt, president of the company, and signed by the respondent, be rejected, we must not lose sight of the overwhelming evidence in writing showing that the company acted pursuant to the authority given, received the shares, placed them in its treasury and refused to hand them over.

To justify the possession and retention of the shares, the appellant alleges a free gift or donation. It was incumbent upon it to prove its title. *Reus excipiendo fit actor.* It failed to discharge the onus and the appellant having admitted respondent's ownership of the shares before the transfer, the plaintiff's case was complete and he was entitled to judgment. The transaction was either *res inter alios acta,* or is really, as found by the trial judge, part of

(1) (1902) 32 Can. S.C.R. 547.

1934

SISCOE GOLD
MINES LTD.
v.
BIJAKOWSKI.

Cannon J.

the business of the company and has been repeatedly ratified and acted upon by it, as appears in the books of the appellant and its bank account. The appellant, having received both the shares and the full benefit thereof (although it contended it had nothing to do with them), and having failed to prove its title thereto, cannot succeed. The attempt to bring Tebbutt before the Court to prove the contention that no one was bound to return respondent's property proved futile. This verbal evidence of Tebbutt, essential to prove appellant's version, was tendered by it after it had objected to similar verbal evidence on the same point by plaintiff, Hoffman and Pluto. It was allowed by the trial judge, but evidently was not believed.

We, therefore, reach the conclusion that the point raised before us by the appellant cannot prevail.

But, says the appellant, if the conclusion be reached that the act of the company was such as to justify the finding that the company actually received the shares, the respondent, in that event, should recover only the amount for which the shares were sold, viz $9,750.

On the other hand, the plaintiff seeks the application of article 1782 of the civil code. He claims to be entitled to the return of the shares loaned or, in default, to their full value which, under the circumstances of this case, would include the increased value of the shares since the appellant refused to remit them to the respondent.

The trial judge made a special reservation of the rights of the respondent for the losses he might suffer through the fluctuations of the market.

The trial judge fixed the value of the shares on the basis of 30,000 at $1.58 a share, the price of the stock on the day of the judgment. Since that date, the stock may have gone up in price and, by the failure to deliver the stock, the respondent may have been deprived of the opportunity of disposing of the shares at a favourable price. The appellant is given the alternative to deliver the shares or to pay the amount of the judgment. Without the reserve made by the trial judge in favour of the respondent to claim any loss resulting from the company's failure to deliver the stock at the proper time, the appellant to-day would pay the amount of the judgment and not deliver the stock. It could then dispose of the shares which belong to the re-

1934

Siscoe Gold
Mines Ltd.
v.
Bijakowski.

Cannon J.

spondent and profit unduly at the expense of the respondent to the extent of any difference between $1.58 and the price to-day.

This reservation would seem to be within the scope of 1073, 1074 and 1075 of the civil code because, when the company decided to refuse delivery of the stock, it must have known and it knew that the value of the shares would fluctuate and it accepted the risk of paying the highest price between the time of the demand and the delivery.

We, therefore, see no good reason to strike the reservation from the judgment as suggested by appellant's counsel. These remarks are made without prejudice to the rights of either party, should it become necessary for the respondent to take another action to recover over and above the amount of the judgment, in case the company would not return the shares.

We will therefore dismiss the appeal with costs.

Appeal dismissed with costs.

Solicitors for the appellant: *Wainwright, Elder & McDougall.*

Solicitors for the respondent: *Robinson & Shapiro.*

BIBLIOGRAPHY

*SUGGESTED READING

Abraham, Carolyn. *The Juggler's Children: A Journey into Family, Legend and the Genes that Bind Us.* Toronto: Random House Canada, 2013.

Adamczyk, Wesley. *When God Looked the Other Way: An Odyssey of War, Exile and Redemption.* Chicago: University of Chicago Press, 2004.

Angelou, Maya. "Shades and Slashes of Light." In *Black Woman Writers (1950 to 1980): A Critical Evaluation.* Edited by Mari E. Evans. New York: Anchor, 1984.

Ascher, Abraham. *The Revolution of 1905: Russia in Disarray.* Stanford, California: Stanford University Press, 1988.

Avakumovic, Ivan, and George Woodcock. *The Doukhobors.* Toronto: Oxford University Press, 1968.

Avery, D. H., and Fedorowicz, J. K. *The Poles in Canada.* Ottawa: Canadian Historical Association, 1982.

Bachmann, Karen. *Porcupine Goldfields 1920-1935.* St. Catharines, Ontario: Vanwell Publishing / Looking Back Press, 2004.

——— Survivors Offered First-Hand Account of Great Porcupine Fire of 1911. *The Daily Press* [Timmins], July 14, 2023, column.

Backhouse, Constance. *Colour-Coded: A Legal History of Racism in Canada, 1900-1950.* Toronto: University of Toronto Press, 1999.

Basiura, Ewa, and Krzysztof Zarzycki. *Legends of Old Cracow.* Cracow: Translator, 1994.

Beaulieu, Sarah. *Remembering the Forgotten Archaeology at the Morrissey WWI Internment Camp.* Simon Fraser University, 2015.

Bedford, Neal, et al. *Poland*. Fort Mill, South Carolina: Lonely Planet, 2008.

*Bednarska, Hanna. *Poland: The Country and Its People*. Ann Arbor, Michigan: Interpress Publishers, 1979.

Bernhard, Michael H. *The Origins of Democratization in Poland*. New York: Columbia University Press, 1993.

Bhatt, Gira. "Home Away from Home." *Vancouver Sun*, March 23, 2010, p. A11.

Black, Charles. "Babies vs Crones: Red Ribbon Shields." *A Guide to Good and Bad Luck Omens in Poland*. Accessed September 14, 2022, 10.

*Blaisdell, Bob, ed. *Essays on Immigration*. New York: Dover Publications, 2013.

Blum, Jerome. *Lord and Peasant in Russia: From the Ninth to the Nineteenth Century*. Princeton: Princeton University Press, 1961.

———. *The End of the Old Order in Rural Europe*. Princeton: Princeton University Press, 1978.

———. *Our Forgotten Past: Seven Centuries of Life on the Land*. London: Thames & Hudson, 1982.

———. *In the Beginning: The Advent of the Modern Age Europe in the 1840's*. New York: C. Scribner's Sons, 1994.

Braudel, Fernand. *The Structures of Everyday Life: The Limits of the Possible*. Vol. 1, *Civilization and Capitalism, 15th–18th Century*. New York: Harper and Row, 1985.

Brown, Justine. *All Possible Worlds: Utopian Experiments in British Columbia*. Vancouver: New Star Books, 1995.

*Brown, Kate. *A Biography of No Place*. Boston: Harvard University Press, 2004.

Brown, Stephen. "Canada Needs a Revival of Popular History." *Financial Post*, December 19, 2023, p. 10.

*Bujak, Adam. *Krakowskie Pejzaze*. Krakow: KAW Krakow, 1980.

Polskie Krajobrazy. Paris: Editions Spotkania, 1993.

Poland. Lesko, Poland: Bosz, 2004.

*Bujak, Adam, and Janusz L. Dobesz. *Poland: Home of a Thousand Year Old Nation*. Cracow: Bialy Kruk, 2003.

Charzynska, Katarzyna, Marta Anczewska, and Piotr Switaj. "A Brief Overview of the History of Education in Poland." *Bulgarian Comparative Education Society* (2012). www.semanticscholar.org/paper/A-Brief-Overview-of-the-History-of-Education-in-Charzy%C5%84ska-Anczewska/9fb58e4bc969fbd37c81c2e856cd14ea90550038.

Chester, Geoff. "Final Point of the Russian Empire: Liepāja's Half a Million Emigrants." *Deep Baltic*, December 2, 2015. www.deepbaltic.com/2015/12/02/final-point-of-the-russian-empire-the-story-of-liepajas-half-a-million-emigrants/.

Cienciala, Anna M. "Lecture 6: Poland 1864–1914." Lecture for History 557, "Nationalism and Communism in East Central Europe." University of Kansas, Spring 2002 (revised 2004). Accessed October 20, 2023, www.acienciala.ku.edu/hist557/lect6.htm.

*Clarkson, Adrienne. *Belonging: The Paradox of Citizenship*. CBC Massey Lectures Series. Toronto: House of Anansi Press, 2014.

*Coleman, Heather J. "Watson Kirkconnell on 'The Place of Slavic Studies in Canada': A 1957 Speech to the Canadian Association of Slavists." *Canadian Slavonic Papers* 58, 4 (December 2016): 386–397.

Collins, Aileen, Michael Gnarowski, and Sonja A. Skarstedt, eds. *Eternal Conversations: Remembering Louis Dudek*. Montreal: DC Books, 2003.

Curtis, Glenn E., ed. "Education." In *Poland: A Country Study*. Washington, D.C.: GPO for the Library of Congress, 1992. www.countrystudies.us/poland/42.htm.

Czerny, Zofia. *Polish Cookbook*. Trans. by Christina Cękalska and May Miller. Warsaw: Paristwowe Wydawnictwo Ekonomiczne, 1975.

Dakiniewicz, Iwona. "How the Tsar Decimated the Polish Nobility." *Rodziny* 40, 4 (Fall 2017): 3–4.

Dauvergne, Catherine. *The New Politics of Immigration and the End of Settler Societies*. Cambridge: Cambridge University Press, 2016.

Davies, Norman. *God's Playground: A History of Poland*. Vol. 1, *The Origins to 1795*. New York: Columbia University Press, 1982.

——— . *God's Playground: A History of Poland*. Vol. 2, *1795 to the Present*. New York: Columbia University Press, 1982.

Davis, Wade. *Light at the Edge of the World: A Journey Through the Realm of Vanishing Cultures*. Vancouver: Douglas & McIntyre, 2007.

——— . *The Wayfinders: Why Ancient Wisdom Matters in the Modern World*. CBC Massey Lectures Series. Toronto: House of Anansi Press, 2009.

Dias, Brian G., and Kerry J. Ressler. "Parental Olfactory Experience Influences Behavior and Neural Structure in Subsequent Generations." *Nature Neuroscience* 17, 1 (2014): 89–96. www.doi.org/10.1038/nn.3594.

Dillingham, William Paul. *Reports of the Immigration Commission*. 41 vols. Washington, D.C.: Government Printing Office, 1911.

Dinesen, Isak. "The Cardinal's First Tale." In *Last Tales*. New York: Random House, 1957.

Dudek, Louis. *All These Roads: The Poetry of Louis Dudek*. Selected with an introduction by Karis Shearer and an afterword by Frank Davey. Waterloo, Ontario: Wilfrid Laurier University Press, 2008.

    In Defence of Art: Critical Essays & Reviews. Edited with an introduction by Aileen Collins. Kingston, Ontario: Quarry Press, 1988.

Farkas, Endre, and Carolyn Marie Souaid, eds. "Louis Dudek: Autobiography." *Poetry Quebec Biographies*, no. 1 (July 2010). www.web. archive.org/web/20120507121606/, www.poetry-quebec.com/pq/biography/printer_6.shtml.

Ficowski, Jerzy. *The Gypsies in Poland: History and Culture*. Warsaw: Interpress Publishers, 1989.

Fiddick, Thomas. "The 'Miracle of the Vistula': Soviet Policy versus Red Army Strategy." *The Journal of Modern History* 45, 4 (December 1973): 626–643.

Foran, Charles. "Tales of Our Shared Exodus Narrative May Just Be How Democracy Fights Back." *Globe and Mail*, December 29, 2018. www.theglobeandmail.com/arts/books/article-tales-of-our-shared-exodus-narrative-may-just-be-how-democracy-fights/.

Francis, Daniel. *Selling Canada: Three Propaganda Campaigns that Shaped the Nation*. Vancouver: Stanton, Atkins & Dosil Publishers, 2011.

Francis, Diane. "Health System Can't Support Immigrant Influx." *Financial Post*, November 30, 2022. www.financialpost.com/diane-francis/canada-health-system-cant-support-immigrant-influx.

Friedman, Gabriel. "All the Reasons Why Canada Needs Immigration—and More of It." *Financial Post*, October 8, 2019. www.financialpost.com/news/economy/all-the-reasons-why-canada-needs-immigration-and-more-of-it.

Glinski, A. J. *Polish Fairy Tales*. Trans. by Maude A. Bigg and illus. by Cecile Walton. New York: John Lane Publishing, 1920; U.K. Registered Office: Sandycroft Publishing, 2015.

Glinski, Mikołaj. "A Foreigner's Guide to Polish Surnames."
Culture.Pl. Last updated February 18, 2021. www.culture.pl/en/
article/a-foreigners-guide-to-polish-surnames.

*Gorski, Waclaw, Marek Zak, and Michal Wozniak. *Piekny Stary Gdansk*.
Poznan: Malaczynski, 1993.

*Grady, Patrick, and Herbert Grubel. "A Mawkish View of Immigration
Overlooks the Facts." *Vancouver Sun*, June 6, 2011, p. A2. www.fraserinstitute.
org/article/mawkish-view-immigration-overlooks-facts.

Hamilton, Douglas L., and Darlene Olesko. *Accidental Eden: Hippie Days on
Lasqueti Island*. Qualicum Beach, British Columbia: Caitlin Press, 2014.

*Hammond, Holly. "The Timeline and History of Yoga in America."
Yoga Journal (blog), August 29, 2007. www.yogajournal.com/yoga-101/
yogas-trip-america/.

Hari, Johann. *Lost Connections: Uncovering the Real Causes of Depression—and
the Unexpected Solutions*. New York: Bloomsbury Publishing, 2018.

Harley, Maria Anna (Maja Trochimchyk). "The Briefest History of Polish
Music." *Polish Music Centre at the University of South California*. Accessed
February 8, 2024. www.polishmusic.usc.edu/research/publications/essays/
briefest-history-of-polish-music/.

Hearne, Samuel. *A Journey to the Northern Ocean: The Adventures of Samuel
Hearne*. Foreword by Ken McGoogon. Surrey, British Columbia: Touchwood
Editions, 2007.

Henderson, Keith. "Not as Crazy as You'd Think: Fenians and Thomas
D'Arcy McGee." *Personal Thoughts and Views* (blog), March 25, 2021. www.
thespecialcommittee.com/blog/history/not-as-crazy-as-you'd-think/.

Henrich, Joseph. *The WEIRDest People in the World: How the West Became
Psychologically Peculiar and Particularly Prosperous*. New York: Farrar, Strauss
and Giroux, 2020.

Henrich, Joseph, Steven J. Heine, and Ara Norenzayan. "The Weirdest People in the World?" *Behavioral and Brain Sciences* 33, 2–3 (2010): 61–83. www.doi. org/10.1017/S0140525X0999152X.

Heydenkorn, Benedykt. "Polish Canadians." *The Canadian Encyclopedia*, July 31, 2019. www.www.thecanadianencyclopedia.ca/en/article/poles.

Hildebrand, George, ed. *Louis Dudek: Essays on His Works*. Montreal: Guernica Editions, 2001.

*Hillmer, Norman, and J. L. Granatstein. *Land Newly Found: Eyewitness Accounts of the Canadian Immigrant Experience*. Toronto: Thomas Allen Publishers, 2006.

Hume, Stephen. "Canada's Bigots Grant Themselves Permission to Vent." *Vancouver Sun*, March 28, 2015. www.vancouversun.com/opinion/columnists/ stephen-hume-canadas-bigots-grant-themselves-permission-to-vent.

Ignatieff, Michael. Foreword to *Passages: Welcome Home to Canada*. Toronto: Doubleday, 2002.

*Jackowski, Aleksander, and Jadwiga Jarnuszkiewicz. *Folk Art of Poland*. Warsaw: Arkady, 1968.

Jewitt, John R. *The Adventures and Sufferings of John R. Jewitt*. Annotated and illustrated by Hilary Stewart. Vancouver: Douglas and McIntyre, 1995.

Jonas, George. "Trudeau's 'Cultural Mosaic' a Failed Cultural Experiment." *Vancouver Sun*, September 21, 2011. www.pressreader.com/canada/ vancouver-sun/20110921/288535904413710.

*Karafilly, Irena F. *Ashes and Miracles: A Polish Journey*. Toronto: Malcolm Lester Books, 1998.

Kasinitz, Philip, et al. *Inheriting the City: The Children of Immigrants Come of Age*. New Haven, Connecticut: Russell Sage Foundation Books at Harvard University Press, 2009.

Kasprzyk-Chevriaux, Magdalena. "Polish Food 101—Goose." *Culture.pl.*
December 2014. www.culture.pl/en/work/polish-food-101-goose.

Kaur Sekhhon, Gagandeep. "Reverse Migration from Canada: Here Are the
Top 5 Reasons." *Immigration News Canada*, June 12, 2023. www.immigra-
tionnewscanada.ca/know-about-reverse-migration-from-canada/.

King, Hayden. "Indigenous Cultures Rivalled Those of Many Other
Civilizations." *Globe and Mail*, October 29, 2008. www.theglobeandmail.
com/opinion/indigenous-cultures-rivalled-those-of-many-other-civilizations/
article716632/.

King, Thomas. *The Truth about Stories: A Native Narrative.* CBC Massey
Lectures Series. 9th ed. Toronto: House of Anansi Press, 2003.

*Klein, Shelley. *Stufflebeem, Brockway & Sturt: The Origins of Our Surnames.*
London: Michael O'Mara Books, 2002.

Knab, Sophie Hodorowicz. *Polish Customs, Traditions, and Folklore.* New
York: Hippocrene Books, 1993.

      Polish Herbs, Flowers & Folk Medicine. New York: Hippocrene
Books, 1995.

*Knowles, Valerie. *Forging Our Legacy: Canadian Citizenship and Immigration,
1900-1977.* Ottawa: Citizenship and Immigration Canada, 2000.

      *Strangers at Our Gates: Canadian Immigration and Immigration
Policy 1540-2006.* Toronto: Dundurn, 2007.

Kojder, Apolonja Maria, and Glogowska, Barbara. *Marynia, Don't Cry:
Memoirs of Two Polish-Canadian Families.* Toronto: Multicultural History
Society of Ontario, 1995.

Koropeckyj, Roman. *Adam Mickiewicz: The Life of a Romantic.* Ithaca, New
York: Cornell University Press, 2008.

Kukushkin, Vadim. *From Peasants to Labourers: Ukrainian and Belarusian Immigration from the Russian Empire to Canada*. Montreal: McGill-Queen's University Press, 2007.

*Leach, Catherine S., ed. *Memoirs of the Polish Baroque: The Writings of Jan Chryzostom Pasek, a Squire of the Commonwealth of Poland and Lithuania*. Oakland, California: University of California Press, 1976.

Lewicki, Roy J., et al. *Essentials of Negotiation*. 6th ed. Toronto: McGraw-Hill, 2016.

Life as a Miner: A Day in the Life. Charlotte, North Carolina: Discovery Education, Social Studies Techbook, n.d. www.joliet86.org/assets/1/6/Life_as_a_Miner.pdf.

*Makowski, William. *The Polish People in Canada: A Visual History*. Toronto: Tundra Books, 1987.

McGoogan, Ken. *Celtic Lightning: How the Scots and the Irish Created a Canadian Nation*. Toronto: HarperCollins Canada, 2015.

"En-lightening Genealogy." *Vancouver Sun*, September 26, 2015, p. F.7.

Mead, Margaret. *Coming of Age in Samoa: A Psychological Study of Primitive Youth for Western Civilization*. New York: Modern Library, 1953.

Mensah, Joseph. *Black Canadians: History, Experience, Social Conditions, Revised Edition*. Winnipeg: Fernwood Publishing, 2010.

*Michener, James A. *Poland*. New York: Fawcett Crest, 1983.

*Mikanowski, Jacob. *Goodbye, Eastern Europe: An Intimate History of a Divided Land*. New York: Pantheon Books, 2023.

Milner-Gulland, Robin. *Cultural Atlas of Russia and the Former Soviet Union*. New York: Checkmark Books, 1998.

*Milosz, Czeslaw. *The History of Polish Literature*. Oakland, California: University of California Press, 1983.

Mitchell, Penni. "Women Led Freedom Quests." *Herizons*, March 22, 2015. www.thefreelibrary.com/Women+led+freedom+quests.-a0415108684.

Moodie, Susanna. *Roughing It in the Bush*. Edited by Carl Ballstadt. Ottawa: Carlton University Press, 1995.

*Moran, Michael. *A Country in the Moon: Travels in Search of the Heart of Poland*. London: Granta Books, 2008.

*Morton, Wendy. *What Were Their Dreams? Valley of Hope and Pain: Canada's History*. Windsor, Ontario: Black Moss Press, 2009.

Meyer, John. "International Migration: A Disaster Coming Soon…to a Neighbourhood Near You." *Humanist Perspectives* 204 (Spring 2018): 17–24.

Muller, Robert T. "Trauma from Back Home Has Long-Lasting Effects on Migrants." *The Trauma and Mental Health Report* (blog), July 25, 2022. www.trauma.blog.yorku.ca/2022/07/ trauma-from-back-home-has-long-lasting-effects-on-migrants.

Nafisi, Azar. *Reading Lolita in Tehran: A Memoir in Books*. New York: Random House, 2003.

*Niezabitowski, Michal, Teresa Kwiatkowska, and Aleksandra Jaklinska. *Cracow Past and Present*. Cracow: Parma Press, 2007.

*Nicholas, Jeremy. *Chopin: His Life and Music*. Chicago: Source Books MediaFusion, 2007.

*Obolensky, Chloe, with an Introduction by Max Hayard. *The Russian Empire: A Portrait in Photographs*. New York: Random House, 1979.

Obolensky-Ossinsky, V.V. "Emigrations from and immigration into Russia." In *International Migrations*. Vol. II, *Interpretations*. Edited by Walter

F. Willcox. Cambridge, Massachusetts: National Bureau of Economic Research, 1931.

Orwell, George. *Animal Farm*. London: Secker and Warburg, 1945.

Ostrowski, Henry J. *My Life and Work*. Mississauga, Ontario: Self-Published, 1987.

*Ostrowski, Jan K. *Wawel: Castle and Cathedral*. Cracow: Karpaty Publishing House, 1996.

Ostrowski, Paul F. "Who Discovered Vitamins?" In *The Polish Review*, Vol. XXXI. Editor-in-chief Ludwik Krzyzanowski, New York, New York, 1986.

Phelan, Josephine. *Ardent Exile: The Life and Times of D'Arcy McGee*. Toronto: The Macmillan Company of Canada Limited, 1951.

Piotrowska, Irena. *The Art of Poland*. New York: Philosophical Library, 1947.

Piotrowski, Tadeusz. *Vengeance of the Swallow: Memoir of a Polish Family's Ordeal under Soviet Aggression, Ukrainian Ethnic Cleansing and Nazi Enslavement, and Their Emigration to America*. Jefferson, North Carolina: McFarland and Company, 2009.

Pitsula, James. *Keeping Canada British: The Ku Klux Klan in 1920's Saskatchewan*. Vancouver: UBC Press, 2014.

*Poponowski, Iwo Cyprian. *Poland: An Illustrated History*. New York: Hippocrene Books, 2000.

Porter-Szucs, Brian. *Faith and Fatherland: Catholicism, Modernity and Poland*. Oxford: Oxford University Press, 2011.

*Portes, Alejandro, and Rumbaut, Ruben G. *Legacies: The Story of the Immigrant Second Generation*. Oakland, California: University of California Press, 2001.

*Preston, Diana. *Eight Days at Yalta: How Churchill, Roosevelt, and Stalin Shaped the Post-War World*. New York: Atlantic Monthly Press, 2019.

Province of Ontario, Department of Mines. *Report on the Mining Accidents in Ontario in 1928, Bulletin No. 67*. Toronto: Printed by Order of the Legislative Assembly of Ontario, 1929. www.geologyontario.mndmf.gov.on.ca/mndm-files/pub/data/imaging/B067/B067.pdf.

Radomski, Jaroslaw K. *The Magnificent 100*. New York: Blurb Incorporated, 2019.

Rostworowski, Marek, ed. *The National Museum in Cracow, the Czartoryski Collection: A Historical Outline and Selected Objects*. Warsaw: Arkady, 1980.

Rukeyser, Muriel. "The Speed of Darkness." In *The Speed of Darkness*. New York: Random House, 1968.

Saul, John Ralston. *A Fair Country: Telling Truths about Canada*. Toronto: Penguin Canada, 2008.

Sek, Lukasz, ed. *Malopolska A Hundred Years Ago 1890–1914*. Tarnow, Poland: District Museum in Tarnow, 2006.

Sicherman, Claire. *Imprint: A Memoir of Trauma in the Third Generation*. Halfmoon Bay, British Columbia: Caitlin Press, 2017.

Silko, Leslie Marmon. "Love Poem." In *Sisters of the Earth: Women's Prose and Poetry about Nature*. Edited by Lorraine Anderson. 2nd ed. New York: Vintage Books, 1991.

Siscoe Gold Mines Ltd. v. Bijakowski, [1935] S.C.R. 195. www.decisions.scc-csc.ca/scc-csc/scc-csc/en/item/8658/index.do.

*Smedman, Lisa. *Immigrants: Stories of Vancouver's People*. Vancouver: The Vancouver Courier, 2009.

Snyder, Timothy. *Bloodlands: Europe between Hitler and Stalin.* New York: Basic Books, 2010.

Sobel, Dana. *A More Perfect Heaven: How Copernicus Revolutionized the Cosmos.* New York: Walker Publishing Company, 2011.

*Stearns, Anna. *New Canadians of Slavic Origin: A Problem in Creative Reorientation.* Winnipeg: Ukrainian Free Press Academy of Sciences, 1960.

*Steiner, Edward A. *On the Trail of the Immigrant.* New York: Arno Press and The New York Times, 1969.

Stone, Daniel, ed. *The Polish Memoirs of William John Rose.* Toronto: University of Toronto Press, 1975.

Stopka, Krzysztof. "History of the Jagiellonian University." *Jagiellonian University in Krakow.* Accessed February 8, 2024, www.en.uj.edu.pl/en_GB/about-university/history.

Stromberg-Stein, Susan. *Louis Dudek: A Biographical Introduction to His Poetry.* Ottawa: Golden Dog Press, 1983.

Sulimirski, Tadeusz. *The Sarmatians.* London: Thames and Hudson, 1970.

*Syrop, Konrad. *Poland in Perspective.* London: Robert Hale, 1982.

*Szabados, Stephen. *Memories of Dziadka: Rural Life in the Kingdom of Poland.* San Bernardino, California: CreateSpace Publishing, 2014.

        My Polish Grandmother: From Tragedy in Poland to Her Rose Garden in America. Columbia, South Carolina: CreateSpace, 2018.

Szewczyk, Sana. *Under a Ginkgo Tree and Other Stories.* San Bernardino, California: CreateSpace, 2012.

Szkuta, Magda. "Polish Mathematicians and Cracking the Enigma." *European Studies Blog*, January 2, 2018. www.blogs.bl.uk/european/2018/01/polish-mathematicians-and-cracking-the-enigma.html.

*Szyf, Moshe. "Epigenetics with Dr. Moshe Szyf, Part 1." YouTube, January 11, 2020, www.youtube.com/watch?v=OEAJmDPJz_I.

Szymczak, Joanna. "Polish Folk Art." *Reflective Journal*, May 20, 2014. www.joannaszymczak.wordpress.com/2014/05/20/polish-folk-art/.

Szyszko, Feliks. "History's Impact on Polish Art: A Talk by Feliks Szyszko." *Info Poland, University of Buffalo*. Accessed October 30, 2023, www.info-poland.icm.edu.pl/classroom/Szyszko.html.

*Taylor, Lynne. *Polish Orphans of Tengeru: The Dramatic Story of Their long Journey to Canada 1941–1949*. Toronto: Dundurn Press, 2009.

Terles, Mikolaj. *Ethnic Cleansing of Poles in Volhynia and Eastern Galicia 1942–1946*. Toronto: Alliance of the Polish Eastern Provinces, 1993.

Thomas William I., and Florian Znaniecki. *The Polish Peasant in Europe and America*. Vols. 1–2. Chicago: University of Chicago Press, 1918.

       The Polish Peasant in Europe and America. Vols. 3–5. Boston: Gorham Press, 1919.

*Times Books. *History of Europe*. New York: Harper Collins Publishers, 2001.

Todd, Douglas. "Ethnic Mapping Conclusion: As Enclaves Grow, Will Metro Residents' Trust Fade?" *Vancouver Sun*, October 20, 2011. www.vancouversun.com/news/staff-blogs/ethnic-mapping-conclusion-as-enclaves-grow-will-metro-residents-trust-fade.

       "Vancouver Ranks Fourth for Foreign-Born Residents, but Is It 'Cosmopolitan?'" *Vancouver Sun*, July 21, 2013. www.vancouversun.com/opinion/columnists/vancouver-ranks-fourth-for-foreign-born-residents-but-is-it-cosmopolitan.

"Ethnic Diversity's 'Inconvenient Truths.'" *Vancouver Sun,* February 9, 2014. www.vancouversun.com/news/staff-blogs/ethnic-diversitys-inconvenient-truths.

"We Must Stand on Guard for Canada." *Vancouver Sun,* July 10, 2014. www.vancouversun.com/opinion/columnists/douglas-todd-we-must-stand-on-guard-for-canada.

"The Floating Life of Affluent 'Transnational' Migrants." *Vancouver Sun,* August 2, 2014. www.vancouversun.com/news/metro/douglas-todd-the-floating-life-of-affluent-transnational-migrants.

"The Pros and Cons of Diversity." *Vancouver Sun,* January 21, 2017. www.vancouversun.com/opinion/columnists/douglas-todd-canada-needs-strong-dose-of-cultural-curiosity.

"Radical Environmentalists Have Strong Views on Immigration." *Vancouver Sun,* October 22, 2018. www.vancouversun.com/opinion/columnists/douglas-todd-how-radical-environmentalists-view-immigration.

"10 Surprising Lessons about Migration from Economists." *Vancouver Sun,* May 11, 2019. www.vancouversun.com/opinion/columnists/douglas-todd-immigration-may-lift-economy-but-not-peoples-wages-plus-other-economists-lessons.

Trevor-Roper, Hugh. *From Counter-Reformation to Glorious Revolution.* Chicago: University of Chicago Press, 1992.

Vandenborre, Katia. "Antoni Jozef Glinski or the Making of a Polish Tale Teller." *Pegasus Oost-Europese Studies* 31 (2018): 79–103.

Varvounis, Miltiades. *Jan Sobieski: The King Who Saved Europe.* Bloomington, Indiana: Xlibris Publishing, 2012.

Vronsky, Peter. *Ridgeway: The American Fenian Invasion and the 1866 Battle That Made Canada.* Toronto: Penguin Canada, 2012.

Walesa, Lech. *The Struggle and the Triumph: An Autobiography*. New York: Arcade Publishing, 1991.

Watters, Ethan. *Crazy Like Us: Globalization of the American Psyche*. New York: Free Press, 2010.

——— *Urban Tribes: Are Friends the New Family?* London: Bloomsbury Press, 2004

Welsh, Jennifer. *The Return of History: Conflict, Migration, and Geopolitics in the Twenty-First Century*. Toronto: House of Anansi Press, 2016.

Wieniewski, Ignacy. *Heritage: The Foundation of the Polish Culture*. 2nd ed. Toronto: Polish-Canadian Women's Federation in Canada, 1981.

Wilson, V. Seymour. "The Tapestry Vision of Canadian Multiculturalism." *Canadian Journal of Political Science* 26, 4 (1993): 645–669.

Wolynn, Mark. *It Didn't Start with You: How Inherited Family Trauma Shapes Who We Are and How to End the Cycle*. New York: Penguin, 2017.

"Worst Case on Record." *The American Marine Engineer* 7, 1 (January 1912): 20. Gjenvick-Gjønvik Archives. Accessed November 9, 2023, www.gjenvick. com/Immigration/Steerage/WorstCaseOfAbuse-SteeragePassengers-1912.html.

Wynn, Graeme. "On the Margins of Empire." In *The Illustrated History of Canada*. Edited by Craig Brown. Toronto: Key Porter Books Limited, 2002.

Yezierska, Anzia. "Children of Loneliness." In *Children of Loneliness: Stories of Immigrant Life in America*. London: Cassell and Company, 1923. www.gutenberg.org/cache/epub/71361/pg71361-images. html#CHILDREN_OF_LONELINESS.

Zajaczkowski, Wieslaw. *Biskupin: A Guide to the Archaeological Reservation*. Trans. by Alicja Petrus-Zagroba. Wroclaw, Poland: ZET Publishers, 1994.

Zalas, Zbigniew. "Powiat dziśnieński województwa wileńskiego w latach 1919–1939" [Today's district of Vilnius voivodeship in the years 1919–1939]. *Lituano-Slavica Posnaniensia: Studia Historica* 13 (2008): 169–215.

Zamoyski, Adam. *The Polish Way: A Thousand-Year History of the Poles and Their Culture.* New York: Hippocrene Books, 1987.

The Last King of Poland. London: Phoenix Giant, 1998.

*Zembaty, Wojciech. "The Elegant Downfall of the Polish Sarmatians." *Culture.pl.* Last updated February 25, 2021. www.culture.pl/en/article/the-elegant-downfall-of-the-polish-sarmatians.

Zielinski, Jaroslaw. *Warsaw.* Warsaw: Festina Publisher, 1994.

*Ziemak, Ryszard. *The Tatra Spell.* Warsaw: Wydawnicatwa Artystyczne I Filmowe, 1994.

Zubrzycki, Bernarda. "Polish Immigrants in Argentina." *Polish American Studies* 69, 1 (Spring 2012): 75–98.

IMAGE CREDITS

Figure 1 (p. 44) Map of Poland in the 1600s. Used with permission of Euratlas, www. euratlas.net/history/europe/1600/

Figure 2 (p. 45) Hetman's Guard. Painting of W. Pawliszak. Scan of old postcard from the private collection of Moonik. Produced by Warszawa Salon Kulikowskiego. Wikimedia Commons, www.commons.wikimedia.org/wiki/File:Straz_hetmanska.JPG

Figure 3 (p. 46) Polish Castle Interior circa 1750. Photo 224623631 . © Mitzobs | Dreamstime.co. Used with permission

Figure 4 (p. 49) Portrait of John III Sobieski (1629–1696), King of Poland . Wikimedia Commons, www.commons.wikimedia.org/wiki/File:Schultz_John_III_Sobieski.jpg File:Schultz John III Sobieski.jpg. Attributed to Daniel Schultz (1615–1683), National Museum in Warsaw, MP 4377

Figure 5 (p. 54) Map of Central and Eastern Europe in 1900 showing the extent of the three empires that partitioned the Polish-Lithuanian Commonwealth. Source: Topographic Maps of Eastern Europe, www.easteurotopo.org. This work is licensed under a Creative Commons Attribution-NonCommercial-ShareAlike 3.0 Unported License. Used with the permission of Henry ("Hap") Ponedel (www.easteurotopo.org)

Figure 6 (p. 59) Map showing location of Folwark Rozpaszka . Photo © Danuta Pawłowska www.radzima.net/eng/Figure_miejsce/rozpaszka.html?id_galley=2929. Printed in 1933 by Wojskowy Instytut Geograficzny, Warszawa. Direction given by Kanstancin Shastouski that it is not under copyright law.

Figure 7 (p. 63) Manor House (Dwor). Used with permission of Henry Piscotta, Penn State University Libraries on June 5, 2023.

Figure 8 (p. 65) Photo of Henry and his grandfather, Ignacy Ostrowski, at the Ostrowski cottage home in Rozpaszka, 1934. Used with permission from the H. J. Ostrowski estate.

Figure 9 (p. 70) Photo of a street in Warsaw, 1979, by author.

Figure 10 (p. 73) Village in Russia 1889. Alamy 2F4P5NR. Artefact/Alamy stock Photo. Permission purchased.

Figure 11 (p. 113) Canada West – the New Homeland. CRHA/Exporail, Canadian Pacific Railway Company Fonds (Canada West). Used with permission.

Figure 12 (p. 119) Map of Railway Lines in Eastern Europe and Russia, 1905. J.J. Arnd Railroad Atlas. Permission received May 25, 2023.

Figure 13 (p. 119) Emigrant Train Station in Libau (now Liepaja, Latvia), 1910. www.ebay.com/itm/255904709809 (item purchased). Used with permission.

Figure 14 (p. 122) Libau Osta Port Bridge. www.shorturl.at/otMOS. Permission purchased.

Figure 15 (p. 123) People carrying materials from the train to the ship at Libau. Mennonite Heritage Archives. CA MHC 744-4. Permission purchased.

Figure 16 (p. 124) The S. S. Kursk. Dunkert, A., Steamship "Kursk" in the port of Libau, Estonian Maritime Museum. Used with permission

Figure 17 (p. 135) Ships docked at Pier 2, the Deep Water Terminals. W.R. MacAskill/Nova Scotia Archives/1987-453 no. 2625. Permission purchased.

Figure 18 (p. 138) Campbell River Road after the Halifax Explosion. Gauvin & Gentzel, Nova Scotia Archives Photo/negative: No. N-201. Permission purchased.

Figure 19 (p. 142) Waverley Hotel, Barrington St., Halifax. Nova Scotia Archives Photographic Collection. Permission purchased.

Figure 20 (p. 147) 160–162 Spruce St. N., Timmins, 1935. Used with permission of the H. J. Ostrowski Estate

Figure 21 (p. 152) Photo of Joseph Pluto, 1933. Used with permission of the H. J. Ostrowski Estate

Figure 22 (p. 154) The Siscoe Gold Mines, May 1930. Photographer: Conrad Poirier, Bibliotheque et Archives Nationales du Quebec. Permission purchased.

Figure 23 (p. 166) Photo of Joanna Dudek and Vincent Dudek, Florida. Used with permission of the H.J. Ostrowski Estate

Figure 24 (p. 172) Photo of Lakeside Cabins. Used with permission of the H. J. Ostrowski Estate

Figure 25 (p. 174) Photo of John Pietkiewicz, Joanna and Vincent Dudek, Rose and Wladek Radek (Pietkiewicz). Used with the permission of H.J. Ostrowski Estate

Appendix A (p. 220-223) S.S. Kursk Manifest, April 25, 1914. Public Domain

Appendix B (p. 224-228) Siscoe Gold Mines Ltd.v. Bijakowski [1935] S.C.R. 193. (Dec. 21, 1934). Used with permission from the Supreme Court of Canada

ACKNOWLEDGEMENTS

You would not have this book in your hands right now if it was not for Keith Henderson, Ph.D., Managing Editor of D.C. Books in Montreal, who took a copy of my manuscript with him on a holiday to Italy in October 2022. I was pleased that my writing had the setting of sunshine and Mediterranean food for its presentation. Keith is a former professor of English literature, the author of six novels and a prize-winning book of short stories, and the former leader of the Equality Party (Quebec). I was delighted when I heard from him while he was in Italy that D.C. Books would publish my manuscript. He has been a god-send to me for his valuable advice on every chapter of this deeply personal journey that I needed to write; up until that point, the greater part of my recent experience had been the writing of tribunal decisions with strict format and content. I appreciated, though struggled, with his encouragement in many places to include personal and family information. And, to my surprise, my sons agreed with him. Much gratitude to you Keith. And thank you to Giuliana Pendenza, Communications Director for DC Books, for your enthusiastic interest in my work.

There are many who assisted me along the way that I must graciously acknowledge. Many thanks to Dr. Bozena Karwowska, UBC professor in the Department of Central, European and Northern Studies and author who, in the early days, arranged for me to meet the Polish Consul General in Vancouver, who was at that time Andrzej E. Mankowski. Consul Mankowski is also a Polish historian and showed me his thick textbook of the history of eastern Poland, albeit in Polish; he sent me many e-mails of suggestions, corrections and commentary that were very helpful in my putting together a simplified version of the history of Poland. He also was very interested in my Polish family as he was writing a book on the Polish in British Columbia. I was very lucky and I am very thankful to have had his counsel.

I must tell you about Dr. Chester Sadowski, Ph.D. in Chemistry. I thank my high school friend, Helen Sadowski, for referring me to her brother. Chester is a well-read lover of Polish history and was very generous with his time and expertise. He provided many valuable recommendations for my Polish history chapters as well as suggesting Polish artists, scientists and theorists for inclusion. He shared many interesting facts that I would not have known – I was delighted to incorporate them into my work.

The books written by Jerome Blum, professor and historian, were invaluable. His book, *Our Forgotten Past: Seven Centuries of Life on the Land*, was pivotal for me. After reading that book, I knew I *had* to research my heritage. I am indebted to him for his interest, perseverance and excellence in highlighting the importance of our past.

I admit that I knew very little about the history of Poland, so I read many books and I greatly depended on those books to instruct me on the basics. The history of Poland is very complex. In my footnotes, I have attempted to recommend readers to authors of extraordinary sources such as Norman Davies, Fernand Braudel, Wade Davis, Daniel Francis, Thomas King, Sophie Hodorowicz Knab, Valerie Knowles, Brian Porter-Szucs, John Ralson Saul, Miltiades Varvunis, Adam Zamoyski, as well as many others. I have attempted to give all sources full credit for their work as I had no background whatsoever in the historical topics that I touch on. Thank you to all the authors who wrote those books. You are so appreciated.

I am indebted to Susan Stromberg-Stein for our wonderful chats over the years about the Dudeks. Susan, the author of the biography of Louis Dudek published in 1983, has been very interested in my story of my grandmother's marriage to Louis's father and her financial support of Louis. Susan is also a renowned sculptor.

And I had help from various libraries and museums and also had legal assistance. Thank you to Steven Schwinghamer at the Canadian Museum of Immigration at Pier 21 for the important information you shared and the photos you sent of Pier 2 in Halifax. I hadn't known there was a Pier 2. Thank you to Karen Backmann and Karina Douglas at the Timmins Museum—you both were very interested and supportive of my work. I am grateful for the services at the Vancouver Public Library, the University of British Columbia Library, and the librarian at the Ottawa Archives who sent me microfiche of ships' manifests that I pored through. And appreciation to Cliché Avocates, Val D'Or, Quebec for help with mining claims history research and to Nexus Law Group LL.P. for copyright advice.

I am very grateful to have known Janina Freyman (nee Runcewicz) whom I met many years ago at meetings of the Polish Canadian Women's Federation. It was wonderful to be welcomed by all there, especially by Janina and Maria Karulis. I enjoyed being a part of a group of women who shared my heritage and being invited into such homey gatherings. Janina was and is a great leader in the Polish community. She is a warm, intelligent, hard-working, very energetic Polish immigrant who loves people and loved my project.

Thank you to Dana Sheldon for your help in the early days of this book. Your feedback was very supportive. Much appreciation goes to Terri Rothman for her exceptional work in organizing and obtaining copyright permissions for my images in the book. I was very needy of help as this was new to me and you were wonder-ful. I loved researching the history for the book but I had no idea how complicated footnote citations could be. A big hug to Beth McAuley of The Editing Company for correcting all my footnotes and for copyediting my manuscript. I'm so grateful to you. Thank you Ryan Thompson, designer and typesetter, for your time and enthusiastic response to my book, and for your great cover design for which I have received many compliments.

I thank all who have helped bring this book into print, and I take full responsibility for all errors.

My brother Paul has been a lifeline to me over the years. You shared many good stories and insights about your several summers living with Joanna, Vincent Dudek and Aunt Stef. You are very appreciated. My sister Mary Hogan also must be thanked for sharing her memories of my grandparents that I might have been too young to have noticed. Gratitude to cousin Stanley Pietkiewicz for telling me the story of his family, a story that included Joanna's brother. And to my other surviving brothers, Peter and Tom, I appreciate you both for being part of my family and I understand that we are survivors of a country that has endured much abuse. I hope you and your children enjoy reading this book.

And thank you to my husband and best friend, Chris Holmes, for being one of the proofreaders of the manuscript and coming to understand and appreciate the outstanding legacy of my Polish heritage. Now you know who you married.

Above all, there are my beloved sons, Simon and Kevin, who have never failed to support me in all my pursuits. Much love and gratitude! You both give me light and hope for the future.

Margaret Ostrowski was the fifth of seven children in a Polish/Canadian Catholic family. Her father was a Polish immigrant from the Russian Partition of Poland, and her mother's family came from the Austrian-Hungarian Partition. Margaret has had a lifetime passion for exploring her world, learning how things work, and looking under proverbial stones. As time went by, her interest in family legacy became a passion. Astonished by the richness of her heritage, she became convinced that most others have similar treasures to be unlocked – deeply enriching knowledge that makes the world much easier to understand.

Margaret Ostrowski holds an Honours Science Degree from the University of Toronto, a Masters Degree in Social Psychology from the University of Western Ontario, and a Law Degree from the University of British Columbia. A retired Registered Psychologist and a retired Lawyer, having practiced law for 35 years in B.C., she was elected President of her provincial bar association as well as a member of the B.C. lawyers' governing body. She particularly enjoyed her time as a decision-maker for the Immigration and Refugee Board of Canada. She wrote hundreds of decisions in that capacity as well as hundreds of decisions for seven other decision-making entities. Always a very active volunteer in whatever community she found herself, she received the Queen Elizabeth II Diamond Jubilee Award for volunteerism, a K.C. for her legal work, and the 2009 YWCA Women of Distinction Award for Business and the Professions. She has travelled to more than 45 countries and has visited Poland three times. Her artwork is displayed in various local venues. She and her husband raised two sons and she has six lovely grandchildren.